CUMBRIA HERITAGE SERVICES
LIBRARIES
COUNTY COUNCIL
This book is due to be returned on or before the last date above. It
may be renewed by personal application, post or telephone, if not in
demand.

C.L.18

THE
STARVATION
BLOCKADES

THE
STARVATION
BLOCKADES

by

NIGEL HAWKINS

LEO COOPER

First published in Great Britain 2002 by
LEO COOPER
an imprint of
Pen & Sword Books Ltd
47 Church Street
Barnsley
South Yorkshire
S70 2AS

ISBN 0 85052 908 5

A catalogue record for this book
is available from the British Library.

Typeset in 10.5/12.5pt Plantin by
Phoenix Typesetting, Burley-in-Wharfedale, West Yorkshire

Printed in England by
CPI UK

'It was a frightful starving match, and for nearly a year we were running neck and neck, or at least seemed to be.'

George Bernard Shaw

Contents

Preface

During the First World War Great Britain, France and later the USA struggled to deprive Germany and the Austro-Hungarian Empire of all supplies, including food, by the imposition of a naval blockade. The Germans on their side, after a brief war against Allied commerce with cruisers, imposed a counter-blockade with U-boats. Neither side could have attempted such a huge undertaking had it not been supreme at sea, the one on the surface the other under it. This is the story of how those two simultaneous campaigns waxed and waned and of the battles, naval and political, which determined the outcome.

No one could have guessed, when the Royal Navy began its blockade, how the chain of events would unfold, until, while the bloodied armies slogged it out on land, all the brittle rules of International Law had been broken at sea, and all the neutral countries of Europe and many outside had become enmeshed in the conflict. But both sides knew that victory depended on who won the naval battle.

In telling the story as actions led to reprisals and further escalation, I have tried to keep the pace of the narrative going by relegating many details to endnotes, which I trust the reader will not find too distracting.[1] Because this cannot pretend to be a work of deep scholarship, I have not given the references for all the facts and figures, though I have given them for all quotations, to whose authors I acknowledge a debt.

I am also indebted to the staff of the London Library, British Library, Public Record Office, Imperial War Museum, Library of the Greenwich Maritime Museum and the Naval Library for their courtesy and help, and to those friends, John Talbot, Keith Reid and Geoffrey Malone who read the manuscript and provided useful comments and encouragement and to John Hunter, who worked with such skill on the photographs. Any errors are of course my own. Lastly, like all authors, I am grateful to my wife for her patience and understanding while I pursued the unsocial business of writing.

Notes

1. The disease of pedographophilia, a morbid love of footnotes, was recently identified by Ben Macintyre of the *Times*, though it may not yet be recognized by all psychiatrists.

Introduction

On 23 June 1914 a powerful British naval squadron of four modern battleships and three light cruisers under the command of Vice Admiral Sir George Warrender, steamed round Denmark into the Baltic Sea and entered Germany's great naval port of Kiel. This was no act of war. On the contrary, the ships were on a courtesy visit, timed to coincide with the annual regatta at Kiel. Only a few decades before, Kiel had been better known for its sprats than its warships, but Kaiser Wilhelm II had prepared a proud future for Kiel and now it was the German Empire's finest naval base. 'There on the still waters of our fjord or bay, they lay, the beautiful ships, one next to the other, each made fast to its buoy,' wrote one of her sons, 'and through the streets of our town came the boys in blue, red-cheeked and bare-throated . . . the cranes of the ship yards arose where the proud ships were being built. Money flowed into the town. And each year (since 1895) in the month of June, trim, slim, tall-masted, sharp-sailed yachts from all the world slipped into the harbour for the "Kiel Week" races. What nobler, what finer sport than a yacht race?'[1] As an attraction to the sailing fraternity the regatta was the rival of England's Cowes week. Like much in Germany then, it showed that, as the Kaiser had declared, her future lay upon the water, the element where Britannia had long held undisputed sway.

Prince Otto von Bismarck, who had dominated German politics for twenty-eight years until 1890, had not been interested in overseas possessions; he was too busy at home, drawing the German states together under Prussian hegemony. To do this he had embarked on three short, crushing wars within seven years. First, in alliance with

1

Austria, Prussia defeated Denmark in 1864, prising from her the Duchies of Schleswig and Holstein, through which the Kiel Canal was to run. Two years later Austria herself and her German allies were overwhelmed, and lastly in 1870 France had yielded to the fearsome military organization of her neighbour. A fifth of the country was quickly occupied and Paris put under siege. At the end of the war the provinces of Alsace and Lorraine were stripped from her and, to rub salt into the wound a new German Empire, the second Reich, was formally proclaimed at Versailles in 1871. When, in 1890, the thirty-year-old Kaiser Wilhelm II dropped Bismarck, the old pilot, a new period of expansion of the German Empire (now an industrial giant of twenty-five semi-autonomous states) was to be introduced, but this time it would be overseas, and 'a place in the sun' became the watchword.

There were German colonies in Africa and Polynesia and on the seaboard of China, but their extent and value was felt to be less than those of states whose wealth and population were inferior to hers, and the Kaiser was rebuffed when his colonial ambitions came up against those of the old established empires. When Lord Salisbury was the British Foreign Secretary, the young Kaiser had innocently asked him to put his finger on the map and show him where he could have a colony which would not interfere with British aspirations. 'And what do you think he replied to me,' the Kaiser complained later to a British admiral, 'We don't want you anywhere.'[2] He received a more forceful check when he sent warships down to Delagoa Bay, in the south of Portuguese Mozambique and at the end of the railway line to Pretoria, at the time of the Jameson Raid into the Transvaal. The raid had been ignominiously repulsed by the Boers, and Kaiser Wilhelm had rashly sent President Kruger a congratulatory telegram, which infuriated the British. They sent their Cape Squadron reinforced by two cruisers from the Mediterranean. The Kaiser backed off. 'I then realised,' he told the admiral, 'that unless I had a navy sufficiently strong that even you would have to think a little bit before you told me to "Go to hell out of it" my commerce would not progress as I wanted it to, and so I determined to build a navy which would at least command respect.'[3] Resentment against British obstruction of their imperial aims was widespread in Germany, although for a time the British were generally unaware of it. Indeed on the surface relations were generally good and in 1890 Germany had acquired from Britain the sparsely inhabited island of Heligoland, lying approximately forty miles from the German coast in the centre of the bight which bears its name. Many German colonialists denounced the trade-off of Uganda and Zanzibar for the 'bathtub' of Heligoland. But their Kaiser was more far-sighted. When fortified, Heligoland was to be the key to the defences of all the German North Sea ports and estuaries; it was worth another fleet. Britain, which had held the island since the eighteenth century, was the party that would rue the bargain. It would be turned into a base for an untried weapon, the submarine. Might that small craft nullify the supremacy of the battleship?

Wilhelm's enthusiasm for a strong navy had been reinforced by reading *The Influence of Sea Power upon History*, written shortly after his accession by the prolific US Admiral, Alfred T. Mahan. It might have been dedicated to the German Kaiser. The book demonstrated that many events of war, which seemed on their face to be purely military, were in fact dictated by the naval situation. Why for instance had Hannibal crossed the Alps at the end of a 1,500 mile trek round the Mediterranean coast, which lost him half his 60,000 veterans? Because the Romans commanded the sea. Why did the British surrender to Washington at Yorktown? Because they had lost command of the sea. A second volume, *The Influence of Sea Power upon the French Revolution and Empire*, hammered the message home. What stifled the hopes of Napoleon's army in Egypt? Nelson's victory of the Nile. And so it had been throughout history. 'The miseries resulting from the overweening power of Spain in days long gone by seemed to be forgotten:' Mahan wrote, 'forgotten also the more recent lesson of the bloody and costly wars provoked by the ambition and exaggerated power of Louis XIV. Under the eyes of the statesmen of Europe there was steadily and visibly being built up a third overwhelming power, destined to be used as selfishly, as aggressively, though not as cruelly, and much more successfully than any that had preceded it. This was the power of the sea, whose workings, because more silent than the clash of arms, are less often noted, though lying clearly enough on the surface. It can scarcely be denied that England's uncontrolled dominion of the seas, during the whole period chosen for our subject (from 1660), was by long odds the chief among the military factors that determined the final issue.'[4] Germany must be able to challenge that power.

A few years later the Kaiser found his man. On 18 June 1897 Rear Admiral Alfred von Tirpitz, then forty-eight years old, was appointed Secretary of State of the Navy Office. The sea was not in his blood – he was the son of a judge – and he had never commanded more than a cruiser squadron, but during the next nineteen years he was to turn the German navy into the second most powerful fleet in the world, one that would 'at least command respect' as his imperial master wanted. A few

3

days after Tirpitz took office the Kaiser appointed the suave, subtle and sycophantic Count Bernard von Bulow, Secretary of State for Foreign Affairs and charged him with keeping the country out of a war with Britain while the fleet was being built. Tirpitz worked fast and lobbied hard among politicians and publicists. Within six months of taking office he introduced the first Navy Bill which provided for a large programme of warship construction. Tirpitz described the possession of a powerful fleet as 'a question of survival' for Germany. Besides, regular placements of naval shipbuilding contracts would counteract trade cycles. The Bill was passed on 10 April 1898.

Protected by its huge battle fleet, the United Kingdom was the most secure of all the belligerents at the start of the First World War. While other countries were invaded by their neighbours, the Grand Fleet's unparalleled might kept the islands safe. However, in the preceding century demographic changes and trade policy had introduced a new and terrible risk which had not existed since the last great wars which Britain had fought in Europe. The nation could no longer feed itself and if Britain failed to match or counter the next revolution in naval technology, if it failed to be supreme at sea for more than the briefest period, the spectre of starvation by blockade would arise.

Advances in public hygiene, the provision of clean water, the construction of sewers and developments in medicine had rapidly increased the number of mouths to be fed. At the same time the doctrine of free trade had resulted in massive imports of food from whichever country provided it cheapest. France was the tenth by value in the list of countries from which Britain imported food, behind distant New Zealand. Germany sent less produce than Australia. At the top of the exporters list was Argentina. The roast beef of Edwardian England would probably have been bred on the pampas, while eighty per cent of the wheat for the nation's bread came from abroad, mostly from the prairies of North America. These imports had to be paid for with exports of coal and a formidable range of manufactures, all of which were generally carried in ships flying the Red Ensign of the British Merchant Navy. At that time over half the steamships of the world flew the 'Red Duster'.

The men who served under the Red Ensign gave the United Kingdom enormous depth of manpower in wartime. As Mahan pointed out, when considering naval power it is not only the size of the population 'but the number following the sea, or at least readily available for employment on ship-board and for the creation of naval material, that must be counted . . . for a great shipping afloat necessarily employs, besides the crews, a large number of people engaged in the various handicrafts which facilitate the making and repairing of naval material . . .'.[5]

In the last decade of the nineteenth century however, a few energetic officers were questioning whether the men who served under the White Ensign of the Royal Navy were ready and equipped to meet a modern foe, such as Germany might be. Foremost of these was Admiral Sir John Arbuthnot Fisher, who was appointed First Sea Lord in 1903 at the age of sixty-two.[6] He served on the Board of Admiralty from February 1892 until he retired in 1910, with a three year absence as Commander-in-Chief of the Mediterranean Fleet. While Tirpitz had to turn a small fleet into a great and modern navy, Fisher set himself to transform the largest navy of the day into the most modern and best prepared fleet of the next generation. Both admirals set about their tasks with demonic energy. The steely resolution that fast drove 'Jackie' Fisher up the ladder of promotion set him at his desk in the Admiralty at five o'clock in the morning day after day until he was well into his seventies. The attention to detail which made his operations on board ship ('evolutions' in naval parlance) a marvel of efficiency, now ensured that his reforms would not be attacked on minor issues.

As a friendly critic wrote, 'Then emerges slowly to the front a man of ideas. He had no social backing and no exceptional attractions of personality; but he had the energy of a steam engine, the pertinacity of a debt collector and no reverence for the past or for anything but facts. Five years ago he became the head of the Navy, and in five years the Navy has been revolutionized. There is hardly a stone that has been left unturned. There is hardly an idea that has not been reversed. Ships, guns, gunnery, strategy, tactics, instruction and training, diet and rewards – all have suffered a literal "sea change". No wonder that he is not loved. No wonder that the Navy writhes like a frog under the harrow.'[7] Fisher expected opposition and knew that if he was to push his reforms through, he would have to outwit the opposition. His method was to keep his plans to himself and a few of his closest associates, until he was ready to launch them on the world all together and all complete. 'A reform thus introduced doesn't grow up like your shore-going reforms, with such accretions and abstractions that its own father does not recognise it. No! It emerges like Minerva out of the head of Jupiter! full-grown, armed, ready for work at once, in its prime.'[8]

Then in 1906, secretly and in record time, the revolutionary battleship *Dreadnought* was launched. The idea of a battleship whose major armament was composed of fewer big guns, but of the same calibre, instead

5

of many guns of a variety of sizes, was not Fisher's. The Constructor to the Italian Navy, General (*sic*) Cuniberti came out with the first designs, and they were officially published in Jane's *Fighting Ships* of 1903. The principle was that one or two strikes at the vital organs of a foe were more efficient than 'the progressive dismemberment of the enemy'.[9] (Also, ranging was much easier with guns of only one calibre. There was only one set of splashes falling short or over the target.) The Japanese had laid down two battleships based on Cuniberti's ideas, and the United States had authorized the building of the USS *South Carolina* and USS *Michigan*, both carrying eight 12-inch guns. However, Fisher was the first to have one completed. When HMS *Dreadnought* slipped out of Portsmouth Harbour for sea trials a year and a day after her keel had been laid, all older battleships were rendered obsolete. (The phenomenal speed of construction was due to standardization of parts, such as the steel plates, but was to some extent rigged too, because much of the material had been quietly stockpiled in advance.) Not only did the *Dreadnought* have ten 12-inch guns, firing a broadside twice the weight of any previous battleship, but she was the first warship of her size to be powered by turbine.

Then Winston Churchill, who was appointed First Lord of the Admiralty in 1911, introduced his own revolution, which was to make his battleships almost as far ahead of the first *Dreadnought* as she had been ahead of her predecessors. They were 'all big gun' ships, turbine driven as before, but with bigger guns and greater speed. The Queen Elizabeth-class created a fast division of five battleships, the other ships being *Warspite*, *Barham*, *Valiant* and *Malaya*. They carried an awesome novelty – 15-inch guns. The greater weight of the ammunition and turret machinery of this weapon system meant that one turret had to be sacrificed, but eight guns in a broadside could throw shells weighing seven tonnes twenty miles – where the standard German 12-inch guns of the day fired a shell weighing only half as much.[10] The 15-inch guns were very reassuring, but how would they perform in battle? How dangerous would the young, enthusiastic, well-armed and well-trained German High Seas Fleet be and what use would be made of the small submarine flotillas which the Kaiser now honoured with a visit?

It was against this background that the Kiel Regatta was held in 1914. The programme began with the reopening of the Kaiser Wilhelm Canal, connecting the Baltic to the North Sea and now made wide enough to take the biggest battleships, and was due to continue for two weeks, but on 28 June the festivities were paralysed by an event far away in the Balkans.[11] The Archduke Franz-Ferdinand, heir to the Dual Monarchy which ruled the collection of eleven nations, comprising the Austro-Hungarian Empire, was assassinated in Sarajevo, the capital of the recently annexed province of Boznia-Herzogovina. News of the Archduke's death was soon cabled to Kiel and the message was taken out to the Kaiser, sailing on the *Meteor*. The race was stopped and the Kaiser returned to shore, ordering 'Flags half-mast, ensigns half-mast. Austrian flag at main-mast for murder of Austrian heir.' All receptions were cancelled as the news spread round the fleets. Lieutenant Stephen King-Hall from HMS *Southampton* was at a tea-dance on board a German battleship. At about 5 p.m. the band stopped abruptly and the Captain announced the news. The eyes of an Austrian countess with whom King-Hall had been sitting filled with tears. 'We shall never meet again,' she said. 'This will mean war.'[12] The British squadron's commander, Vice Admiral George Warrender, had no doubts about the consequences either. 'This crime,' he foretold, 'will mean war between Serbia and Austria. Russia will be drawn in and thus Germany and France cannot remain lookers-on.'

There was a final quiet lunch on board the *King George V*, attended by Tirpitz, Ingenohl and other admirals. Admiral Warrender then went ashore to drop in on a party which British bluejackets were giving for their German hosts. Warrender's arrival was greeted by thunderous stamping from the British sailors. The Admiral climbed up onto a table and made an enthusiastic speech about the friendship of the two nations, and ended with three cheers for the German navy. *Konteradmiral* Mauwe replied with three cheers for the British navy. The Admirals shook hands amid great stamping.

The fleet visit wound down. It had been 'a great success and gave fine proof of naval comradeship the world over and of German hospitality,' the *Times* reported.[13] As the British squadron steamed out of Kiel harbour gentlemanly George Warrender radioed a parting message back to his hosts and brothers in arms. In the light of the critical international situation it must go down as one of the most unguarded signals of all time: 'Friends in past and friends forever!'[14] It was 30 June 1914. In five weeks the two navies would be at war.

Notes

1. Salomon, Ernst von, *The Answers*, Putnam, 1954, p17. Until 1864 Kiel had been under the control of Denmark.
2. Kerr, Mark, *Land, Sea and Air*, Longmans, Green, 1927, p166
3. ibid. p.167. In an inexplicable piece of double perfidy, the British

government in 1898 made a secret agreement with Germany providing for the eventual partition of the Portuguese colonies and then in the next year secretly guaranteed Portugal that it would not be carried out. German disgust on finding out about the latter treaty can be imagined.

4. Mahan, Captain A.T., *The Influence of Sea Power upon History*, Samson Low, Marston, 1892, p.63

5. ibid. pp.45–6

6. The quaint, archaic nomenclature of these offices may be confusing. The First Sea Lord was the senior naval professional on the Admiralty Board. He answered to the politician responsible to parliament for the Navy, who then was called the First Lord of the Admiralty. All these 'Lords' were usually commoners.

7. Bacon, Admiral Sir Reginald H., *Life of Lord Fisher of Kilverstone*, Hodder & Stoughton, 1929, Vol. II p. 1. When William Goodenough repeated Fisher's remark that he, Fisher, had not got a friend left on the Flag Officers' List, a respected C.–in–C. flatly told him, 'Captain Goodenough, what he said is quite true.' (Goodenough, Admiral Sir William, *A Rough Record*, Hutchinson & Co., 1943, p.61)

8. ibid. Vol.1, p.281. Bacon wrote a two-volume biography of the great naval administrator. A lighter, if partial portrait is *Fisher's Face* by Jan Morris.

9. Cuniberti's article is reprinted in Jane, Fred T., *Fighting Ships*, Samson, Low, Marston, 1914, p.138

10. As battle conditions were to show, in range and penetrating power the greater muzzle velocity of the German projectiles largely made up for their smaller size.

11. 28 June was notable as the anniversary of the Battle of Kosovo in 1389, in which Sultan Murad I destroyed the Serbian Empire by defeating and killing the Serbian King Lazar.

12. King-Hall, Commander Stephen, *My Naval Life*, Faber & Faber, 1952, p.90

13. *Times*, 8 July 1914. The symbol was frequently invoked. For instance, King Edward VII dressed in the uniform of the Kiev Dragoons when he visited Reval (Tallinn) in June 1908, and he and the Russian Emperor made each other Admirals of the Fleet of their respective navies.

14. Hase, Commander Georg von, *Kiel and Jutland*, translated by Chambers and Holt, Skeffington & Son, 1921, p.62

THE BRITISH ISLES AND THE NORTH SEA

Atlantic

Ocean

Shetland Is.

NORWAY

Orkney Is.

Scapa Flow Kirkwall

Lewis

Stavanger

Cromarty

Moray Firth

Kinnairds Head

The Naze

Aberdeen

SCOTLAND

Skagerrak

Dundee

Jutland
Bank

Rosyth *Firth of Forth*

Edinburgh

Glasgow

DENMARK

Londonderry

Horns Reef

Belfast

Newcastle

Is. of
Man

Sunderland

Dogger

Scarborough

Bank

Heligoland

Irish Sea

Flamborough Head

Dublin

Manchester

Hull

Borkum

Holyhead

Liverpool

R.Humber

Wilhelmshaven

ENGLAND

St.
George's
Channel

Birmingham

Yarmouth

Broad
Fourteens

Lowestoft

HOLLAND

Swansea

Harwich

GERMAN
EMPIRE

Bristol Channel

Bristol

London

The
Downs

Zeebrugge

Southampton

Portsmouth

Dover

Bruges

Land's
End

Plymouth

I. of Wight

Calais

BELGIUM

Falmouth

Scillies

English Channel

FRANCE

CHAPTER ONE

The British Blockade

At 7 a.m. in the misty morning of 29 July 1914 the British First Fleet disappeared from Portland Harbour, bound for a destination known only to its Flag Officers, the admirals of the squadrons. That day artillery of the Austro-Hungarian Empire bombarded the Serbian capital, Belgrade, from across the Danube. They were the first shells to be fired in what soon developed into the Great War.[1] For three weeks after the murder of Archduke Franz-Ferdinand it appeared that the terrible event would pass without further bloodshed, but on 23 July the Austrian ambassador in Belgrade delivered a note, which made several demands in terms which were intended to be unacceptable to the Serbs. All bar one of the stipulations were none the less accepted by them. That, however, was not enough for the Austrian government, which immediately declared war. Aware that the interlocking alliances of the major European powers and the timetables of the mobilization of their armies could cause the powder keg of European tension to explode at any moment, Sir Edward Grey, Britain's eminent and peaceable Foreign Secretary, called for a conference of the powers, while all Europe prepared for war. The German High Seas Fleet broke off manoeuvres and the British Third Fleet was stopped from dispersing after being reviewed by King George V.

On 29 July Sir George Callaghan, the Commander-in-Chief of the First Fleet, had been summoned to the Admiralty, so Vice Admiral Sir George Warrender took the ships from the shelter of Portland harbour north towards the bleak anchorage, surrounded by the southernmost islands of the Orkneys and known as Scapa Flow. As the fleet steamed

11

through the Channel and up the east coast of Britain for two nights and a day, Commander Usborne recalled, 'all attention was fixed on the urgent problem of defending ourselves against a night attack . . . Nobody really knew how we stood in this matter, for we had never fired at night at real live destroyers attacking at full speed. We had engaged hundreds of floating targets, and with certain precautions towed targets, but what would the situation be like when some twenty or thirty destroyers charged down upon us in a mass and loosed their torpedoes?'[2]

By the time that the Fleet had anchored in Scapa Flow, Austria and her ally, Germany, and Russia and her ally, France, were all fully mobilized. Germany had declared war on Russia. That, she knew, would involve her in a war on two fronts, in which case her plan was to defeat France first. Germany therefore issued a request and an ultimatum to neutral Belgium requiring free passage of German troops through their country in order to outflank the French fortifications. Until the last moment, in spite of the unwritten Entente Cordiale binding the United Kingdom morally to France and the similar arrangement with Russia, it had been unclear what the country would do, but in the afternoon of 3 August Sir Edward Grey, in a speech which former Prime Minister Arthur Balfour described as 'probably the most historic speech which has been made for one hundred years,'[3] persuaded the House of Commons of the danger ahead and as German troops crossed the Belgian border, Britain delivered her ultimatum for them to withdraw.

At Scapa Flow the Fleet was joined by the man who, some years previously and unknown to himself, had been earmarked by Admiral Sir John Fisher to be Commander-in-Chief in the event of war. Vice Admiral Sir John Rushworth Jellicoe was then fifty-four years old and had had a distinguished career, culminating in the post of Second Sea Lord. He had seen action as a lieutenant in the Naval Brigade in Egypt, fighting at the battle of Tel-el-Kebir, and again as Chief of Staff to Sir Edward Seymour during the Boxer Rising, when he was severely wounded. Jellicoe had been assistant to Fisher, when Director of Naval Ordnance, and later himself held that position, so important in an age when big guns commanded the seas. He was noted for the brilliance of his mind, hard work and quiet, gentlemanly character, which endeared him to all who served under him. Winston Churchill, as First Lord of the Admiralty, had appointed him at the end of July to be Second-in-Command of the Fleet under Sir George Callaghan, and indicated that he might 'in certain circumstances' be made C.-in-C. This came upon the modest John Jellicoe as a great and shocking surprise. He protested against 'such an appointment being made on what might possibly be the very eve of war'[4] and sent several telegrams to the First Lord and First Sea Lord dwelling on 'the danger of substituting, at such a juncture and at such short notice, an admiral who was not in touch with the Fleet for a Commander-in-Chief with long experience of command'.[5] Jellicoe wanted nothing more than to be Chief of Staff to the man with whom he had served for seven years in China, and was embarrassed at the prospect of taking over from an old friend at *the* moment of his life. Many of the Flag Officers were very upset at the time too.[6]

As he took his seat in the train which would take him north to Scotland, Jellicoe had been handed an envelope which was not to be opened until he received an order from the Admiralty. It contained his appointment to the command of The Grand Fleet, a new name for the huge armada which was to be his country's first line of defence. The order came at 4 a.m. on 4 August, and at 11 p.m. that night Britain's ultimatum to Germany to withdraw from Belgium expired.

Far from planning a sudden onslaught on the Royal Navy, the High Seas Fleet had itself been expecting an immediate attack, and so to hamper the forces emerging from the Thames estuary and east coast bases the Germans planned to lay a line of mines across their path. At 11 a.m. on 5 August, when the United Kingdom and Germany had only been at war for a few hours, a flotilla of British destroyers was sweeping along the Dutch coast. A lone trawler had informed Captain C. H. Fox in HMS *Amphion* that a suspicious vessel had been 'throwing things overboard' twenty miles north-east of the Outer Gabbard light ship (about one third of the way across the North Sea on a line from Lowestoft on the East Anglian coast to Rotterdam). The destroyers *Lance* and *Landrail* went ahead to investigate, while HMS *Amphion* followed. It was the passenger ferry, *Königin Luise*, which had quietly left Heligoland a few days before, and on the eve of war had embarked on a secret errand. By noon, before she had finished her task, the destroyers had caught and sunk her, taking her crew aboard the *Amphion*. Few of the prisoners were to reach shore, however. If it had been first blood to the British, the sunken vessel was soon to take her revenge. Captain Fox set a course home round the area where he thought the mines might have been laid, but just when he believed that he was clear, the *Amphion*'s bows were shattered by a huge explosion. As she drifted and men were abandoning ship, a second mine exploded and she sank almost at once. Most of the German seamen, who had been held in the forecastle, perished along with 150 of the *Amphion*'s crew.

13

To many, not only the British, it seemed inhuman that mines should have been laid, not in the approaches to a naval base, but well off the Suffolk coast, outside British territorial waters and in international shipping lanes 'regardless of neutrals and the time-honoured customs of the Sea'.[7] This first naval action was an indication that the war at sea was to be conducted on different lines from anything previously known in Europe. The indiscriminate scattering of mines, imperilling even neutral merchantmen, was, as Churchill pointed out in the House of Commons, a new fact calling for the attention of nations.

The United Kingdom government had no intention of sowing mines in international waters in those early days. They wanted to keep the moral high ground, and it was possible for British naval forces to put economic pressure on their enemies without risking the lives of neutral citizens. They would isolate the Central Powers, which were already cut off from the east by the great land mass of the Russian Empire and from the south by France and the Mediterranean, which was controlled by the French and British navies. The enemy ports would be blockaded, their commerce and communications strangled. The Royal Navy had up its sleeves several cards which were played quickly.

An immediate attack was made on enemy communications. German companies had laid five telegraph cables from Emden down through the English Channel and on to Vigo in north-west Spain, Tenerife in the Canary Islands and to the Azores. These then joined up with transatlantic cables and others leading round Africa to German colonies and consulates. When the warning telegram was sent out to British authorities, the Post Office and the Royal Navy prepared to sever these cables. On 5 August, as soon as the British ultimatum expired, the cable ship *Telconia* cut all five cables.[8] For the rest of the war, with the British commanding the seas, Germany would have great difficulty in communicating abroad without the risk of interception of her messages. There was of course an international cable service in other countries available to belligerents and neutrals alike, but agents were to become adept at intercepting cabled messages from their enemies. A small bribe to someone in the telegraph office would usually do the trick. Germany had also built a very powerful radio transmitter at Nauen, west of Berlin, but radio transmissions could be received by anyone tuned to the right wavelength (though breaking the code in which messages were usually sent was another matter).

On the first day of the war the Royal Navy also started rounding up enemy merchant ships, wherever they were found. In the Irish Sea the German steamer *Wilhelm Behrens* was captured. A shot across the bows stopped her, and a prize crew from HMS *Grafton* took her and her cargo of timber into the Clyde, while HMS *Gibraltar* sent another merchantman into Liverpool. Two German sailing trawlers were captured, much to the surprise of the fishermen who had been at sea for three weeks. Others were sunk after their crews had been taken off. In the English Channel the steel-hulled German schooner, *Else* was taken into Falmouth and adjudged a prize.[9] Within hours twenty German vessels had been captured in British waters.

At the same time the Royal Navy began its blockade of Germany. After the war scare of 1911 – the 'Agadir Crisis', the Committee for Imperial Defence had considered the actions required to blockade the German North Sea coast in the event of war. At first they had thought in terms of a close blockade with ships steaming just outside the Heligoland Bight. But times had changed since the days when Nelson's storm-tossed men-of-war could ride out the gales off Toulon for months on end (or when the US Government, stretching the concept considerably, had blockaded the southern ports in the Civil War). The submarine had made it too dangerous for battleships to exercise a close blockade by waiting offshore, and without the support of capital ships smaller warships would too easily be sunk by cruisers emerging from the ports. However, with the increased speed of warships, much the same result could be achieved by battleships and cruisers hundreds of miles away. Each year in the lead-up to the war, as the range of submarines increased, the radius of the blockading force from Heligoland was enlarged, until it was recognized that the only safe but almost equally effective solution was for ships to block the north and south entrances of the North Sea.

Wherever the blockading ships took up station the objective would be the same. As McKenna, the First Lord of the Admiralty in early 1911, trusted, 'The enemy . . . would neither be able to transport his forces nor continue his trade, and the result of the economic pressure of the destruction of overseas trade in almost any modern state would be so serious as, I believe, to constitute something even more than a crippling blow'.[10] A quick result was not expected, but much might be anticipated from the combination of Britain's naval power and her dominating geographical situation. The position of the British Isles, lying like a breakwater across the North Sea, gave her a great advantage in a war with Germany, as opposed to one against France or Spain. Every ship proceeding to Germany from any of the oceans had to pass Great Britain. It was easy to seal off the narrow straits between Britain and France. All vessels passing Dover for London and other ports beyond were directed to be examined for contraband in the waters between the east Kent coast and the Goodwin Sands – the historic anchorage known as the Downs. (The Goodwins are sufficiently exposed at low spring tides for an annual cricket match to be played there, and these shallows formed a good protection against marauding submarines.) The 270 miles separating Scotland from Norway posed a problem of a different order, but that too was solved in practice by the Tenth Cruiser Squadron, which was assigned to intercept all maritime traffic passing round the northern route. On 1 August, as the storm clouds gathered, Rear Admiral Dudley de Chair had been ordered to mobilize Cruiser Force B, as it was first called, from the scattered ships of the Training Squadron. They had gathered at the Orkneys by 6 August and soon began searching ships for contraband and shepherding suspect vessels into harbour at Kirkwall, the Orkadian capital. With the Dover Patrol, the Tenth Cruiser Squadron formed the arms of the great undertaking which came to be called 'the British Blockade', 'the Great Blockade' or 'the Starvation Blockade', depending on the nationality of the speaker. Similar limbs of the organization were to be found at Gibraltar and Alexandria, sifting all traffic passing through the Mediterranean.

The backbone of the blockade was the Grand Fleet with its overwhelming fire power. Since the building of Germany's Navy Britain could no longer maintain the 'two-power standard', meaning a fleet larger than those of the next two naval powers combined, but she still had fifty per cent more capital ships than the High Seas Fleet, and she had not sacrificed quality. This material superiority was reinforced by a feeling of supreme confidence in the invincibility of the Royal Navy, which had prevailed since Nelson's great victory at Trafalgar. Their enviable morale was heightened scarcely three weeks after the outbreak of war by the Battle of Heligoland Bight. British submarines under Commodore Roger Keyes had observed a pattern of enemy patrols and Keyes, ever keen to get into action, had hatched a plan to destroy the German torpedo boats in an attack by the Harwich destroyers under Commodore Reginal Tyrwhitt. In the scrappy fight which ensued the British came to be hard pressed by light cruisers emerging from Heligoland, but were saved by Vice Admiral Sir David Beatty, commanding the Battlecruiser Force, who risked his capital ships by coming right into the Bight to join the fray. The Germans, gallant but outgunned, lost three light cruisers and a destroyer and suffered over 1,200 casualties as against thirty-five dead and fifty wounded British.

In Scapa Flow the crews prepared for an imminent fight. Surely the

German battle fleet would not stand by while their trade was suppressed? Ships were stripped of wooden fittings and inflammable upholstery, wardroom pianos were dumped on shore or overboard, and life was made generally less comfortable, but as it was expected that the great battle would be fought any day and that the war could not last more than six months, if only because of the worldwide financial disruption which economists forecasted, this temporary inconvenience seemed no trouble. The Fleet made a sweep into the North Sea and down towards the Heligoland Bight, hoping to catch enemy patrols, but was frustrated that the enemy's battle fleet did not oblige by coming out to meet the Royal Navy's superior squadrons.

However, other units of the High Seas Fleet did emerge. Ten *Unterseeboote* (submarines) were patrolling northwards, spread out seven miles apart combing the seas up to the Orkneys in that first week. When on the fourth day of the war the battleship, HMS *Monarch*, reported a U-boat south of Fair Isle, over 500 miles from Heligoland, where the huge warship had been leisurely towing a target without any screen or escort, it was generally thought to be a case of the 'jim-jams'.[11] But there were two other reports of German submarines about the same time and next day, 9 August, the light cruiser HMS *Birmingham* rammed one, and then at the second attempt sliced it in half. It was the *U-15*, which had only narrowly missed HMS *Monarch* with the first torpedo ever to be fired in anger. From then on battleships were instructed to steer a zig-zag course.

One other U-boat failed to return, probably striking a mine, so that the German Imperial Navy, the *Kaiserliche Marine*, had lost twenty per cent of that first patrol (a loss rate which the Royal Navy was unable to maintain). The losses did not, however, deter the Germans from pursuing their *Klein Krieg* or little war. The objective would be to snipe at any warships which could be found, gradually sapping the Royal Navy's strength until the High Seas Fleet could take on the Grand Fleet on something like equal terms. If the Grand Fleet could be whittled down and then beaten, not only would the blockading squadrons be swept from the seas, but the country would be open to invasion and liable to be starved into submission.

Once he realized that U-boats would have reported that the Grand Fleet was based at Scapa Flow, Jellicoe became extremely anxious. He was acutely aware that the anchorage was completely and scandalously unprotected. When, only a couple of years before, the Committee for Imperial Defence had considered measures needed to defend the east coast of Britain in view of a possible war with Germany, they had decided that the anchorage in the Cromarty Firth was the furthest north that should be considered, and had not protected Scapa Flow either with guns or booms. Since then Churchill too had failed to recognize the omission. Some small calibre, 12-pounder, guns had been landed from the ships by Admiral Callaghan, but he could not spare search-lights from the ships and so they were of no use at night. There were no breakwaters, nor net defences (other than those carried by the ships themselves) and the only protection to prevent hostile submarines from entering the Flow by any of three or four channels were the vicious currents, which ripped round between the islands and the mainland, making underwater navigation extremely erratic and dangerous. Paradoxically, in this disgraceful situation the Grand Fleet may have been in less danger of a torpedo attack from the Germans, than they would have been from a less efficient enemy. As Jellicoe wrote, 'It may have seemed impossible to the German mind that we should place our Fleet, on which the Empire depended for its very existence, in a position where it was open to submarine or destroyer attack'.[12] How he must have envied the German ships sheltering off Wilhelmshaven in a wide horseshoe bay at the mouth of the River Jade, protected by a string of fortified islands, mine fields and waters often so shallow that a submerged submarine could be observed from the air.

Depth charges and echo location had not been invented, so there was no really effective way of attacking a U-boat after it had submerged, even if one was found. In exercises shortly before the war, Commander William Boyle had been ordered to take his division of destroyers and torpedo boats and clear the fleet's intended anchorage of submarines. He proceeded to look businesslike, while realizing that he 'had no means wherewith to attack an enemy submarine and no clear notion of how to set about doing so'.[13]

In the early days of the war U-boat scares were frequent – hardly surprising, when the only method of detecting them was to have men stationed on either side of the ship straining their eyes for a periscope. At dusk on 1 September a light cruiser, HMS *Falmouth* suddenly opened fire at what, through the grey mist and driving wind, appeared to be a periscope, and soon reported that she had sunk a submarine. The whole fleet raised steam and prepared to leave the Flow. Another sighting was reported, other ships opened fire and destroyers criss-crossed the water in a vain attempt to spot and ram the intruders. While steam was being raised in the battlecruiser *Invincible*, two colliers were called up to make fast on either side of her, but not to coal ship. The faces of the colliers' masters 'fell several fathoms and their dismay and disgust were indescribable, when it was explained that their presence alongside was merely to provide a buffer in the event of a torpedo attack'.[14] The fleet spent the night at sea, where its manoeuvrability gave a feeling of security, and returned at daylight to anchor. The 'Battle of Scapa Flow', as it came to be called, had almost certainly been a false alarm. Perhaps it was a seal or the lookout had mistaken some flotsam in the water.

The precautions were not unreasonable, however. *Kapitänleutnant* Otto Hersing took *U-21* up to the Forth Bridge before being detected and driven off. Then on 3 September not far from the mouth of the river he struck HMS *Pathfinder*, a flotilla leader (half way in size between a destroyer and a light cruiser). Hersing's torpedo had probably blown up the destroyer's magazine, because she went down in just four minutes with nearly all her crew of 260 men. She was the first warship ever to be sunk by a submarine. But the record would not stand for long.

Although there were many unfounded scares and mistaken 'sightings' of periscopes, bold patrols were beginning to be made by the German submariners all round the British Isles and on 21 September 1914 three elderly armoured cruisers wandered into a tragedy that startled the world. HM ships *Aboukir*, *Hogue* and *Cressy* were patrolling at a leisurely speed off the Dutch coast, when they were sunk one after the other by a single submarine. As the *Hogue* and *Cressy* stood by to rescue the crew of the *Aboukir*, which they thought had been struck by a mine, *Kapitänleutnant* Otto Weddigen in the relatively old *U-9* reloaded his torpedo tubes and struck each in turn. Thirty German sailors had sunk three large warships and killed 1,459 of their enemy in one hour.

No wonder the Commander-in-Chief was apprehensive. Until Scapa Flow was made safe (which was not until February 1915), it was only the expanse of the sea that saved the ships from constant attacks. The Fleet would regularly be ordered out to cruise at night. Next Jellicoe retired them to Loch Ewe on the west coast of Scotland, and, to vary the base again, to Lough Swilly on the north coast of Donegal. 'What were we to think now?' wrote one officer. 'Where was the vaunted stranglehold of the British fleet over Germany? Scapa Flow had been bad enough, but how could we hope to pounce upon the enemy's fleet, should it emerge, from the distant harbours of northern Ireland and western Scotland? I think everybody must have felt, and I certainly did, that we had suffered a strategic defeat.'[15] It was fortunate that the move was not known in Berlin, for the one consideration which kept the High Seas Fleet in its bases was the fear that it would be unable to retire home again before the Grand Fleet arrived in overwhelming force. (Von

Hennig boldly took the *U-18* up to the entrance of Scapa Flow on 2 November, and was disappointed to find that 'the nest was empty! There was not a single large vessel in harbour'[16], but the news did not get back, because he was rammed and forced to surrender.)

One part of the Grand Fleet kept to its allotted station come hell or high water, however. The Tenth Cruiser Squadron steadfastly maintained its Northern Patrol – but not without loss. On 15 October, scarcely three weeks after the three Cressy-class cruisers had met their fate off the Dutch coast, five of the Squadron were spread out at ten mile intervals steaming in line abreast. At 1.20 p.m. HMS *Theseus* reported that she had been attacked, and all ships of the squadron were ordered to turn to the north-west at full speed. No acknowledgment was received from the *Hawke*. Three hours earlier she had been hit almost amidships, under her foremost funnel, and had sunk without time to get off a radio report. The thirty-nine-knot destroyer, HMS *Swift*, was immediately dispatched to the scene and after searching for two hours she picked up a raft with twenty-two of the crew on board. A Norwegian steamer found another three officers and forty-six men in a sea boat and took them into Aberdeen, but nearly 500 sailors were lost. It was thought that another full sea boat had been crushed when the stricken cruiser turned turtle before sinking bow first. When, shortly afterwards, another division of cruisers steaming in line abreast outside Scapa Flow was nearly struck, the patrol line was withdrawn further north.

Five cruisers steaming in line abreast with visibility at ten miles or more could sight any vessel within a band eighty miles wide. But such clear weather was not common to the north of Scotland. Sometimes merchant ships slipped through in fog, at night or in a storm. At other times they escaped, because the ships at first used by the Navy were not the best for the job. The Squadron was composed of 7,000 ton armoured cruisers of the elderly Edgar type.[17] With two 9.2-inch and ten or twelve 6-inch guns they were well enough armed for the work, but could manage only seventeen to nineteen knots, which was less than some of the ships they might have to intercept. Matters came to a head when three of the cruisers rushed after a suspicious vessel which, after a chase of 130 miles, turned out to be the SS *Bergensfiord*, a liner of 11,000 tons. On board this 'Norwegian Mauretania' they only found six German stowaways, some crude rubber and a consignment of coffee, a catch which hardly justified the cost of the chase, especially when all three cruisers developed engine trouble soon afterwards.

It was soon clear that the Edgars lacked the endurance necessary for the task. With their regular need for coaling and repairs, the blockading squadron was sometimes reduced to three ships out of the ten. So in December 1914 they were replaced by twenty-two merchant ships and four trawlers equipped with wireless. Britain had a hundred passenger liners of 10,000 tons all capable of twenty-seven knots. They could carry provisions for a long period at sea, had large coal bunkers and plenty of accommodation for the extra officers, seamen and Royal Marines who formed prize crews. A few of these ships were found to be particularly suitable when, having swapped the Red Ensign for the White Ensign of the Royal Navy, they were armed with 6-inch or 4.7-inch guns. They were joined by armed freighters of various types and for the remainder of the war the 'Tenth Cruiser Squadron' was something of a misnomer. The assorted ships were soon rechristened 'The Muckle Flugga Hussars' after the northernmost point of the Orkneys, where they battled the winds and waves.

Though life in the spacious liners and even the more humble steamers was better than in a cruiser, the basic task of the Squadron was still hard. Every ship met was a potential enemy, so they kept their ammunition ready in racks round the guns, half of which were manned day and night. An hour in the crow's nest in ice or a blizzard, watching for a smudge of smoke on the horizon, was as much as a man could stand, and boarding intercepted ships was always a risk, as one far from timid officer described: 'Some of these boarding trips were anything but pleasant. To be lowered in a cutter from a height of fifty feet, with the ship rolling heavily, and the boat itself swinging wildly from the davit heads, is bad enough, even when the cruiser is not moving above six knots. And then there is the final drop of some feet that gives you a hearty shake-up as the boat falls on the water. You feel it still more if, by a piece of faulty judgment on the part of the officer lowering her, the boat happens to strike a hollow between two seas.'[18] And that was just the start of the operation. The boarding party's cutters were usually powered by oars. Some had outboard motors, but they were of little use in the mountainous waves, where their propellers often revved wildly out of the water. Keble Chatterton, who also served in the Tenth Cruiser Squadron wrote, 'There is something awe-inspiring both for the onlookers and the handful of men (in the boat) as the boarding party puts off from one tall ship's side to another, over the steep green, white-topped hills, rushing down terrible declivities of an unstable switch-back. One flick of a wave at any moment could send the boat with crew to the bottom: one scend of sea could hurl the wooden craft against the neutral's steel hull and strew the water with splinters; one

21

error of judgment in coming alongside would mean broken limbs, if not instant death.'[19]

Once up the ladder the boarding party first searched the boats and deck houses to see if they hid guns. This was not only to safeguard their own ship. Another vital function of the Squadron was to prevent German armed merchantmen from escaping into the open sea and joining their comrades for, since the outbreak of war, hostile cruisers had enjoyed considerable success attacking Allied commerce on the ocean trade routes.

Notes

1.The First World War was first known as the European War, but before the end of August 1914 publications were already advertising stories of 'the Great War'.

2. Usborne, Vice Admiral C.V., Blast & Counterblast, John Murray, 1935, p.25

3. Riddell, Lord, *War Diary 1914–1918*, Ivor Nicholson and Watson, 1933, p.31

4. Jellicoe of Scapa, Admiral of the Fleet Viscount, *The Grand Fleet, 1914–1916*, Cassell, 1919, p.3

5. ibid. p.4

6. Warrender and his fellow Vice Admiral, Lewis Bayly, even sent a cable to the Admiralty regretting the decision and asking for it to be reconsidered. 'It will be over by Christmas' was the view of most. 'And Sir George would surely last till then!' wrote Beatty's Flag Captain. (See Chatfield p.122.) Lord Kitchener knew better than most and required his volunteer army to enlist for three years or the duration of the war.

7. Corbett, Sir Julian, *Official History of the Great War, Naval Operations, Vol.I*, p.39 The Germans claimed, when trying to win American sympathy in *The Truth about Germany*, that the mines were laid in the mouth of the Thames, which seems stretching a point.

8. ibid. p.42. Since the cables on the sea floor were mostly manufactured and owned by British firms, and the Royal Navy patrolled the seas, cables were a very secure form of communication for the UK forces and government. The Navy used the cabled telegram, but since a ship had to put into port to receive her message, it was superseded by wireless.

9. The *Else* was auctioned and renamed *First Prize* by her purchasers before being requisitioned by the Admiralty for 'special services', as will be told.

10. Committee of the Dominions in Council, 29 May 1911.

11. Some Royal Navy captains did not believe that a submarine could range so far from home, although British submariners had travelled that far across the North Sea in the other direction, and in 1911 three of their C class submarines – less than half the size of the later D and E classes – had steamed to Gibraltar under their own power. (See Edwards, Lieutenant Commander Kenneth, *We Dive at Dawn*, Rich & Cowan, 1939, p.57)

12. Jellicoe, op. cit. p.31

13. Boyle, William H. D., Earl of Cork and Orrery, *My Naval Life 1886–1941*, Hutchinson, 1942, p.74, adding, 'This was all the more extraordinary because as far back as 1902 we had been experimenting with explosive charges and why this was discontinued I have never been able to find out.'

14. Bingham, Commander the Hon. Barry, *Falklands, Jutland and the Bight*, John Murray, 1919, p.39

15. Usborne, op. cit. p.53

16. PROCAT HW 7/1 p.116

17. The Edgars were named after the first ship of that class, launched in 1890. Of her sister ships in the Tenth Cruiser Squadron, the *Royal Arthur, Endymion, Hawke, Grafton, Theseus, Gibraltar* and *Crescent,* the latest was of 1892 vintage.

18. Bingham, op. cit. p.42

19. Chatterton, E. Keble, *The Big Blockade*, Hurst & Blackett, 1932, p.80

CHAPTER TWO

Cruisers on the Outer Seas

As soon as war was declared between the British and German Empires there had begun a brief and unique form of warfare at sea, well outside European waters. 'Commerce destroying' was a new name for an old game. What the French called 'guerre de course' had been practised through the centuries, and had been carried on continuously by both the French and British during the Napoleonic wars, even though for most of the time Britain enjoyed mastery of the seas when it came to fleet actions. Half a century later during the American Civil War the Confederate Navy's British built cruiser, *Alabama*, succeeded in burning or capturing sixty-four northern merchantmen (thereby nearly involving the United Kingdom in the war), even though the Unionist north had blockaded the ports of the south. The difference in 1914 was that this form of warfare was conducted for the first time by iron-clad steamships and according to the rules of international law recently codified at the Hague conferences. The purpose of the rules was to try to ensure that, if wars had to be fought among nations which considered themselves civilized, the destruction of enemy trade should be inflicted with the least harm to neutrals and the non-combatants of the opposing sides. For the first few months of the war, on the outer seas if nowhere else, both sides obeyed the unenforceable rules of international law in a way which subsequent generations, used to the ruthless, wholesale destruction of merchant shipping by submarines from the second year of the First World War and throughout the Second World War, can only view with amazement and respect.

Within two months around the world some 220 German and

Austrian merchant ships were rounded by British cruisers or detained in British ports. Most ships of the German or Austrian mercantile marine made for a neutral port and stayed there, as useless as if they had been interned. If enemy merchant ships were found at sea near any of the many ports of the British, French or Belgian empires, they were captured and, with a prize crew on board, taken in for the vessels and any contraband to be adjudged by a prize court. Contraband would be seized and the goods of neutrals forwarded to their destination in another ship. In the absence of a suitable Allied port, a German merchantman would be sunk but only after any crew or passengers had been taken off. By the end of 1914 nearly half the tonnage of the Central Powers lay immobilized in neutral ports, and almost a fifth was detained in British, Belgian, Russian or French ports or the Suez Canal, so that little more than a third was available for their trade. (But anyhow maritime trade was impossible for the Germans outside the Baltic and the north European coasts and the Austrians dared not venture out of the Adriatic.)

For a time the enemy could play this game too. Dotted around the oceans were twelve German cruisers of varying size, age and armament. All were of 1,000 tons or more, big enough to range the oceans, and all capable of at least sixteen knots, which was fast enough to overhaul most merchant vessels. A similar number of gunboats, largely in the Far East, were ready to attack river and coastal trade. But these were not all. Approximately sixty merchant ships, among them the three largest passenger liners in the world, could be converted into armed cruisers. When the war began, forty lay in foreign harbours and about twenty more in German ports. The Admiralty knew that preparations had been made to convert some of the fast liners into auxiliary cruisers, because there were sheds in German naval ports with the ships' names painted on them and guns and ammunition had been spotted lying inside. Also, when the huge 50,000 ton *Imperator* of the Hamburg-Amerika Line, docked in Southampton, it was noticed that she had had her decks strengthened for gun mountings. (RMS *Lusitania* and others followed suit, some purely for their own protection, others subsidized by the Admiralty for possible conversion to auxiliaries.) For destroying commerce an armed liner was as good as, and in some ways better than, a regular cruiser. The passenger liners were often as fast as warships, and had the space below decks for the provisions and coal needed for a long cruise, as well as accommodation for the crews and passengers of their victims, but they had the disadvantage of their huge fuel consumption. Besides these potential auxiliary cruisers there were many other vessels of the German merchant navy at sea, and those in time of war could be put to use as supply ships or colliers for the raiders.

The Germans hoped, and the British feared, that these eighty or more actual or potential warships would all be free to roam the seas, and cause havoc in the shipping lanes of the world, but in the event few of them, besides the cruisers already on station, posed any threat to the Allied merchantmen. The fast passenger and cargo liners in the ports of Germany were, with one exception, effectively blocked in. They dared not attempt the narrow Straits of Dover, and the northern exit from the North Sea was watched by the Grand Fleet. As for the ships which lay in foreign ports and might have been armed, these were one by one captured, blocked in, or sunk, mostly without striking a blow.[1] War had broken out so suddenly that the *Kaiserliche Marine* found that it could neither deliver guns to the stranded merchant ships, nor put trained naval crews on board. With the Royal Navy's early mobilization, there was not even an hour before the exits from the North Sea were completely blocked.

However, the cruisers of the Imperial German Navy which were outside their home waters when war started, constituted a menace which took some months to eradicate. While they were at large, their exploits, often conducted with quixotic generosity, were the stuff of boys' adventure novels. The captains of the German cruisers were playing a game of cat and mouse with a difference. While the hundreds of mice scattered around were easy to catch, there were a number of terriers loose and the trees in which the cats might find refuge (the German colonies) were being felled one by one. A resourceful commerce raider had a fair chance of evading capture for some time by making use of the vastness of the oceans and the short distance that any interfering British cruiser could see in those days before the invention of radar. However, to capture merchant ships, the raiders could not stray far from the main shipping lanes and their plans were dominated by the problem of refuelling.

There were indeed so many mice that the British Admiralty warned that some losses must be expected. A map of the world showing the volume and distribution of British trade just before the Great War would have dots for shipping deployed all over the tropical and temperate oceans in such profusion that an enemy cruiser at sea could hardly fail to capture one or more merchantmen before being hunted down. Surprisingly to modern eyes, the most congested concentration of traffic was not across the North Atlantic to the USA and Canada, dense though that was, nor across the Channel and North Sea to the continent of Europe. The richest pickings were en route to South America, down the Brazilian coast and on to Argentina. At any time there would be over 200 British ships in or off Buenos Aires and the Rivers Plate and Parana, in Montevideo and the River Paraguay, Rio and the ports and rivers of the east coast of Brazil, while another 120 would be at sea along the line between the Canary Islands and the Plate. True, there were almost as many British vessels in the ports of Canada, the US east coast and the Mexican Gulf, but the routes to them were more spread out.[2]

The general opinion both in the Royal Navy and the Merchant Navy was that the best protection for a merchant ship in time of war was the fact that a steam vessel could sail in whatever direction it pleased and was usually faster than its sailing predecessors. By keeping wide of the standard routes, and varying their course, ships could avoid the hazards of the few cruisers which the enemy would have at its disposal, much better than in a convoy. It was a comforting philosophy, and generally not wrong against surface raiders. In any event, when war loomed the Admiralty vetoed convoying, because they considered that it would take too many escorts. The Grand Fleet had first call on newly commissioned light cruisers, which were so essential for ocean convoys. (It was a different matter for troopships. They were always escorted. The loss of one troop transport would have been a disaster: the loss of a few freighters was a risk which had to be faced.)

So on 4 August 1914 the first of many instructions from the Admiralty was sent out to all the 265 Lloyd's agents and shipping Intelligence and Reporting officers throughout the world: 'Advise British shipping to steer course parallel to and from 30 to 150 miles distant from regular track. Endeavour to fill up sufficiently with coal to avoid bunkering on passage. Reduce brilliancy of lights. When obliged to pass through localities where traffic is most congested, endeavour to do so at night. Use neutral territorial waters where possible. Homeward bound vessels call for orders at any signal-station on South coast of Devon or Cornwall, or on South, North or West coasts of Ireland. Pass this secretly by visual to any British ships met with.'[3]

As the unescorted merchant ships spread out, on either side of the shipping lanes, their predators were forced to do the same, which had the further slight advantage of causing the raiders to steam further and use up more fuel. The repeated need of all steamships to find coal and repair boilers was a serious problem for the German raiders. Not for them the chain of colonies and bases around the globe, which the British enjoyed. Further, international law forbade a warship to return to port in a neutral country more than once in three months (unless unseaworthy), and neutrals strong enough to enforce it would do so. Normally a raider would have to refuel every few days: the period that his propulsion systems could go without attention depended largely on the quality of coal, but it could not be long. In Churchill's words, 'To steam at full speed or at high speed for any length of time on any quest was to use up his life rapidly. He was a cut flower in a vase; fair to see, yet bound to die, and to die very soon if the water was not constantly renewed.'[4] Part of Britain's huge exports of coal would sometimes find its way into the furnaces of the enemy via a captured collier, but for a raider to take the supply organized by German agents was hazardous. 'The extensive organisation of the Admiralty kept the closest watch in every port on every ton of coal and every likely collier. The purchase of coal and the movement of a collier were tell-tale traces which might well lay the pursuers on his track.'[5]

To capitalize on this problem of their enemy and to shut down his communication centres, the forces of the British and French Empires hastened to seize the German colonies and coaling stations and destroy or capture enemy wireless installations. The guiding principle was the defence of Allied maritime communications, but the effect was inevitably the conquest of territory.

The two West African colonies were immediately attacked from the adjoining British and French colonies. Lome, the capital of Togo, surrendered on 7 August, but it took three weeks' campaign to capture the wireless station at Kamina, which lay 100 miles inland through the forest. It was the key to the whole German communication system of the Atlantic, as radio messages from Nauen were picked up at Kamina and relayed to South America and all the ocean in between. Douala, the capital of Kamerun (Cameroon) was next to fall, and nine fine merchant ships and a gunboat were captured by HMS *Cumberland*.

As their wireless stations were closed down, the German raiders had to rely on relayed messages from friendly merchant ships and cables passed by the international network, but few neutral countries would allow cabled telegrams to be sent in code or let merchant ships transmit when in harbour. One of the first objectives of the British cruisers was to have the radio installations of German merchantmen silenced, if they were in some neutral port and so could not be captured as prizes. Sending information to warships was a warlike act, and neutral countries, fearful of reprisals from the belligerents, would take steps to prohibit illegal wireless signalling from inside their ports or territorial waters. The Portuguese and Spanish were even persuaded to dismantle the radio receivers of German ships in their harbours.

Nevertheless, cruisers of the *Kaiserliche Marine* got off to a good start. They were immediately alerted to the outbreak of war by radio, while their first victims, sailing under the prewar orders of their shipping companies, steamed on, blissfully unaware that hostilities had commenced. The first encounter took place on the moonlit evening of 5 August 1914 in the Gulf of Aden, when the SS *City of Winchester* got a rude surprise. The cruiser *Königsberg* approached, trained her guns on the merchant ship, and raised the signal for her to stop. Her papers were seized and, with four armed men on board, she was ordered to proceed in accordance with their instructions. Soon the *Königsberg* was joined by two German cargo liners, the *Zeiten* and *Ostmark*, and the *City of Winchester*, minus her charts and sailing directions, steamed on with them; all had their lights extinguished at night. Two days later the captors took the coal, food and water out of the British ship, and her master and most of the crew were transferred to the *Zeiten*. The rest went later into the *Königsberg*. Anything portable in the captured ship was dismantled and taken; then she was flooded. With three parting shots into her victim, the *Königsberg* steamed away. The *Zeiten* disguised her funnels to look like a British ship and hoisted the Red Ensign before sailing into port in Mozambique, where the British seamen were landed. The master of the *City of Winchester* reported that they were 'treated with every civility and respect by the Germans'.[6] That was the only capture made by the *Königsberg*, which, after surprising and sinking the light cruiser *Pegasus*, was blocked into the Rufigi river in German East Africa (today's Tanzania) and eventually scuttled.[7]

The greatest threat to British commerce was the Cruiser Squadron commanded by *Graf* von Spee in the Far East. It was to join this force that the *Dresden*, a light cruiser, slightly larger and faster than the *Königsberg*, but with the same main armament of ten 10-centimetre guns (4.1-inch), was steaming out of the Caribbean, when she met the SS *Drumcliffe*, also unaware that there was a war on. The British ship was on her way to Trinidad to refuel, and, unfortunately for the Germans, had no cargo. Worse than that, the master had his wife and child on board. This set *Kapitän* Lüdecke a problem. To comply with his naval prize code he must either put a prize crew on board and send the *Drumcliffe* into harbour – but there was nowhere at hand – or he could order the master to follow him. He was not permitted by the rules to sink her unless it was necessary for the safety of his own ship, which it clearly was not. The only alternative was to persuade the officers and crew to sign a declaration that they would not do any service in the British Navy or Army, nor would they give any assistance to the British government against Germany for the duration of the war, and then let them go. Fearing for his family, Captain Evans made the declaration and his crew followed his example. After dismantling her wireless, Lüdecke sent the *Drumcliffe* on her way.

In the course of her progress south, round Cape Horn and into the Pacific, the *Dresden* met eight more British steamers and a sailing ship. Three of the steamers and the sailing ship were sunk, four were dismissed and one escaped into the terrifying, then uncharted, straits between Tierra del Fuego and Chile. The *Dresden* wisely turned back to join von Spee at Easter Island.

Fortunately for British trade few ships of the German merchant marine were able to escape from foreign ports, and if not already armed, take on guns and engage in raiding. The armed merchantman, *Spreewald* got out into the Caribbean Sea and met up with a collier and a supply ship chartered for her, but on 12 September HMS *Berwick* found the three ships at their rendezvous and captured them all. Two days later the *Cap Trafalgar*, an 18,710 ton German liner, was sunk in the only battle between two converted passenger ships. She had come out of the River Plate and had met a gunboat, which transferred its 4.1-inch guns and pom-poms and its naval crew to her. However, the SS *Carmania*, a British converted liner of much the same size, caught her coaling and attacked with 4.7-inch guns. With the high sides and cabined superstructures of both ships, their gunners could hardly miss, and neither had armour plating. They shelled each other as the range decreased to two miles, at which distance even the *Cap Trafalgar*'s pom-poms could hit. The German liner was holed along the waterline and on fire, with a heavy list and her captain was killed. Eventually she sank and her crew were rescued by her colliers. The *Carmania* had suffered badly too and only just made port.

Only one armed merchant ship managed to escape from Germany and reach the Atlantic as the war started. She was the *Kaiser Wilhelm der Grosse*, a 14,349 ton liner, whose speed had won her the Blue Riband on her maiden voyage across the Atlantic in 1897. On 4 August before the British declaration of war, she sailed fast northwards, hugging the Norwegian coast, and when her captain felt secure from the British patrols, turned west and round the north of Iceland, sinking a trawler on the way. A week later she had worked her way south to the Canaries where she encountered bigger game, the *Galician*, a Union Castle passenger liner of 6,762 tons on her way home from South Africa. The raider was flying no colours. When she hoisted the German Navy ensign, the *Galician* hoisted the Red Ensign and was promptly warned, 'If you communicate by wireless, I will sink you'. The *Galician* was then required to circle round, with the cruiser behind her hoping to see some other prey, whose crew would have been transferred to the liner. Unfortunately for the German captain nothing turned up that day and so in the early hours next morning he sent the message: 'To Captain Day: I will not destroy your ship on account of the women and children on board – you are dismissed – good-bye'. Day replied: 'Most grateful thanks from passengers and crew – good-bye'. Beyond breaking up the radio apparatus and appropriating the British ship's supply of quinine, the raider and her crew had taken nothing. Passengers reported that German sailors had said, 'We do not want to fight; we have no grudge against your English ships'.[8] They wanted to buy some cigarettes, but this trading with the enemy was stamped on. However, as they could easily have been taken, Captain Day gave 300 cigars and 1,200 cigarettes, later reporting that the German officers were most courteous throughout.

A New Zealand cargo vessel was sunk and another, even larger liner was dismissed on account of having women and children on board. Then the *Kaiser Wilhelm der Grosse* turned south-east along the West African coast, where she caught and dynamited her last victim before being sunk by HMS *Highflyer* on 26 August. Called to give herself up, her captain replied curtly, 'German warships do not surrender'. In the unequal action which followed, the British prisoners were unharmed, because the German captain 'with the humanity which distinguished him throughout'[9] sent them on board a collier before the firing started.

These acts of restraint, even courtesy, shown by the seamen of two nations at war, were appreciated but in those early days of the war not considered remarkable. They were expected of the officers who had decisions to take within the guidelines of the prize codes issued to them by their Admiralties. The maritime laws of the nations may have differed slightly, but the prize codes of each required that the safety of passengers and crew should be paramount, and the captains of surface warships found no difficulty in complying.

As it was becoming clear that voyages were very infrequently interrupted by the enemy, confidence rose among British shippers. Premiums for War Risks insurance, which had been set on the day after war was declared at five per cent of the values insured, soon fell back to near their pre-war levels, though there were raiders still at large.

The German cruisers, which share the record for sinking the largest number of merchant ships in the first months of the war, were the *Emden* and the *Karlsruhe*. The tactics of *Fregattenkapitän* Erich Köhler in the *Karlsruhe* were simple, as he marauded on the Brazilian coast. His victims became his eyes and ears. An American on board one of the captured British ships recorded, 'The five merchant steamers (captured or otherwise) spread out, and scouring in zigzag, in touch by wireless with the *Karlsruhe*, formed a net impossible to evade, no matter what course we might have made. *Karlsruhe* has no intention of fighting; her mission is to destroy shipping. She can easily escape anything so far sent after her.'[10] In the centre of her web the raider quickly reached any vessel which her consorts had radioed were possible prey. Seeing the innocent merchant ship which was scouting for the *Karlsruhe*, the victim would be unaware that danger was over the horizon, and as soon as the cruiser was discernible as a warship, it was too late to flee. No chase would last more than half an hour before the German guns brought the quarry to a halt.

The great quantities of coal exported from Britain to South America meant that the raider had no difficulty in keeping herself supplied with fuel. Nearly 20,000 tons of coal were seized from colliers or other victims, and so, it seemed to her 500 bored prisoners, the game might have continued indefinitely. However, after they had been landed, the *Karlsruhe* accidentally met her end. On 4 November 300 miles from Barbados, while the band was playing to the crew, one of her torpedoes exploded, tearing away the fore part of the ship and killing the captain and 260 men. A month later the *Rio Negro*, which had been in attendance throughout the *Karlsruhe*'s escapade, evaded the North Sea blockade and brought the survivors home. Her demise was kept secret, and as a ghost ship the *Karlsruhe* occupied the attentions of Allied cruisers for some three more months, before news of her fate leaked out.[11]

A more real threat to Allied shipping was based on the northern coast of China opposite Korea. The Chinese had yielded to pressure in 1898 and granted Germany a ninety-nine-year lease of 400 square miles of the land behind the great bay of Kiaochow, (just as in the same year, for the same period and under similar pressure, they had granted the British a lease of the New Territories of Hong Kong.) In the wide bay the Germans had developed and defended the port at Tsingtau, furnished it with a floating dock and coaling station, and made it the base for their East Asiatic Cruiser Squadron under Vice Admiral Maximilian, *Graf* (Count) von Spee.

When war broke out von Spee was at sea. He knew that if he returned to Tsingtau he would be blocked in by the British and so, since the German Naval Staff, the *Admiralstab*, wisely gave him no detailed orders, he proceeded to gather his forces at the German colony of the Mariana Islands in the western Pacific. There his powerful cruisers, the *Scharnhorst* and the *Gneisenau*, were joined by the light cruisers, *Nürnberg* and *Emden*, and the armed merchant ship, *Prinz Eitel Friedrich*. Of the eight supply ships which were to have joined him four were captured or sunk by French or British cruisers before they could link up. Eight thousand tons of coal were in two of the captures, but German commercial agents were able to arrange for other supply ships to rendezvous with him. Two more light cruisers, the *Leipzig* and the *Dresden* were on their way from American waters to join him, but when all were assembled he could hardly expect to win a fleet action against any concentrated force of his opponents. Vice Admiral Sir Martin Jerram, commanding the China and East Indies Stations could muster two battleships, the *Triumph* and *Swiftsure*,[12] two armoured cruisers and four light cruisers. Two French cruisers and two older Russian ones were put under Jerram's command, and to the south lay the battle-cruiser *Australia* and the light cruisers *Melbourne* and *Sydney*, leading the Dominion forces. Then on 15 August the Japanese entered the ring. Using the same words with which the Germans had demanded Japanese withdrawal from Port Arthur in 1895, they gave the Reich an ultimatum to surrender Tsingtau, and on the 22nd they declared war.[13] *Graf* von Spee now had another powerful adversary to the north.

To avoid these forces the German Admiral set off across the Pacific. Coaling was a major factor in his decision. The Reich had no colonies or coaling stations in the Indian Ocean, as opposed to the Pacific, and he had been advised by Berlin that Chile was a friendly country. Germany had strong trading connections there and many agents, who could arrange fuel supplies. Meanwhile as he disappeared in the vast ocean, he would tie down a disproportionate number of Allied ships in the search for him. This might allow Germany's eastern trade to continue for a while, and would hamper the sailing of the Imperial troop convoys from Australia and New Zealand to Europe. Further, von Spee's ships could inflict damage along the way: the *Nürnberg* severed the telegraph cables on Fanning Island in mid Pacific, and the squadron bombarded the French colony of Tahiti.

As von Spee set off, the *Emden* was detached. At a conference aboard von Spee's flagship the forty-one-year-old captain of the *Emden*, Karl von Müller, had suggested that a light cruiser of the squadron should break away and harass the plentiful British shipping which plied the Indian Ocean. As he had the fastest ship and was an outstanding commander, von Müller was given the task. The world was to hear more of him.

Von Spee took two and a half months on his journey across the Pacific. While he was doing so the colonies and communication stations along his route were falling into the hands of his enemies. 'The outburst of Imperial enthusiasm in the self-governing Dominions', as the Official History expressed it,[14] led to the rapid mopping up of the numerous small German outposts in Oceania. German Samoa surrendered to New Zealand troops on 29 August, so that when von Spee's squadron made a detour there two weeks later, his presence was reported. The five German wireless stations in the Pacific had all been destroyed or occupied by mid-September and by the end of the month the German colony in north-west New Guinea had been captured by an Australian expeditionary force. The Japanese had been active too. They took possession of the Marshall, Caroline, Mariana and Palau Islands in October 1914. Finally Tsingtau, which had been blockaded for two months, fell to Japanese forces (with some British involvement) on 7 November. There were still many isolated islands where German warships could hide, but if von Spee wanted a base for coaling and communications, he would now have to capture one from his enemies.

On 12 October the German squadron, having crossed three quarters of the Pacific, halted at Easter Island, where it was joined by two light cruisers from the west coast of America. One was the *Dresden* and the other the *Leipzig*, under *Fregattenkapitän* Haun, who had claimed only two victims in the ten weeks since the war had begun.[15] Now *Graf* von Spee's squadron was complete, with the two heavy cruisers, three light cruisers and an armed merchant ship. A week later they sailed on towards Chile.

Meanwhile Rear Admiral Sir Christopher G.F.M. Cradock had come round from the Atlantic and was off the west coast of Chile in search of the *Dresden*. He flew his flag in the armoured cruiser *Good Hope* and was accompanied by another armoured cruiser, the *Monmouth*, the light cruiser *Glasgow* and an auxiliary, the *Otranto*. The pre-dreadnought battleship *Canopus* joined him and the cruiser, *Defence*, was promised, but did not arrive in time. Immediately Cradock heard that the German squadron had arrived off the west coast of Chile, he concentrated his ships and proceeded to intercept.

The five assorted British vessels stood to the north up the Chilean coast, but the *Canopus* could not keep up with the cruisers and so limped behind. Twelve hundred miles up the coast the *Glasgow* was sent into the coaling station of Coronel, south of Valparaiso, to pick up any cabled messages, and her presence was reported to von Spee.[16] The Germans passed all their signals through the *Leipzig*, and so when the British heard wireless signals from a German cruiser, they were led to believe that there was only one ship that far south. Cradock pressed north to engage without the *Canopus*. He was rash to do so. The unrestrained ardour, which had won him fame leading the land attack on the Taku forts during the Boxer Rebellion, served him ill now. His two armoured cruisers were older, slower and less well armed than von Spee's *Scharnhorst* and *Gneisenau*. The British had only 6-inch guns except for two 9.2-inch guns in the *Good Hope*. Against these the two main German ships had between them sixteen 8.2-inch guns firing salvos almost three times as heavy as the British 6-inch projectiles, and with a longer range. Slow though the *Canopus* was, brave 'Kit' Cradock needed her 12-inch guns.

When the two forces sighted each other at 16.40 on 1 November, it was a clear spring afternoon. Von Spee knew the *Monmouth* well – he had been friends with her previous captain[17] – and was confident of the superiority of his ships, knowing that his well-trained crews would give a good account of themselves. The *Scharnhorst* and *Gneisenau* had rivalled each other for first and second place in the Kaiser's prize for gunnery in 1913 and 1914, and the crews of the squadron had worked together for many months. (The crew of the *Monmouth*, on the other hand, were largely reservists and, to the shame of her captain, had only fired four practice rounds from their guns.) Von Spee was alert too. He quickly summed up where the advantage of the sunlight would lie and made a dash to put his ships between Cradock and the coast. This ensured that as the light faded his enemy would be silhouetted against the glow of the sunset, and his own ships would become increasingly difficult to see against the dark of the mountainous shoreline. But he did not want the action to start too soon, because the setting sun would be directly in the eyes of his gun-crews and spotters.

His stratagem was an outstanding success. It took less than an hour to decide the issue. The British fire soon became ragged as the crack German gun-crews struck home. An internal explosion soon silenced the *Good Hope* and at 19.57 she sank. The *Monmouth* struggled gamely on. The *Glasgow* had stood by her, suffering miraculously little damage at the hands of the *Leipzig* and *Dresden*, but the captain of the *Monmouth* gallantly refused an offer to be taken in tow, knowing that it would have sealed the light cruiser's fate to no avail. The *Glasgow* then made off to the west, patching up a hole in her stern with wood, and circled round

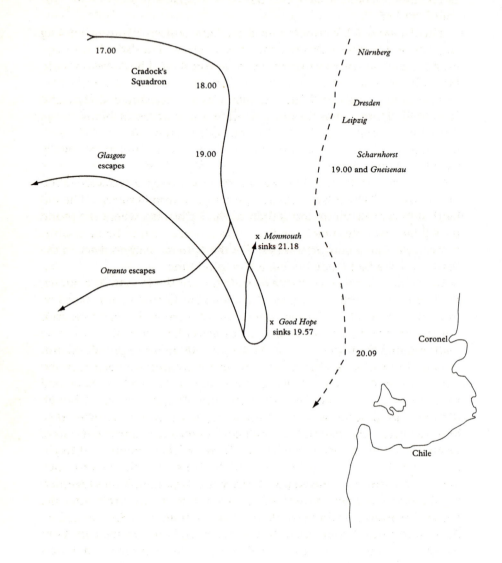

17.00

Cradock's
Squadron

18.00

Glasgow
escapes

19.00

Otranto escapes

x *Monmouth*
sinks 21.18

x *Good Hope*
sinks 19.57

Nürnberg

Dresden

Leipzig

Scharnhorst
19.00 and *Gneisenau*

20.09

Coronel

Chile

The Battle of Coronel
1 November 1914

36

as fast as she could to arrive at the Falkland Islands before von Spee could cut her off.

The *Monmouth* lay crippled until the light cruiser *Nürnberg*, coming late into the action, delivered the *coup de grâce*. The British ship was listing to port so severely that her guns were useless. The *Nürnberg* could fire with impunity. She ceased firing for a while to allow the *Monmouth* to surrender, but her White Ensign was never hauled down, and remained flying defiantly until another salvo at point-blank range caused her to capsize at 21.18. Not one of her crew survived. The seas were high, and the *Nürnberg*, seeing smoke on the horizon, immediately went off to investigate.

On the way back south the *Glasgow* met the *Canopus* and warned her of the disaster which had befallen the two armoured cruisers. The old battleship turned about and retired to the Falklands, where she found the *Otranto* waiting. Once the two cruisers were seen to be in trouble, it was clear that a converted liner, like the *Otranto*, had no place in the battle and she had made her escape in good time.

Why Cradock accepted battle on such unfavourable terms is a puzzle. Had he turned back as soon as he became aware that he was faced by four and perhaps five German ships, two of them with clearly superior armament, he might have avoided the catastrophe, before the oncoming night hid him from view. The *Canopus* was 300 miles to the south, but, steaming towards each other, the squadron could have been reunited before morning. The old battleship was not fast enough to catch and hold her foes, but the four 12-inch guns of the *Canopus* (though described as antiques with a maximum range which was actually three hundred yards less than the 8.2-inch guns of the German cruisers) were protected by up to twelve inches of Harvey-nickel armour and might have held them at bay. (Besides that she bristled with twelve 6-inch guns.) Von Spee recognized this. 'If they had kept their forces together, we should most likely have come off second best,' he wrote after the battle.[18] However, waiting would not have brought von Spee to action. Arthur Balfour, when unveiling a memorial to Cradock in York Minster, credited him with the belief that if he damaged von Spee's squadron at all in those distant waters, far from any German naval base, his sacrifice would not have been in vain. 'There never was a nobler act,' Balfour believed, 'unsuccessful though it was.'[19] But 'unsuccessful' is an understatement: the British lost 1,600 men; von Spee had three men wounded on the *Gneisenau*. Two shells hit the *Scharnhorst* but failed to explode. For all that, Cradock's sacrifice of men was not quite in vain. The fight had used up forty-three per cent of the irreplaceable ammunition for von Spee's 8.2-inch guns. At the end of another battle he would be left almost defenceless. The German admiral recognized this: 'I am quite homeless. I cannot reach Germany; we possess no other secure harbour; I must plough the seas of the world doing as much mischief as I can, till my ammunition is exhausted, or till a foe far superior in power succeeds in catching me.'[20] And a superior force was soon to be assembled.

Notes

1. Of forty-two ships of Albert Ballin's Hamburg-Amerika Line, which were out of their home ports when war was declared, only five returned; the rest, including the massive 50,000 ton *Vaterland*, rusted abroad.
2. The Panama Canal did not open until 16 August 1916.
3. Hurd, Sir Archibald, *Official History of the Great War – The Merchant Navy*, John Murray, 1921 Vol.I, p.214
4. Churchill, W.L.S., *The World Crisis 1911–1918*, Odhams Press, revised in two volumes, 1938, p.251
5. ibid. p.251
6. Hurd, op. cit. Vol.I, p.139
7. Von Lettow, who led the British on a four-year fruitless safari in East Africa, used the *Königsberg*'s guns.
8. Hurd, op. cit. pp.149–50
9. Corbett, op. cit. Vol.I, p.135
10. Hurd, op. cit. Vol.I, p.168
11. The fifteen ships sunk by the *Karlsruhe* totalled 72,805 tons, which was just more than the aggregate tonnage of the *Emden*'s sixteen victims, but the *Emden*'s other exploits and her gallant death ensured that she was better known.
12. But these two ships, originally built for the Chilean Navy, had only 10-inch guns.
13. The Japanese, who intended to turn China into a vassal state by their 'Twenty-one Demands', rushed to forestall the possible return of Tsingtau to the Chinese.
14. Corbett, op. cit. p.131
15. Bennet, Geoffrey, *Coronel and the Falklands*, Pan, 1967, p86. Haun was thought by the crew of the British sloop *Shearwater*, to have deliberately avoided her, because his men had made so many friends on the weaker British ship.
16. ibid. See Appendix II for an interesting review of the communication problems facing von Spee and Cradock in Chilean waters.

17. Two years previously, when there had been rumbles of war, the *Monmouth* had been in the Far East and had found herself blocked in by von Spee's squadron. The German Admiral sent a destroyer to find the *Monmouth* and warn his friend, 'I have had many scares before. But it would be well if you got out of the Gulf. I should be most sorry to have to sink you.' (See Copplestone, Bennet, *The Secret of the Navy*, John Murray, 1918, p.128)

18. Corbett, op. cit. Vol.I, p.355

19. ibid. p.356. Balfour became First Lord of the Admiralty in 1915 on Churchill's resignation.

20. Bennet, op. cit. p.115

CHAPTER THREE

Von Spee Meets Disaster

When the news of the disaster at Coronel reached London on 5 November 1914, the desk of the First Sea Lord had a new incumbent. Prince Louis Battenberg, a loyal, efficient and greatly respected officer, had resigned in October, writing to Winston Churchill, 'I have lately been driven to the painful conclusion that at this juncture my birth and parentage have the effect of impairing in some respects my usefulness on the Board of Admiralty'.[1] He had succumbed to the clamour arising from his German name. There was little else against him, but in the popular rooting out of all things Teutonic he became one of the many victims. To fill the void Churchill brought back his old mentor, Admiral of the Fleet 'Jackie' Fisher. At the venerable age of seventy-three Fisher, now a peer, was still capable of starting his day at five o'clock in the morning and working long hours.

For the Royal Navy to have lost two cruisers in a surface action was a humiliation which it had not had to endure for a hundred years. The truculent old admiral did not take long to decide what to do. He had found the solution eight years before. When Cuniberti had designed the first 'all-big-gun ship', he had argued, 'this squadron or division, however "invincible", will not be really and truly *supreme* if it cannot also catch hold of the enemy's tail.'[2] Fisher had therefore laid down at the same time as the *Dreadnought* three of another new type, the battle-cruisers, the first of which was confidently called HMS *Invincible*. These ships carried the same 12-inch guns, but only four turrets, and were of roughly the same length, beam and draught as the *Dreadnought*, but with 7-inch armour instead of 11-inch, which enabled them to carry more

40

boilers and engines with less displacement. Their turbines now delivered almost twice the horse-power (41,000 as opposed to 23,000). Consequently, while the *Dreadnought*'s nominal speed was twenty-one knots, the *Invincible*'s was twenty-five, and after shaking down she and her sister ships all exceeded twenty-eight knots. They could overhaul any battleship in the world, and crush any armoured cruisers marauding on the sea lanes. In a fleet action they could destroy any lesser scouting cruisers, and so keep the opposing admiral in the dark. More questionably, it was thought that they could engage and hold the enemy's capital ships, until the heavily armoured Dreadnoughts came up to destroy them. The downside for fleet purposes was their insufficient armour, and for trade protection was the enormous quantity of fuel they burnt. (When at speed, *Indomitable*, the fastest of the class, burned about 500 tons of coal a day as well as 120 tons of oil.)

Lord Fisher immediately ordered two battlecruisers, the *Invincible* and the *Inflexible* to Devonport, where they were given three days to have their bottoms scraped for maximum speed, take in six months' stores, coal ship and prepare themselves for the voyage. Speed and secrecy were essential. The officers were only told that they were going south and would need tropical kit. If the ships were not ready, the dockyard hands were to sail with them to complete the work. 'We stored and provisioned all day and most of the night,' one officer recalled, 'and finally coaled from 2 p.m. on one afternoon until noon of the following day. . . . At the end of it one and all were completely exhausted. Officers and men, begrimed all over from top to toe, unshaven, haggard, and weary, were staggering about like drunken flies.'[3]

Vice Admiral Sir Frederick Doveton Sturdee, the fifty-five-year-old Chief of Staff at the Admiralty, was summoned from his desk and put in command, largely because he was not, in Churchill's understatement 'a man with whom Lord Fisher could have worked satisfactorily'.[4] Vengeance was to be exacted. Not only was Britain humbled by the defeat at Coronel, but ill-tidings had been arriving regularly from the Indian Ocean where von Müller seemed to be as daring as his cruiser *Emden* was elusive.

The success of *Fregattenkapitän* Karl Friedrich Max von Müller was largely due to the surprise which he managed to maintain. In mid September shipping companies were beginning to report the late arrival of ships sailing from Calcutta. One or two delays might be put down to problems of mechanics or the elements, but more absent vessels would have needed a typhoon – or a hostile cruiser. If the latter, which could it be? The *Königsberg* was off the African coast and von Spee was in the middle of the Pacific. The *Emden* had been last heard of at Tsingtau where she had captured a Russian steamer, but as von Müller avoided the usual sea traffic routes, and was helped by several days of squally drizzle, he had found his chosen station in the Indian Ocean without being observed.

The raider was accompanied by the modern Hamburg-Amerika liner *Markomannia*, carrying 6,000 tons of coal and 1,000 tons of provisions. First he haunted the dense shipping lane along the east coast of India, and had sunk or captured seven ships in as many days, before the maritime authorities were aware of his presence in their midst. He captured the Greek ship *Prontoporus*, with a cargo of coal for Karachi, and kept her with him. Then the *Indus*, *Lovat*, *Killin*, *Diplomat* and *Trabboch* were caught and sunk. They had been completely unsuspecting, not troubling to extinguish their lights at night. Their masters, seeing a cruiser approaching with a merchantman steaming on either side, would think that it was a British warship with a couple of prizes. They were not alarmed until the German ensign was unfurled and a blank shot or a shell across the bows was accompanied by the order 'Do not use wireless. Stop at once'. If the victim attempted to send radio signals, he would be jammed. Thus no news of this new danger to British shipping escaped until a neutral vessel, the Italian *Loredano*, was approached and asked to take the *Emden*'s captives to safety. The master refused, saying that he had no room for them all and, when it was safe to do so, informed the authorities of the *Emden*'s presence.

The crews of the first victims were put aboard the *Markomannia*, but when the *Kabinga* was caught, and her crew were mustered, the boarding party discovered that the master had his wife and child on board. Von Müller decided that the sea was too rough for the woman and child to go across that night, and so the *Kabinga* was released, filled with the captives from all the ships, and told to steam to Calcutta. With typical thoughtfulness von Müller warned her captain to 'take care when approaching Sand Heads, as the lights are out'.[5]

One more ship was sunk and then von Müller, conscious that the Indian authorities would by now be sending warships to find him, turned back away from Calcutta. His journey south took him past Madras, where there were tempting oil tanks by the harbour. On the night of 22 September the *Emden* approached the city which had all its lights blazing as in peacetime. A dummy funnel, made out of canvas, had been rigged up to make the raider appear to be a typical four-funnelled British cruiser. Von Müller suddenly switched on searchlights and fired ranging shots at the oil tanks. Then the searchlights were switched off and a concentrated fire of 125 shells was aimed at the harbour and oil installations. The burning oil soon lit up the scene, and guns opened up ineffectively from the shore. The *Emden* turned round, her lights now burning so that she could be seen heading north-east back to Calcutta, but as soon as she was out of sight the ship was darkened again and she resumed her course towards Sri Lanka. Photographs of holed oil tanks of the Anglo-Persian Oil Company under billowing black smoke did nothing for British prestige in India.

Two days later von Müller was off Colombo and in the following four days he captured six more ships. Five were sunk and their crews put into the other. Eventually, she was released, the master saying in his report, 'I wish to say that I appreciate very much the courtesy shown to us by the officer in charge of the prize crew, and also the good behaviour of the men; they one and all performed their duties with every consideration for everyone on board'.[6]

What the *Emden*'s crew now wanted was 'good Cardiff coal' and newspapers, not just because they read the reports of their own activities with the avidity of stage performers, but because the papers gave details of the departures and arrivals of merchant shipping. They were lucky that the next ship to be stopped was the *Buresk*, a UK government collier sailing from south Wales to Hong Kong.

So far all the *Emden*'s exploits had been off the east or south-west coasts of India, and to maintain the surprise von Müller now headed her south into the middle of the Indian Ocean but nothing was found and his crew carried out firing practice, coaled ship, scrubbed down, painted and repaired where possible. When he turned back north and resumed raiding in mid October off the south-west coast of India, there had been an interval of over two weeks since the previous losses of merchant ships, and British consuls in Middle Eastern ports were not alerting shipping to any danger there. Consequently five vessels were soon sunk, three of them in one day. Another ship which was carrying American goods was sent on her way with more captives on board, and then the *Emden* turned east.

Von Müller then tried another bold stroke. If there were British cruisers about, the *Emden* would disguise herself like one of them again. The canvas funnel was erected and she steamed into Penang harbour, Malaya. The guard boat did not challenge her and she passed right up to the Russian light cruiser, *Zhemchug*. Von Müller raised the German ensign and at 380 yards loosed off a torpedo. It exploded by the engine room. As the *Emden* went past she raked the *Zhemchug* with gunfire. 'The surprise was complete and resistance hopeless.'[7] Two French destroyers and numerous merchant ships were caught equally unprepared, but von Müller ignored them, turned and fired another torpedo at the unlucky *Zhemchug* to make sure. 'A few seconds later there was a frightful report, and the Russian cruiser was literally torn into two parts. Huge pieces of metal flew about in the air and fell back noisily into the water. The spectacle only lasted for a few seconds, when a thick cloud of yellow smoke hid the scene of destruction, looking like a mountain spouting fire, with green and yellowish flames darting out from it, followed by detonations. It was a wonderful and awful spectacle.'[8]

As he steamed out of Penang von Müller met a munition ship, but he was distracted by another small French destroyer, the *Mousquet*, which bravely engaged him and was sunk too. The valiant French captain's legs were shot off, but he would not leave his post during the fight, and had himself lashed to the bridge. The *Emden* rescued thirty-six of the crew, and then, as another destroyer was approaching, made off to sea, and disappeared in a squall of rain.

Admiral Jerram had by now gathered his forces to seek out the raider. Off Sumatra HMS *Yarmouth* found and sank the *Markomannia* and recaptured the *Prontoporos*, which were both awaiting von Müller with supplies of coal. It was the first stroke of luck for the British. Captain Grant in the *Hampshire* had been less fortunate. Having searched in vain, he had followed a hunch and steamed south to Diego Garcia. There he learned that von Müller had left only five days before. On another occasion HMS *Hampshire* had been searching the creeks of an island while the *Emden* had been on the opposite side.

The German cruiser had now put 30,000 nautical miles behind her. Sooner or later her luck was bound to turn. On the night of 8 November 1914 she was approaching the Cocos-Keeling Islands, which lie in the middle of the seaway running from Fremantle, Western Australia to Colombo. Von Müller's purpose was to cut the oceanic telegraph cables and destroy the wireless station there. His position was unknown to any of the Allied forces searching for him, but, as it chanced, his own activities and the threat of von Spee's ships had delayed a troop convoy from Australia by three weeks, and the transports, escorted by the cruisers *Melbourne* and *Sydney*, were now approaching the islands at the very same time. The Australian ships kept wireless silence, and the Germans were totally unaware of their presence too. The *Emden*, sporting her false funnel again, and accompanied by the collier, *Buresk*, approached the islands at half past six in the morning, three hours ahead of the convoy. Von Müller landed forty men who began to demolish the station.

Jerram had guessed that the Cocos Islands might attract von Müller's attention, and had warned the staff of the telegraph station, giving them the call signs of all the Allied ships. And perhaps the *Emden*'s crew were getting overconfident. The dummy funnel had not looked quite right this time. As soon as she hove in sight, news of the approach of a strange cruiser had flashed out by radio and telegraph. When Captain Silver commanding the convoy in HMAS *Melbourne* received the signal, he did not know whether the warship was the *Emden* or the *Königsberg* or whether both were at hand, so he sent the *Sydney*, under Captain Glossop, to report back. If the signals ceased, Silver would know that the *Sydney* was in trouble and come to her aid. The wireless station on the island also kept on sending messages as the German sailors landed, and everyone knew what was afoot when they suddenly went silent.

A lookout on the *Emden* spotted the Australian cruiser approaching, and von Müller had to make a quick decision. Leaving his men on shore, he quit the harbour to attack what he soon recognized was a more powerful ship. The *Sydney*'s eight 6-inch guns would quickly account for the ten 4.1-inch guns of the *Emden*. What was more, the *Sydney* came fresh out of harbour and was fast, while the *Emden*, three months at sea, could not get the best out of her boilers. So the *Sydney* could choose her moment to fight at a range which would make her almost immune to the fire of her opponent. However, all was not lost for the Germans. Though the *Emden* had been sighted while the *Sydney* was 20,000 yards from her, Glossop continued to approach until the range was nearly halved, when he turned north to run parallel with the *Emden*. Both ships were broadside on within the extreme range of the 4.1-inch armament. Glossop, who had never fought before, had thrown away his advantage and was astonished to find von Müller opening fire with great accuracy. The *Emden*'s first salvo fell short, the second went over and the third hit. 'At the long range the *Emden*'s shells fall steeply – at an angle of thirty degrees – rarely burst and never ricochet from the sea. They whine overhead in torrents, plop into the sea on all sides, and now and then smash on board. One reaches the upper fore bridge, passes within a foot of (Gunnery) Lieutenant Rahilly's head, strikes the pedestal of the big range-finder, glances off without bursting, cuts off the leg of the operator who is sitting behind, and finishes its career overboard.'[9] Minutes later a shell struck the after control too. Both rangefinders were now out of action: Lieutenant Rahilly had to judge the distance by eye.

However, Glossop had learnt his lesson and, using his speed, opened the range. The *Sydney* had suffered ten hits in the first quarter of an hour. One entered an ammunition hoist and burning cordite might have destroyed the ship, if a seaman had not courageously thrown it aside, burning his arms severely. Another shell burst against her 2-inch armour, doing no damage. Then the danger passed. Rahilly had the range with his third salvo too, and the *Sydney*'s 6-inch shells, each weighing 100 pounds, were taking their toll. The *Emden* was on fire aft and amidships, her steering was gone and the men in her gun control killed. Most of the ammunition hoists had been shot away and the shells had to be laboriously brought up by hand. Some of the guns were being served by only one man. Finally, when his ship was holed below the waterline, von Müller made for Keeling Island and grounded her. She looked and was a shambles. 'Everything was lying tossed together; what was destructible destroyed, two funnels completely demolished, and the foremast thrown over the port side by a full hit, lying across the railing with its point in the water. . . . Everywhere lay the wounded and dead, and the groaning and cries of the former caught at one's heart.'[10]

Eventually nine out of the *Emden*'s ten guns were out of action. Still her captain would not lower the ensign in surrender. To the crew of the *Sydney* it seemed to be obstinacy or gallant, but foolish bravado. (According to the *Emden*'s Second Torpedo Officer, *Prinz* Franz Josef of the royal house of Hohenzollern, they had forgotten about the flag.) Glossop held off for a while, signalling to the wrecked ship by morse and flags of the international code, which were not understood. When no answer was received he came in to 4,000 yards and poured fire into the *Emden*. The German ensign came down at last, and a white flag went up. She had had 122 officers and men killed, nearly forty per cent of her crew, many losing their lives in those last minutes of hell. Over fifty more were wounded. The worst was on the quarterdeck, where fires had been burning and the deck itself was red-hot, so no one could approach the wounded. After the battle only bones were to be seen there; the rest had been burnt.

So ended the most famous German raider of all time. No ship in the First or Second World Wars achieved as much or won such universal respect as that little cruiser. Von Müller earned the admiration of his crew and the gratitude of his victims. His leadership was exemplified by the way in which his officers would give the best food to the men, who had the heavier work; his chivalrous conduct to the passengers and crew of his victims is proved by the three cheers for the *Emden* given by the 200 captives in the *Kabinga* as they sailed away. 'This unexpected ovation gave us great pleasure,' wrote *Prinz* Franz Josef.[11]

Meanwhile *Graf* von Spee had taken over a month slowly journeying

46

down the Chilean coast and round Cape Horn, while Admiral Sturdee had come south. The two battlecruisers, *Invincible* and *Inflexible*, had left Devonport on 10 November, so secretly that no wives and sweethearts, except Lady Sturdee and her daughter, had been on the jetty to wave them off. In spite of the urgency of their departure, however, Sturdee had progressed at a leisurely and economical ten knots, and his ships had made frequent use of wireless. Off the Brazilian coast he had been joined by three cruisers, the *Carnavon*, *Kent* and *Cornwall* and the light cruiser, *Bristol*, plus the two survivors from Coronel, the *Glasgow* and the armed liner *Otranto*. Now maintaining radio silence and steaming in line abreast ten miles apart, the eight ships had combed a path down the coast of South America, and had reached the Falklands on 7 December. It was most fortunate timing.

True to their traditions, the first thing the British ships did was to coal ship. Never was this discipline to bring a greater reward. In HMS *Bristol*, after a delay because some of the coal was too hot to be safely handled, they began again from a fresh collier next morning at 2.30 a.m. 'Naturally, the fact that it was daylight here at this time was not favourably commented on,' wrote Leading Signalman Buchan. 'We continued coaling, but the fates decided that we should not take in the amount we intended to. It became known about 8 a.m. that strange ships were in sight. Immediately hands ascended the mast in all ships as high as possible, and oh, joy! it was reported that German cruisers were in sight. Two closing the shore and three more coming up on the horizon. Raise steam for full speed (our fires were out by the way) was the next order, pack up coaling, prepare for sea at once.'[12]

Von Spee's leading ships, the *Gneisenau* and *Nürnberg*, came on and had trained their guns on the Falklands' wireless station, when a junior officer in the spotting-top of the *Gneisenau* reported that there were two battlecruisers and five other cruisers in the harbour. He was not believed, until his senior went aloft and confirmed it. Even then the ships were assumed to be Japanese. When the old *Canopus*, moored resting on the mud as a floating fortress, fired her 12-inch guns over the spit of land hiding her from view, the Germans turned sharply away, but as the projectiles fell short they came round again towards the entrance of the harbour. There they saw clouds of black smoke as several ships got up steam, and to their dismay and disbelief descried the tripod masts which could only be British battleships or battlecruisers. Soon Sturdee's squadron was out in hot pursuit of *Graf* Spee's ships, just visible above the horizon.

Chance favoured the British that day. It had been lucky that no inkling of the dispatch of the battlecruisers had filtered through to von Spee. In spite of the secrecy there must have been many people in Devonport aware of their destination. Not all were discreet. J.C. Silber, the busy German spy in the censor's office in London, had read that, 'A married woman had written to her relatives (in Canada) informing them that her husband employed by Vickers engineers was now busy day and night on the battle/armoured cruiser *Invincible*, and might have to go with the ship to the Falklands, if the repairs were not finished by the day the ship had to sail'.[13] Silber looked up the *Invincible* and compared its tonnage, speed and armament with *Graf* Spee's squadron. All became clear and he sent off the ill tidings to Germany by devious routes and also to the USA, but he had to use the mail and if his missives arrived, they were too late. News also got out as the great warships coaled at Ascension Island, but though this found its way into US papers and was known in Rio, the German agents did not pass it on.

Another piece of luck was the weather. As the action began it was one of those clear, calm summer days, which are so rare in the southern ocean, and there were several hours of daylight ahead of them. Sturdee ordered 'general chase'. The *Invincible* and the *Inflexible* led the way with the fast light cruiser *Glasgow*, all at reduced speed, while the *Kent*, *Cornwall* and *Carnavon* did their best to keep up. During the chase, the admiral signalled that the men could take a meal and clean themselves up after the coaling to avoid fighting while black from the coal dust. Then, not to lose the advantage of the fine weather, the battlecruisers pressed on ahead. In the early afternoon the straggling *Leipzig* came within range. Von Spee recognized that the only hope for his squadron to be of any use to the Fatherland was for the light cruisers to escape, while the *Scharnhorst*, flying the admiral's flag, and the *Gneisenau* engaged in a hopeless battle against their pursuers. Following his orders the *Dresden*, *Nürnberg* and *Leipzig* turned back towards South America.

The main battle began around 13.20. At first, to enable the British battlecruisers to take advantage of the range of their guns, Sturdee kept the distance to about 14,000 yards. However, whether from the long range, or because the smoke of their own ships blowing towards the enemy impeded the spotters, few hits were recorded in the first hour of the struggle. The main armament of both the *Scharnhorst* and the *Gneisenau* concentrated on *Invincible* and had obtained hits from the third salvo.[14] But Sturdee was keeping his distance like a boxer with the longer reach, until von Spee tried to come in close to make use of the one advantage which his ships had, their secondary armament. The Germans had six 15-cm guns (5.9-inch), to which the British, if their

48

main armament were ever knocked out, could only reply with 4-inch. To get in range with their secondary guns von Spee had to close to 12,500 yards or less. Sturdee allowed the distance to shorten, but never less than the extreme range of the 5.9-inch guns, where they were ineffective. After erratic shooting at the start, the 12-inch guns of the battlecruisers found their mark. Hits on the distant enemy ships were shown by a little red glow or a cloud of yellow smoke from the lyddite high explosive. After ten minutes of this hot action the *Gneisenau* began to list and the *Scharnhorst* was on fire. The flagship was the first to go. Her upper deck became a twisted mass of metal, while the dull red glow of flames could be seen below. She kept on firing, but at 16.00 she had the attention of both battlecruisers and 'suddenly shut up as when a light is blown out'.[15] Like the *Monmouth* five weeks before, the *Scharnhorst* turned on her side and disappeared beneath the waves; like the *Monmouth* too, she went down with her flag still flying, and as with the *Monmouth*, not a soul was saved.

The *Invincible* and *Inflexible* steamed straight on in pursuit of the *Gneisenau*, which now had to contend with two battlecruisers, either of which could have destroyed her easily. By then the armoured cruiser, *Carnavon*, had caught up and joined in. Courageously the German cruiser fought on. At 17.30 she was scarcely moving. Two funnels had gone and fires were blazing in several places. Finally all her 8.2-inch ammunition (depleted by Coronel) was exhausted. 'Some 600 of her men had been killed or wounded, she could no longer fire a gun, but even so there had been no thought of surrender.'[16] She, too, heeled over onto her beam ends and men were seen walking on her side plates. At 18.00 she slipped below. Great efforts were made to rescue the crew, but only 200 were plucked from the icy water and many of them died from exposure.

The British on the other hand had not lost a single life in the battle between the big ships; in that the Falklands battle had been the reverse of Coronel. Twenty-two shells from the two heavy German cruisers had struck the *Invincible*, but amazingly the only casualty was the Commander with an ankle wound. The *Inflexible* had but a few scratches and the *Carnavon* had none. Sturdee was to incur some criticism for the large amount of ammunition which had been expended, but he was able to bring his capital ships back home in good order, and later engagements were to make senior naval officers understand the great difficulty of obtaining hits in war conditions at the enormous ranges at which the big ships fought.

When at 13.20 von Spee had ordered his three light cruisers to escape,

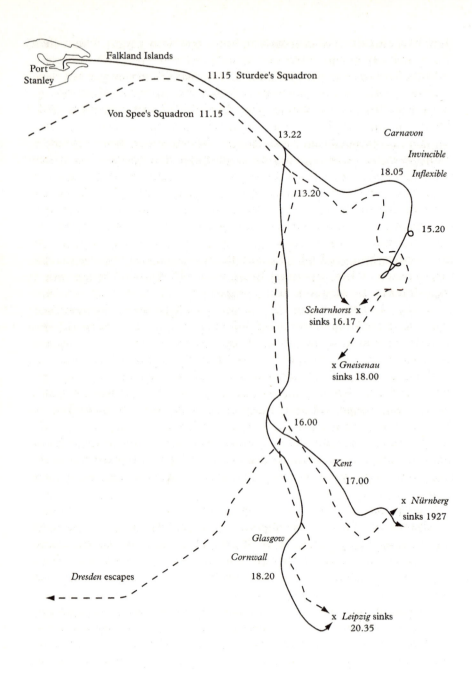

Falkland Islands

Port
Stanley

11.15 Sturdee's Squadron

Von Spee's Squadron 11.15

13.22

Carnavon

Invincible

18.05 Inflexible

/13.20

15.20

Scharnhorst x
sinks 16.17

x Gneisenau
sinks 18.00

16.00

Kent

17.00

x Nürnberg
sinks 1927

Glasgow

Cornwall

Dresden escapes

18.20

x Leipzig sinks
20.35

Battle of the Falkland Islands
8 December 1914

they had all turned south, making for Tierra del Fuego where they hoped to be able to hide and find coal. Sturdee detached the armoured cruisers *Kent* and *Cornwall* and the light cruiser *Glasgow* in pursuit. The *Glasgow*, being the fastest, caught up with the *Leipzig* and opened fire at 14.50 in the hope of delaying her until the heavier cruisers arrived. This running fight lasted for nearly an hour and a half before the *Cornwall* came up, firing ranging shots for some twenty-five minutes until she was close enough to turn to starboard and give the *Leipzig* her whole broadside of nine 6-inch guns. This turn, while the *Leipzig* continued her straight flight, opened the range again and *Cornwall*'s Captain Ellerton had to turn head on again to catch up. So the battle continued for two more hours – with the *Cornwall* turning to fire broadsides and turning back again – until the *Leipzig* was ablaze. By 19.30 the German had fired off all her ammunition and as a desperate last throw loosed off her torpedoes. None reached the mark. Captain Haun then ordered the seacocks to be opened and called the men onto the forecastle. 'Everywhere lay heaps of ruins with bodies of the dead and dying upon them,' his navigating officer later said. 'The bearing of the men was splendid; several of the dying asked whether the flag was still flying and were comforted by the assurance that it would be kept flying till the ship sank.'[17] The Captain spoke briefly to the survivors, and then they cheered the Kaiser and sang the *Song of the Flag*. Tragically, while the German ensign still flew, Ellerton could not risk the possibility of further action by the crippled ship and fired another salvo which inflicted terrible slaughter among the men on deck. Captain Luce in the *Glasgow* came up to save life but only seven officers and eleven men were rescued from the water. Haun went down with the *Leipzig*, her flag still flying.

The *Glasgow* had suffered damage to one of her boilers, and so had no chance of catching the *Dresden*, especially as drizzle was now reducing visibility. That, so far as Sturdee knew, left two of the German light cruisers at large, for the *Kent* had not replied to his signals. As it turned out, signalling was the one thing that the *Kent* could not do. Her radio had been hit as she chased the *Nürnberg*, but she had otherwise got off lightly. Her pursuit of the faster German light cruiser was to become one of the navy's oft-told stories. The *Kent*, completed in 1903, was five years older than the *Nürnberg* and had a nominal speed of twenty-two and a half knots, one knot less than her opponent. On many occasions during the war that one knot difference made it impossible to catch an escaping quarry. However, on this day the *Kent*'s engine room hands achieved the impossible. 'All available wood, such as accommodation ladders, hen coops, wooden lockers, capstan bars, etc., was broken up and passed down into the stokeholds to be used in the furnaces,'[18] Captain Allen reported, adding, 'The stokers responded magnificently'. Or as he put it more racily to his friend Commander the Hon. Barry Bingham, 'We sat on the safety valves and forced the boilers fit to bust'.[19]

In the *Nürnberg* two of her boilers did indeed burst from the exceptional and prolonged pressure. She could now manage only nineteen knots and opened fire while she was being gradually overhauled. Her 4.1-inch guns had a greater range than the *Kent*'s old 6-inch armament at their maximum elevation, and for ten minutes accurate salvos fell all around the British cruiser. Sometimes a shell would hit but as the range closed, the *Kent* scored. Her shooting was good too, and the end was inevitable as the distance fell to 4,000 yards. Both ships were firing as fast as the guns could be loaded. 'We could see the shells bursting all over the *Nürnberg*, and we could see that she was on fire,' Captain Allen reported. 'There was a tremendous noise, guns firing and shell bursting, with a continuous crash of broken glass, splinters flying, things falling down, etc. It was hard to understand how the *Nürnberg* could survive it so long . . . At 6.10 she turned towards us, steaming very slowly, and we crossed her bow, raking her with all our starboard guns as she came end on.'[20] Two 6-inch shells destroyed her forecastle guns and twenty-five minutes later she ceased firing altogether, but, as with the *Leipzig*, her ensign was still flying. The *Kent* closed and fired another broadside. Minutes later the flag came down and the *Nürnberg* was obviously sinking. It was then a race to save lives.

All the *Kent*'s boats had been damaged by shellfire and for twenty minutes while the two viable ones were being repaired nothing could be done. When at last the boats were lowered, most of the Germans were too exhausted to hang onto a rope. British sailors shouted encouragement and some went down over the ship's side to tie ropes round them, but few could be rescued from the freezing water. 'Search for survivors was kept up till 9.0, when it was quite dark,' the Official History records. 'A few men were found floating lashed to hammocks, but many of these were dead from cold, and albatrosses were attacking even the living. In the end only seven men were saved alive.'[21] These made a total of twenty-five survivors from the 580 crew of the two light cruisers.

Though the *Kent* had received thirty-eight hits, only four men were killed and twelve wounded, and the damage to the ship was slight. Such was the advantage of her armour. Nonetheless she was lucky to escape destruction. One shell had struck a gunport and the flash from its explosion ignited charges in the casemate, sending a flame down the hoist into the ammunition passage. She would almost certainly have blown up, had not Sergeant Charles Mayes RMLI[22] quickly thrown away the charge at the bottom of the hoist and flooded the compartment.

Early in the day two ladies in Port Darwin had telephoned to say that three merchant vessels were following behind von Spee's warships. Two of these (which turned out to be colliers rather than troop transports) were sunk after the crews had been taken off. The other escaped south among the icebergs.

Sturdee had avenged the defeat at Coronel. He could justly, if immodestly, say to his officers, 'Well, gentlemen, that was one of the most decisive actions you will ever experience'.[23] Though Lord Fisher blamed 'that ass Sturdee' for not bagging all five cruisers, he returned to a hero's welcome. The Germans saw *Graf* Spee as a hero too. Twenty years after his death the renascent *Kriegsmarine* named one of its finest pocket battleships after him. It was a posthumous reward for his victory, but was he not a failure overall? That may seem a harsh judgement on a man as courageous as he was courteous, quick thinking, yet cool in battle, who succumbed to overwhelming odds. Nonetheless his mission was one of the wasted opportunities of the German Navy. His mandate was to destroy Allied commerce wherever he could find it, but what had his powerful squadron (the *Emden* excepted) achieved? He sank two British warships, but the propaganda effect of his victory was soon overshadowed by his own disastrous defeat. While von Spee kept the East Asiatic Squadron together they destroyed only one enemy merchantman, a sailing vessel.

Why did he do it? Had he forgotten the teaching of the American master, Admiral Mahan, the German Navy's bible? Writing about 'commerce destroying', Mahan had declared, 'This operation of war, being directed against peaceful merchant vessels which are usually defenceless, calls for ships of small military force'. He contrasted it with regular fleet actions. 'The essence of the one is concentration of effort, whereas for commerce destroying diffusion of effort is the rule. Commerce destroyers scatter that they may see and seize more prey.'[24] From this point of view the reputation of von Spee's squadron was redeemed only by the exploits of one light cruiser under the enterprising von Müller.

In defence of the German Admiral, he had been warned that, because of the British patrols, cruiser warfare in the Atlantic could only be carried on by ships operating in groups, and had been advised to try and break through with all his ships and return home. He had received advice from Berlin, not an order, and so he held a conference, to decide whether to attack merchant shipping off the Plate, to dash for home via the centre of the Atlantic or to capture the Falkland Islands. Von Spee decided to draw the remnant of Cradock's squadron out from the Falklands and destroy them, and then occupy the islands, destroying the W/T equipment. A landing party had already been detailed off.[25] This had the advantages that the moral effect of military action would be greater than the sinking of merchantmen, and the loss of the only British coaling station in the South Atlantic would cripple squadrons searching for him.

There may, however, be another fascinating explanation for *Graf* von Spee's actions – that he was following specific orders – but those orders emanated, not from the *Admiralstab*, but from Captain Reginald Hall, RN, the Director of the Naval Intelligence Division in London. This most powerful of spy masters, known as 'Blinker' Hall from his fluttering eyelids, had, so the story goes, an agent in Berlin who had obtained or copied the forms and stamps which were used to send telegrams from the *Admiralstab*. Hall, already possessing the appropriate German code, composed a message which was sent by his agent to von Spee. This instructed him 'to leave immediately for the Falkland Islands and destroy the wireless station at Port Stanley'. So in due course he kept the fatal appointment with Admiral Sturdee and the British battle-cruisers. The only source for this tale of intrigue is the memoirs of the German agent, Franz von Rintelen. No evidence of the telegram remains, because, according to Rintelen's account, it was addressed to 'The Admiral Commanding Squadron – Personal', and was lost with von Spee and his ship.[26]

Whatever the cause of von Spee's actions, the Battle of the Falkland Islands was the Royal Navy's most conclusive victory of the whole war. The destruction of the East Asiatic Squadron had at a stroke virtually cleared German warships from the outer seas. Except for their losses at Coronel, it had been a good month for the British. On 8 November the gunboat *Geier* had been interned by US authorities in Honolulu, as the auxiliary cruiser, *Cormoran*, had been at Guam. (Neither had succeeded in capturing any vessels.) On the 9th the *Emden* had been destroyed and the next day the *Königsberg* had been blocked in the Rufigi River. Nothing more was to be heard from the *Karlsruhe*. That left only the *Dresden*, the *Prinz Eitel* and the *Kronprinz Wilhelm*. These were widely scattered and attended by little success, though it was another three months before any of them was put out of action.

The *Dresden* was the first to go. She had only one more victim after the Falklands, but she performed a service by disappearing for three months among the islets and inlets of the south Chilean coast. Watching out for her were no less than eight cruisers, including for a short while the battlecruisers *Inflexible* and *Australia*. As she did not appear off the Argentine coast, it was guessed, correctly, that she was hiding in the Straits of Magellan or the islands, rocks and treacherous channels of the south Chilean coast, and it was left to the *Glasgow* and *Kent* and an armed liner to trawl through these dangerous waters. Eventually she was discovered, chased until she had nearly exhausted her coal and found again on 14 March 1915 in the neutral harbour of Juan Fernandez, Robinson Crusoe's island. When the German warship had overstayed her legal time in Chilean waters, the *Kent* and *Glasgow* were ordered to open fire.[27] Two minutes later the *Dresden*'s flag came down. A boat came out to parley, but the German sailors had already been sent ashore and shortly afterwards Captain Lüdecke blew up his ship.

The auxiliary cruiser *Prinz Eitel Friedrich* had left von Spee's squadron just before the Falklands battle. By March 1915 she had been cruising for seven months and had sunk five vessels. But she now had to put into Newport News for repairs. When it was discovered that she needed completely new boilers, that no relief was coming from any other German cruisers and no support from the US, her Captain delivered the ship and the crew for internment.

During March only two ships were destroyed by German cruisers, both by the converted liner, *Kronprinz Wilhelm*, roaming the eastern coast of South America. After seven months at large she had sunk nine vessels and released one, a slow rate of destruction, but more than any other auxiliary cruiser had achieved until then. This last of the original corsairs was given up to internment in the USA on 25 April.[28]

There were to be no more victims of surface raiders until 1916. It had been an extraordinary episode of naval history, conducted in such a gentlemanly manner, that at times it seemed more like a romantic film than warfare. Some sixty-three merchant vessels had been sunk; another thirteen had been captured but released. Not a single life had been lost among the crews and passengers of the victims. But nothing had come of the great threat which the British had expected. For years, the *Times History* noted, 'we had been told of the elaborate preparations in progress by Germany for preying upon our commerce, more especially by means of fast merchant vessels converted into warships: and it had come to be regarded as at least a possibility that, in the event of war, we should immediately be plunged into a condition of semi-famine, with prices rising to a figure prohibitive except to the wealthy'.[29]

Now the outer oceans were clear. Trade and troops could pass throughout the scattered empires of Britain, France and Belgium without fear of molestation. Tirpitz had been proved right, when he wrote that commerce raiding was 'so hopeless because of the shortage of bases on our side and the great number on England's side, that we must ignore this type of war against England in our plans for the constitution of our fleet'.[30] Germany had lost the freedom of the seas for the duration of the war, and the British were to exploit their control of the surface of the oceans with an increasingly severe blockade, forcing their enemy to rely on weapons deployed under the waves.

Notes

1. Churchill, op. cit. p.359
2. Jane, op. cit. p.142
3. Bingham, op. cit. p.48
4. Churchill, op. cit. p.362. In fact Fisher exploded to Churchill that he would not have that 'd—d fool as Chief of Staff' a day longer. Sturdee had long ago angered Fisher by refusing to report on the doings of his chief, Lord Charles Beresford, when the latter was C.-in-C. in the Mediterranean. (See Bennet, op. cit. p126)
5. Hurd, op. cit. Vol. I, p.192
6. ibid. p.196
7. Corbett, op. cit. Vol.I, p.337
8. Hohenzollern, Prinz Franz Josef of, *Emden*, Herbert Jenkins, 1928, p.177
9. Copplestone, op. cit. p.180
10. Hohenzollern, op. cit. p.214
11. ibid. p.87
12. Buchan, W., *The Log of HMS Bristol*, The Westminster Press, 1916, p.79
13. Silber, J.C., *The Invisible Weapons*, Hutchinson & Co., 1932, p.49
14. The German 8.2-inch guns were capable of firing 16,500 yards, but at that range the shells fell almost perpendicularly. The battlecruisers' guns had a higher muzzle velocity, and the shells had a flatter trajectory, giving a greater 'danger space'.
15. Corbett, op. cit. Vol.I, p.423

16. ibid. p.425

17. Bennet, op. cit. p.160. Survivors said there was an order that no ship should haul down her colours.

18. Bennet, op. cit. p.163

19. Bingham, op. cit. p.79

20. Chatterton, E. Keble, *Gallant Gentlemen*, Hurst & Blackett, 1931, p.113

21. Corbett, op. cit. p.428

22. The Royal Marine Light Infantry and the Royal Marine Artillery merged in 1920.

23. Bennet, op. cit. p.154

24. Mahan, op. cit. p.31

25. According to a chief stoker and a writer from the *Gneisenau*; see Report of Vice Admiral Sir F.C.D.Sturdee on the 'Action off the Falkland Islands'. (PRO ADM 186/566, p.58) Accounts of the conference differ. Some say only von Spee, and two other officers wanted to attack the Falklands. However, two officers from the *Gneisenau* at dinner in the *Carnavon* informed their hosts that 'Vice Admiral Graf von Spee did not wish to approach the Falkland Islands, but was persuaded to do so by his staff officers and the Captain of the *Gneisenau*'. According to them, his original plan was for his ships to have scattered and stopped all enemy trade in the Atlantic, and they considered that 'if they did so for a fortnight – which they thought they could do – they would have done their duty'. (PRO ADM 186/566)

26. See Rintelen, Captain von, *The Dark Invader*, Lovatt Dickson, 1933, pp. 209–12. You would have thought that, if this triumph of naval intelligence were true, it would be mentioned in Admiral James' revealing biography of Hall, *The Eyes of the Navy* or in Geoffrey Bennet's *Coronel and the Falklands*. The author's researches in the Public Record Office and the Naval Historical Library have so far revealed nothing to corroborate it. Von Rintelen described how after his arrest, Hall and his private secretary, Lord Herschell, unbuttoned themselves while dining with him at a London Club. There are inaccuracies in von Rintelen's book, and it is incredible that such a circumspect old hand as Reginald Hall would have spilt the beans in this way to a notorious German agent, who might, and indeed did for a while, escape. On the other hand it is an extraordinary story for von Rintelen to invent. After the war he became a firm friend of Hall, so it is possible that he was told of the entrapment later, but, using artist's licence, he slipped it into the period covered by his book.

27. An agent of British naval intelligence in Chile relayed an enemy

cipher message, which when decrypted at the Admiralty revealed the *Dresden*'s next rendezvous with a collier. The Admiralty sent back, 'You sink the *Dresden*, and we shall attend to the diplomatic side'. (Rintelen, op. cit. p.99)

28. The decision may have been influenced by the appearance off New York the day before of a liner disguised as the battlecruiser *Queen Mary*. If so, it was the only action of any importance by a 'dummy dreadnought'. Compare the bluff of the cruisers off Montevideo persuading the pocket-battleship *Graf Spee* to scuttle herself, twenty-five years later.

29. *The Times History of the War*, Vol.II p.27

30. Memorandum of June 1897.

CHAPTER FOUR

Mines!

In its attempts to strangle British trade during the first months of the war the German Navy evinced a split personality. While its cruisers were conducting a campaign on the seven seas with punctilious regard for the Hague Conventions and the sanctity of human life, minelayers in the North Sea and the Channel were depositing their deadly cargoes in waters where they inevitably took a toll of civilian lives from belligerent and neutral nations alike. And as the courteous Dr Jekylls were removed from the surface of the seas, the brutal Mr Hydes increased the threat below.

In the light of subsequent events it is perhaps surprising that in home waters it was only mines, anchored or floating, which worried the British Department of Trade during 1914. Few thought that a submarine, let alone its torpedoes, would be used for the destruction of freighters. A commission, reporting a decade before the war on the best methods of protecting merchant shipping in wartime, paid no attention at all to the submarine; it was then an untried weapon. Anyhow, such a tiny vessel could not possibly be used against merchant ships without a gross breach of the Hague convention. 'It is hardly too much to say,' wrote Archibald Hurd, the official historian of the merchant navy, 'that before the outbreak of war no naval officer, whatever his nationality, seriously contemplated the possibility of vessels being used for attacking ocean-going commerce which could not supply prize crews or make provision, in case the prize was destroyed, for the safety of the crew as well as passengers, if passengers were carried'.[1] At that time the *Admiralstab* would have agreed. The swift march of their armies gave hope that, after the fall of France they would have the French fleet (and perhaps Russian ships later) to join the *Kaiserliche Marine* in a blockade of the United Kingdom, if it continued to fight, but until then they relied exclusively on mines to disrupt trade. On 23 August Tirpitz and Admiral von Müller, head of the Naval Cabinet, discussed 'preparations for air and mine warfare against England'[2] to be begun as soon as the German army had reached the Channel. However, the swift loss of the *Königin Luise* on the first day of the war indicated that minelayers might not be able to escape the Royal Navy's patrols. How then could they lay them?

In the third week of the war German light cruisers patrolling towards the Dogger Bank came across a fishing fleet and sank eight of the vessels. The German ships returned home without being intercepted, taking the crews of the fishing craft back as prisoners. Emboldened by this reconnaissance, they ventured further from their bases a couple of days later. This time the light cruisers *Mainz* and *Stuttgart* carried mines and were accompanied by a purpose-built minelayer, the *Albatross*. The mines were laid thirty miles off the entrances to the Humber and the Tyne. In the middle of the North Sea the Germans again met up with fishing vessels, sinking a further sixteen, but made port without being spotted by the Royal Navy. Almost at once the mine fields made their presence felt, a Danish trawler being blown up off the Tyne and a British fishing vessel catching a mine in its nets off the Humber. Two more neutral vessels and two minesweepers were lost before the extent of the minefields was ascertained. They were then marked and left in place as a protection against German raids on the coast.

The Navy quickly geared up to deal with mines, thanks largely to Admiral Lord Charles Beresford, the great enemy of 'Jackie' Fisher. Always abreast of technical developments, Fisher had recognized the danger of mines to his warships, but it was Lord Charles who took the first practical steps towards creating a defence against them. Germany was known to be building minelayers and manufacturing thousands of mines, and Beresford foresaw that an enemy might lay mines to block the fleet in harbour. What craft could he use to clear them? He had tried tugs and destroyers, and neither were suitable for sweeping mines, but when Beresford talked to some of the men who manned the hundreds of fishing trawlers gathered at Grimsby, he realized that he had found the vessels and crews for the job. The fisherman's trawl ropes were like minesweeping gear and the boats were fitted with steam winches to haul them in. The men spent their lives casting their nets in fair weather and foul, and dragging the trawls, a task needing seamanship, endurance and a good skipper too, if their nets were not to be caught in their propellers.

What was more, the supply of fishing vessels seemed inexhaustible. From the end of the eighteenth century, when Grimsby had been a small haven with 1,000 inhabitants, it had grown to be the largest fishing port in the world with a population of 75,000. An enormous fleet of steam trawlers was registered there, replacing the previous 900 sailing trawlers. English fishing fleets also sailed from Hull, Scarborough, Whitby, Boston, Ramsgate, Yarmouth and Lowestoft, wherever there was a harbour. On the south coast, Brixham and Falmouth flourished; Wales had its fishing ports too, and all along the Scottish coasts there were more major bases. As the war began there were nearly 1,000 steam drifters assembled in Scottish waters for the herring fishing. The trawlers dragged a huge trawl net, scooping up every sort of fish, while the drifter, specially built for the herring fishery, 'shot her nets and then rode, or drifted with them, at the will of wind or tide'.[3] To cater for these fleets there were shipyards along the length of the east coast. A modern yard would have accommodation for a score of trawlers or drifters and Aberdeen might have a dozen trawlers on the stocks being built. Even inland Selby in Yorkshire built fishing craft, launching them sideways into the river.

A small minesweeping force was started well before the war. Sir Arthur Wilson, who succeeded Fisher as First Sea Lord in January 1910, carried on the work. He realized that 'the really serious danger that this country has to guard against in war is not invasion, but interruption of our trade and the destruction of our merchant shipping'.[4] A special Trawler Section of the Royal Naval Reserve was formed and trained. The men took to it easily. They were used to working to a system and under discipline, each fishing fleet having an admiral and vice admiral in control. The Section expanded, so that at the outbreak of war there were eighty-two trawlers and over a thousand skippers and men on the Admiralty list. A month later another 250 fishing boats, steam yachts, paddle steamers, motor launches and other craft had been pressed into service. Still it was only a beginning. By the end of the war the number of these vessels flying the White Ensign would rise to 4,000 and the hands serving in them to nearly 50,000. So, under the aegis of the Royal Navy 'a fortuitous and unorganised assemblage of shipping, with crews undisciplined to the demands of war, developed into what was in effect a supplementary navy'.[5]

On the outbreak of war the crews of the Trawler Reserve came into port, landed their fish, and were provided with minesweeping gear, a month's consumable stores, rifles and ammunition, charts, morse lamps, naval clothes and a week's pay. Next day they set out on their minesweeping assignments, 'one of the most dangerous occupations which, in the whole history of marine warfare, has ever been devised by the wit of man'.[6]

From the autumn of 1914 six of these former fishing boats would emerge from each east coast port every day just before dawn, throwing out their sweeps and trawling for their new type of catch. The fairway they swept down England's east coast was 800 yards wide and 200 miles long. This was cleared twice each day. The freeway was then extended northwards, especially in the firths of Scotland and round the Shetlands where the Grand Fleet lay. Other ex-fishing vessels were dispatched to wait and watch out for minelayers.

It was exhausting, monotonous, uncomfortable and dangerous work, carried out in all weathers. There was not only the peril of a mine exploding against the small craft. Accidents were common. The trawler's immense coils of steel wire might tauten suddenly as the boat yawed, and any man in the way could lose a limb. Down below he risked being thrown against a red-hot furnace or into moving machinery. But these were hazards of pre-war work too, and the more regimented ways of minesweeping may even have been a relief from the yet more arduous life of peacetime. Picture the end of a trawlerman's day: 'Fully dressed, utterly exhausted, the fisherman climbed into the stifling black box he called a bunk, drew the shutter, and in an atmosphere which would suffocate an ordinary person sought forgetfulness in sleep; or he would just stretch himself on the locker or the sodden greasy floor and know nothing till the unwelcome roar of a voice came down that tiny hatch-way, "Haul up your trawl, Boys, haul!" And so, as likely as not, especially in the bitter winter, with torn and bleeding hands that never had the chance to heal, the laborious work of getting the trawl up, cleaning, packing and ferrying the fish, would be done.'[7] This was no seasonal job either. Men might spend only five or six weeks ashore each year – and some had kept that up for fifty years. Often for unmarried men the boat was their only home and held all their possessions. But what an unparalleled knowledge of the sea these hardy folk had!

So the Admiralty had the vessels and the men to sweep the mines, but they did not at first know how the mines were being laid. They were aware that most German warships were equipped to lay mines and most merchant ships could be easily converted to do so, but they imagined, not unfairly, that even if a ship flying the German flag managed to escape the Royal Navy's patrols, it would not be able to linger laying mines without at least being seen by some passing craft. Yet mines had been found round the east coast of England. Minelaying, the Admiralty argued, must be perpetrated by ships flying neutral flags – probably by some of the many fishing vessels which were always around. (Just before war was declared the British embassy in Berlin had reported that Germany was equipping thirty trawlers with searchlights and fitting them out as minelayers. Besides, four drifters, which were reported to have been flying the German flag when fishing a couple of months previously, were seen off the Tyne in September, which was not the season for herring fishing there.) Having reached this conclusion the Admiralty took strong action. From 1 October 1914 all east coast ports of Britain were closed to neutral fishing craft. A war area was declared to exist from the coast to lines running north and south between thirty and a hundred miles from the shore.[8] This was not perhaps a large proportion of the North Sea, but there were objections from the neutral countries. A nation's territorial waters were only three miles wide in 1914, and the freedom of the seas had been breached. Britain and other nations had closed parts of the seas in previous wars, but it had always met with opposition from neutral nations. It was considered high-handed, even in wartime for Britannia to waive the rules in this way. The British Government could respond, however, that the seas were closed in a more deadly fashion by those who strew them with unmarked mine fields.

All neutral fishing craft in the war area were to be treated as under suspicion of minelaying. They were to be warned off and if they did not comply they were to be seized and treated as committing an unneutral act. Any crews found laying mines would be shot after trial by court martial, unless 'in the exclusive employment of the German government,' when they would be made prisoners of war.[9]

There were, nonetheless, other German mines laid around the British Isles. Two efforts to mine the Firth of Forth failed, but the SS *Berlin*, a large liner of 17,000 tons managed on her second attempt to break out of the North Sea, and it was the results of her activities that prompted the British Government to make its next move. Luck turned very much in the *Berlin*'s favour on her second sortie. As she dodged around the northern waters she came within a few miles of squadrons of cruisers and dreadnoughts patrolling or exercising between Scotland and the Faeroes or Iceland. Yet the visibility was so poor that the liner avoided discovery. On the night of 22–23 October 1914 she laid 200 mines about twenty miles north of Tory Island, which lies off the north-west coast of Donegal. The mines were in the path of traffic passing round the north of Ireland towards the Clyde or the Mersey, and on 26 October they claimed their first victim, a freighter. Circumstances delayed the passing of this news to the Fleet till the next day, and so the *Berlin*'s escapade had another piece of amazing luck. Though the Germans were quite unaware of it, the Grand Fleet was sheltering in Lough Swilly, the long, narrow inlet in north Donegal, and the Second Battle Squadron was setting off for target practice, when the new dread-nought, *Audacious*, was struck by a mine on her port quarter and was stopped. The great White Star passenger liner, *Olympic*, (sister to the ill-fated *Titanic*, which had hit an iceberg two years before) was passing the spot four hours later. Had she struck a mine, there would have been an international incident, as there were American citizens on board. The *Olympic* now turned to take the battleship in tow, but the towline parted and the liner was led safely away, HMS *Liverpool* steaming in front as a 'mine-bumper'. The *Audacious* managed to get under way again and it was hoped that she might make port, but then she went further down by the stern till her quarterdeck was awash, and all her crew were taken off. She eventually blew up with a violent explosion and sank. (The Admiralty tried to keep the loss secret, and never admitted that she had been more than damaged, in spite of reports from the Americans on the *Olympic*.)

For a few days the Germans kept the source of those mines secret, for the *Berlin*'s luck had persisted until she rounded Scotland again and made for the Norwegian coast. There she ran out of coal and was interned. The consequence of her miraculous escapes from being sighted was that the Admiralty persisted for some time more in its belief that the mines must have been laid by ships flying neutral flags. Jellicoe had already asked for some regulation of the international traffic along the northern sea lanes, when Prince Louis was First Sea Lord, and now his appeal fell on new and more receptive ears.

As Fisher's reaction to Coronel had shown, the years had not weakened his resolve to deal with problems in the drastic way that he felt necessary. The whole of the North Sea (except for the territorial waters of Norway, Denmark and the Netherlands) was in effect closed off. All neutral shipping from the south and west was required to enter and leave via the English Channel. Announcing this on 2 November 1914 the Admiralty stated, 'During the last week the Germans have scattered mines indiscriminately in the open sea on the main trade route from America to Liverpool via the north of Ireland. Peaceful merchant ships have already been blown up with loss of life by this agency. The White Star Liner *Olympic* escaped disaster by pure good luck . . . (So far correct, but they then disclosed their error.) These mines cannot have been laid by any German ship of war,' it was roundly declared. 'They have been laid by some merchant vessel flying a neutral flag which has come along the trade route as if for the purpose of peaceful commerce and, while profiting to the full by the immunity enjoyed by neutral merchant ships, has wantonly and recklessly endangered the lives of all who travel on the sea, regardless of whether they are friend or foe, civilian or military in character. The Admiralty . . . therefore give notice that the whole of the North Sea must be considered a military area. . . .' After passing the Straits of Dover shipping proceeding to Scandinavia or the Baltic was directed up the English coast as far as the Farn Islands, just short of the Scottish border, and then north-east across the North Sea to the south-west tip of Norway. 'By strict adherence to these routes the commerce of all countries will be able to reach its destination in safety, so far as Great Britain is concerned, but', warned the declaration, 'any straying even for a few miles from the course thus indicated, may be followed by fatal consequences.'[10]

The result of this order was that neutral shipping on its way beyond Britain to northern Europe had to steam two sides of a triangle, but by doing so they would keep between the shore of England and the known minefields, along a coast-wise track which was constantly swept. A well publicized mine barrage had already been laid by the British off the Kent coast and the long minefield laid by the Germans further north off the east coast had been left in place, buoyed and strengthened as a protective shield. But the action was only justifiable as a reprisal for Germany's illegal acts.

Then on two occasions towards the end of the year minefields which destroyed several merchant ships and minesweeping trawlers were laid by the *Kaiserliche Marine* as a by-product of other operations with greater ambitions. Pursuing its *Klein Krieg*, the German High Seas Fleet had begun a game of chess on the chequerboard of the North Sea. Pawns were to be advanced, and perhaps sacrificed, in the hope that more important pieces of the opponent would fall into the trap which was carefully being laid. The game plan was simple. A powerful force of fast battlecruisers, with light cruisers and destroyers in support, would sally forth out of their bases in the evening, cross the North Sea during the night and by dawn the next day would be in position to bombard towns on the east coast of England. The damage which they inflicted was not expected to be significant, but the moral effect of the bombardment on British public opinion and the affront to the pride of the Royal Navy, which would be shown to be unable to protect the shores of Britain, were calculated to bring some of the Grand Fleet's capital ships thundering down to avenge the insult. The British warships would be met by two dangers. The first would be a line of mines laid across their path by the retiring squadron. This it was hoped would sink or at least cripple one or more ships and reduce the squadrons' fighting strength, like banderillas in a fighting bull's neck. The second was the crushing might of the battleships of the High Seas Fleet steaming not far behind the battlecruisers. To some extent the dispositions of the British Fleet laid it open to this plan. Beatty's battlecruisers were based halfway between the Firth of Forth and Scapa Flow, at Invergordon in the Cromarty Firth, several hours' steaming away from the rest of the Grand Fleet at Scapa.

By coincidence, because it had been planned long before, the first sortie by units of the German High Seas Fleet was made on the day after the British had declared the whole North Sea to be a military area. Their target was Great Yarmouth, at the point of the English coast nearest to Heligoland, only 280 miles away. The spearhead was to be the First and Second Scouting Groups, commanded by Rear Admiral Franz Hipper, 'the outstanding sea officer of the war', in the opinion of the American Professor Marder.[11] The First Scouting Group consisted of the modern battlecruisers, *Seydlitz*, *Moltke* and *Von der Tann*, accompanied by the older *Blücher* (the first German ship to be designated a battlecruiser and not in the same class as the others), and three light cruisers in the Second Scouting Group. On their way they swept through a fishing fleet, and at 07.00 on 3 November 1914, were off the Norfolk coast. Challenged by a minesweeping gunboat, they replied with salvos of 11-inch guns. A destroyer's smokescreens saved the gunboat, and the German ships then bombarded the suburb of Gorleston, doing negligible harm. As a German sailor described it, 'Unfortunately the distance (fifteen kilometres) was too great for us to do considerable damage. Some shells fell on the shore, window panes were broken and so on. If only we had been five kilometres nearer the coast Yarmouth would have been in flames. The main object of our enterprise had, however, been gained. In the first place our small cruisers, which were packed full with mines, had strewn the local waters with German mines. When the English submarine *D5* tried to attack us it struck a mine and blew up. In the second place we had shown the Englishman, who is always boasting of his command of the sea, that he cannot even protect his own coast, and that the German navy is not, unlike him, afraid to attack.'[12]

66

At 07.40 the raiders returned home untouched. They had laid a line of mines five miles long as they went. Though Beatty rushed south and Tyrwhitt came out of Harwich with his destroyers, they could not catch the enemy. Nonetheless the Germans lost more than the British from the attack. Two of their armoured cruisers had been out in support, and on their return one of these, the *Yorck*, struck one of their own defensive mines. She took down with her 300 sailors, half her crew. The British had lost only the submarine *D5*, (though just two of her complement survived). A trawler had reported the mines being laid and they were to claim no victims other than two fishing boats with fifteen dead.

Public outrage at the raid was predictable, but muted. It was the first time that English soil had felt the effect of foreign cannon, since the French had landed in Sussex in 1690, but the Germans had not dared stay long enough or get close enough to do real damage, and no doubt the coastal defences would be strengthened.

The next raid, six weeks later was a different affair. It took place a week after news of the Battle of the Falklands had been brought to Germany, and may to some extent have been prompted by calls for revenge in the German press. For Admiral Friedrich von Ingenohl, Commander-in-Chief of the High Seas Fleet, the moment was opportune, because two of Beatty's battlecruisers were known to be absent in the South Atlantic. This time the targets were Scarborough and Whitby in Yorkshire and Hartlepool, just to the north of them. These towns were chosen because they happened to lie on the other side of a gap in the German minefields which lay along the English coast, and Whitby in the centre was only 340 miles from Heligoland, so that on the long December nights they were within the distance which the battlecruisers could steam in darkness from the safety of their own bases. The bombardment was made easier by the steeply shelving shore, which enabled the heavy ships with their deep draught to come in close. The defencelessness of two of the three towns was ignored.[13] Scarborough was a seaside resort at the peak of its elegance. Whitby was famous for fishing. Only Hartlepool, a port with steel, wood and shipbuilding industries, was of any military significance and defended.

The raiding squadron appeared out of the morning mist off the English coast on 16 December 1914, and divided in two. One part assailed Scarborough and Whitby. Scarborough's only ordnance was an old Crimean cannon decorating the Esplanade. Yet it received five hundred shells in half an hour and had seventeen people killed, over half being women and children. Whitby received a few shells, killing three people and wounding two more. The more powerful division, consisting of the *Derfflinger*, *Von der Tann* and *Blücher*, brushed aside the defence of a gunboat and two destroyers, briefly shelled old Hartlepool and directed a volcano of fire over the promontory at industrial West Hartlepool. One of the shipbuilding yards was damaged and the gas works were destroyed. Fortunately someone had had the presence of mind to let the gas out of two gasometers as the firing commenced. But the major injury was suffered by 600 houses, while schools, hospitals, workhouses and churches were also hit. Because of the time of the raid children were in the streets on their way to school. Not surprisingly there was panic. Peace one moment, terror the next. About 1,500 high-explosive shells had been poured into the town in fifty minutes – one every two seconds – killing 119 men, women and children and wounding another 300.[14]

However, all was not lost. The German ships were still 300 miles from their bases and the Admiralty had been alerted. Before the Yarmouth raid the Admiralty had been aware that some activity of the High Seas Fleet was imminent, thanks to the work of a new branch of the Naval Intelligence Division. A small group of picked men had been working for some weeks on intercepted German wireless signals. At first they could make neither head nor tail of the groups of letters, but on 13 October a light came into their world from the direction of Russia. Two months previously the German light cruiser *Magdeburg* had been caught in the Baltic by the Russian Navy and run aground. To avoid the capture of her code book, a sailor had been ordered to take it away in a rowing boat and drop the lead-weighted book overboard in deep water. The sailor was killed in the process and his body, still clutching the book, was washed ashore. The Russians sent the code book to their British ally. A staff of cryptographers had been established in Room 40, Old Building at the Admiralty, under the new Director of Naval Intelligence, Captain W. Reginald Hall.[15] From now on the brilliant, strange mix of men and women of various professions and disciplines, who worked in the greatest secrecy in Room 40 OB, would provide the Naval Operations Division and Chief of Staff with advance warning of German movements. Initially their transcripts were sometimes nonsensical, but they spoke with increasing confidence as they began to understand German naval terms and practices, and soon spread their interests beyond the purely naval sphere.

The team in Room 40 had again intercepted the German signals as Hipper had set out from his bases for the Scarborough/Hartlepools raid. This time the decrypts were better and Churchill and Fisher planned decisive action. By midday on 15 December, the day before Hipper arrived off the north-east towns, Warrender and Beatty had already been ordered to sea. Warrender, as senior officer, passed on to Beatty the amazingly precise information and instructions received from the Admiralty, 'German squadron of four battle-cruisers, five light cruisers and three flotillas leave Jade River daylight today, return Wednesday night. Rendezvous 54.10 N, 3.0 E, 7.30 am 16th.'[16] Though the Admiralty did not know the German objective, the ambush had been directed at a point exactly on a line between Heligoland and the gap in the minefields through which Hipper was to return.

The British squadrons setting out from Scapa, Cromarty and Rosyth, met up that evening and steamed south through the night in a diamond formation. Even as Scarborough and Whitby were about to suffer under the German shells, Sir George Warrender's Second Battle Squadron, comprising six of the fastest dreadnoughts, and Beatty's four battle-cruisers were approaching the German line of retreat. The battlecruisers led the way five miles ahead of the battleships, which were flanked five miles on the port side by the Third Cruiser Squadron and on the starboard side by the First Light Cruiser Squadron, led by Commodore Goodenough in the *Southampton*. The destroyers struggled to keep up astern amid the heavy seas which they encountered as the ships reached open water. It was a mixed force, short on destroyers, but the Harwich flotillas were due to join them from the south. Not only would the German First Scouting Group be outnumbered two to one, but the battleships opposing them had greater weight of armour and longer range of guns.

At 07.00 Warrender and Beatty were at battle stations in high hopes of engaging the enemy, and half an hour later, as it was getting light, they were at the precise spot indicated by the Admiralty's instructions, approximately thirty miles to the south-east of the Dogger Bank and almost exactly in the line which the German ships had taken on the way to the attack. At that time 150 miles to the west the bombardment of Scarborough was just starting. Churchill was in his bath when an officer came hurrying in from the War Room bearing news of the bombardment, which the First Lord 'grasped with dripping hand' as he jumped out of the bath, and, pulling on clothes over his damp body, rushed downstairs to the War Room. Fisher had just arrived from his house next door and Admiral Oliver, the Chief of Staff, 'who invariably slept in the War Room, and hardly ever left it by day, was marking positions on the map. Telegrams from all the naval stations along the coast affected by the attack, and intercepts from our ships in the vicinity speaking to each other, came pouring in two and three to the minute. Everything was now sent to sea or set in motion.'[17]

However, there were other German warships at sea besides those mentioned by the Admiralty. In fact von Ingenohl and his whole High Seas Fleet were, unknown to Room 40, out in close support of Hipper. Soon it would be the turn of Warrender and Beatty to be completely outnumbered. Here, just as the *Admiralstab* had planned, was a chance for von Ingenohl to deliver a crushing blow to an important part of the Grand Fleet, while the main force was too far away to intervene. To destroy Beatty's battlecruisers and Warrender's modern battleships at the same time would have been a victory indeed, at one stroke levelling the strengths of the two fleets. But von Ingenohl lacked vital information too.

British destroyers attending Warrender's fleet were already in action with a heavy cruiser and five destroyers of the High Seas Fleet. The sudden appearance of the British ships made von Ingenohl think that he was faced by the whole Grand Fleet, and, mindful of the Kaiser's instructions not to risk his ships, he returned home, leaving Hipper on his own to face potentially overwhelming squadrons.

As the British destroyers were being hard pressed, Beatty set off to the north-east to intercept, but they turned back when a signal came through from the destroyer *Shark*, that she was being pursued westwards. Still there was no clear information about the German First Scouting Group. Then HMS *Patrol* radioed that she was being engaged by two battlecruisers, but since she did not give her position, and German signals and jamming interfered with the message, Beatty was little the wiser. Finally an Admiralty signal was picked up, saying that Scarborough was being shelled. Lieutenant Filson Young, in Beatty's flagship, *Lion*, received the signal by chart-room telephone. 'It came through first time as Scapa being shelled,' he recalled, 'but even that could not add much to the confusion.'[18]

At least Warrender now knew that he was between the enemy and their base, and he turned west to catch them, but the weather was once again playing on the German side. Mist drove across the sea and visibility fell to five miles and then to scarcely two. It was a cruel stroke of fate, because as Hipper skirted north of the Dogger Bank, Beatty was also taking the northern route towards him, while Warrender went south of the shoals. Beatty, believing too early that he had missed the enemy, turned back and between 14.00 and 16.00 the British and German battlecruisers were on approximately parallel courses, driving south-east towards Heligoland, at times only nine miles from each other, within gunshot range. For over an hour, until dusk fell at 15.45 on that misty winter afternoon, their courses converged, with the British slightly ahead. In another half hour Beatty's battlecruisers would have been directly in the path of Hipper's retirement. However, as darkness fell, Warrender reluctantly called off the hunt and turned his ships home.

There had been but one opportunity for engagement. The German light cruisers had been seen by the *Southampton* and when they failed to reply to the recognition signal, Goodenough had opened fire. The Germans disappeared in the mist with a valuable piece of information. When some time later the huge forms of the British battleships loomed out of the haze towards them, and must with a couple of salvos of their great guns at that short range have blown the light cruisers out of the water, the quick-thinking German captain got in first and flashed the British recognition signal at them. The deception could not have been kept up for long but, in the short time they had won, the German ships turned sharply about and vanished.

Commodore Keyes' submarines were dispatched to intercept Hipper off the German coast, and Lieutenant Nasmith in *E11* managed to get in a shot, but the torpedo went harmlessly under the dreadnought *Posen*.

If the British Admiralty were dismayed at the lost opportunities, so were the German admirals. Tirpitz believed that, 'On December 16th. Ingehohl had in his hands the fate of Germany'. Scheer considered they had 'missed a first rate chance which probably would never be repeated'.[19] However, in Berlin generally there was exultation. 'The world will learn with new astonishment that England is able to make the North Sea a field of death and destruction for all neutral shipping and even for its own shipping, but that it was not able to make the North Sea unsafe for the German Navy.'[20] Naturally, German people did not accept that their fleet had bombarded any unarmed port. They would believe Captain Persius, the Fatherland's best known naval analyst, who, possibly mistaking Scarborough for Harwich, wrote that it was 'the most important harbour on the East Coast of England between the Thames and the Humber' and was 'protected by powerful batteries'.[21]

In Britain this second attack on the English coast, which the enemy had inflicted with, impunity, caused an outcry. The question, 'What is the Navy doing?' had been raised in the press before. It seemed that the public imagined a ring of steel protecting the islands. They might understand how simple it was to cross the North Sea undetected in darkness, but did not realize how easy it was to miss ships in daylight when the visibility was poor. Nor could they be expected to know that the steeply shelving water off the north-east coast of England enabled the enemy to come in close, while the string of islands off the German coast and the shallows stretching from Heligoland to the shore made reprisals impossible. The Admiralty's exercise in public relations only exacerbated the problem (as it was to do on a more important occasion later). Four official messages were issued during the day of the bombardment as information came in. The evening bulletin contained the unfortunate paragraphs:

> The Admiralty take the opportunity of pointing out that the demonstrations of this character against unfortified towns or commercial ports, though not difficult to accomplish provided that a certain amount of risk is accepted, are devoid of military significance.
>
> They may cause some loss of life among the civil population and some damage to private property, which is much to be regretted; but they must not in any circumstances be allowed to modify the general naval policy which is being pursued.

One critic, saying that 'nothing more calculated to depress and alarm the public . . . could be designed by the most irresponsible alarmist', translated the Admiralty's announcement as:

> (1) Open towns on the East Coast must expect to be bombarded, and we cannot help it.
> (2) Those who are killed must be killed, and their relatives who mourn must mourn. We are sorry, but this cannot be prevented.
> (3) Though we are supposed to command the North Sea, we cannot scatter our big ships about to prevent bombardments, which, though deplorable, are devoid of military significance.[22]

For obvious reasons the true story could not be told, and it was galling to Captain Hall and his staff in Room 40 to keep silent, while Sir Walter Runciman, MP for Hartlepool asked: 'What has the Intelligence Department to say to this? Were we caught napping?'[23] Warrender too was criticized and his replacement was considered, but Jellicoe, his Commander-in-Chief, supported him.

Hipper had escaped, but the Royal Navy was determined not to allow such a humiliation to occur again. The seven battlecruisers, and Goodenough's First Light Cruiser Squadron were moved further south to Rosyth, on the north side of the Firth of Forth opposite Edinburgh, where they joined the Third Battle Squadron and the Third Cruiser Squadron.

During the Scarborough raid light cruisers had laid 200 mines. This time they took a greater toll. An hour after the German battlecruisers had disappeared into the haze, the first merchant ship fell victim. It took three weeks to clear the mines and by then eight steamers, (three of them Norwegian) four sweeping trawlers and one patrol trawler had been sunk. Another two merchant ships, a steam yacht and a trawler had struck mines, but been beached.[24]

New Year's Day 1915 brought another blow to the British fleet. *Kapitänleutnant* Schneider in the *U-24* spotted a squadron of pre-Dreadnought battleships exercising in the Channel off Portland. At first they were too far away for him to attack, but as night fell they returned, escorted only by two light cruisers, and Schneider found himself within striking range. There was no moon, and when the sea became too rough to keep the boat at periscope depth, Schneider boldly attacked on the surface. His first torpedo missed, but the second caught HMS *Formidable* amidships. She began to list and in the growing storm foundered, taking 540 men down with her. However, it would not be long before the opportunity came for her to be avenged.

Six weeks after the Scarborough raid Vice Admiral Hipper's Scouting Group was out again, but not supported by the High Seas Fleet. This third time they were not to escape without loss, but a combination of events again saved them from disaster. In the morning of 23 January 1915, Room 40 gave due and exact warning. They picked up instructions from von Ingenohl to Hipper to make a sally to the Dogger Bank, where it was expected that British light forces might be patrolling unsupported. Hipper again took the *Seydlitz, Moltke* and *Derfflinger*, but since the *Von der Tann* was refitting, the slower and lighter armed *Blücher* took her place. Light cruisers and destroyers made up the squadron. The British hoped to ambush them with a force consisting of five battlecruisers, the *Lion, Princess Royal, Tiger, New Zealand* and *Indomitable*, Goodenough's light cruisers from the north and Tyrwhitt's Harwich force of thirty-three destroyers plus three more light cruisers from the south. Their rendezvous was to be thirty miles north of the Dogger Bank. Pre-Dreadnought battleships and three armoured cruisers from Rosyth were to cut off any attempt to flee north, while the Grand Fleet also made a sweep in case the full High Seas Fleet emerged behind Hipper. Finally Keyes and his submarines were sent across to keep watch on the German coast. Beatty and Hipper both set out in the evening of the 23rd, one in full knowledge, and the other ignorant, of his opponent's departure.

The battle commenced next morning at 07.20, when in the early light the scouting forces of the two sides made contact. Beatty turned towards the sound of the guns. So too did Hipper at first, but then he realized from intercepted radio traffic and his cruisers' reports that he might be taking on more than was planned and he turned back, taking a straight line home. Beatty called to Percy Green, his Engineer Commander, 'Get us within range of the enemy. Tell your stokers all depends on them.' 'They know that, Sir,' Green replied.[25] In hot pursuit the battlecruisers put on all speed even though the older and slower *Indomitable* could not keep up. They were gaining on Hipper, who was held back by the *Blücher*. Beatty's battlecruisers opened fire individually at about 09.00 with ranging shots at 20,000 yards, ten sea miles. Fifteen minutes later the Germans replied. Since the *Indomitable* was now well astern, the battle was even. The four German battlecruisers steamed in line ahead in the order *Seydlitz, Moltke, Derfflinger* and *Blücher*, and the four British, led by the *Lion*, flying Sir David Beatty's flag as usual, and followed by the *Tiger, Princess Royal* and *New Zealand*, chased sufficiently wide on the starboard quarter to enable their after guns (and the enemy's forward guns) to bear as well. So the fight continued for an hour and a half, both sides firing huge numbers of shells and scoring few hits.[26]

For the unengaged light cruisers 'it was like sitting in the front row of the dress circle at a play,' Lieutenant Stephen King-Hall remembered. While the firing continued without much visible result 'every one who could get there crowded to the starboard side of the boat deck and sat there smoking their pipes'.[27] The *Cassandra*, a trawler quietly fishing off the Dogger Bank, had an uncomfortably close view of the action. At noon her skipper had just left the bridge to fetch some tobacco, when the mate shouted down that he could hear the sound of big guns. 'I immediately went on deck,' recounted the skipper, 'and there rushing towards us was a big German cruiser accompanied by a torpedo flotilla, steaming about south east. About seven or eight miles to the westward were our Fleet, firing as hard as they could. Immediately we were surrounded by flying shells. You could hear them whistling overhead and see them falling all around us. As the Germans were passing us, the big cruiser fired a shot which passed between our bridge and funnel and hit the water about fifty yards away from us. Simultaneously I saw two shells hit one of their destroyers, and all I saw was a tremendous upheaval of water and then nothing more. This all lasted about fifteen minutes.'[28]

However, the pattern of firing was not the same. Beatty flew the signal, 'Engage the corresponding ships in the enemy's line', but the British battlecruisers did not all engage their opposite numbers. The captain of the *Tiger*, H.B. Pelly, believing that the *Indomitable* was near enough behind to engage the *Blücher*, and that they therefore had a ship over, fired on the *Seydlitz*, leaving the *Moltke* unmolested. The three leading German ships concentrated most of their fire on the two leading British ships, primarily the *Lion*, then the *Tiger*. By 11.00, after two hours of battle, the *Lion* had been hit seventeen times by 11-inch and 12-inch shells. Two of them, striking the main belt armour on the waterline, had not penetrated, but had driven in the plates (nine inches thick and fifteen feet long) so that salt water came in and entered the fresh water tank for the boilers. Both engines were put out of action. As she stopped, Beatty in despair watched the battle receding from him. A destroyer came alongside to take the Admiral off to the *Princess Royal*, where he could resume command, but the fight had already all but ended. Beatty himself had made a fatal error in ordering his ships to turn to port to avoid a submarine attack, which never materialized. As the signal did not indicate that submarines were the cause of the move, his captains might with reason have believed that the action was being broken off. Also, while the flags for 'Course North East' were still flying, his Flag Lieutenant, Seymour, ran up Beatty's order 'Attack the rear of the enemy'. Now, at the rear of the enemy was the unfortunate *Blücher*, which was already on fire and doomed. She should have been left to the *Indomitable* to finish off, but in view of the signal all the British battlecruisers turned on her, abandoning the pursuit of the main force. She went down fighting, riddled with shells and torpedoes. To King-Hall 'It seemed amazing to think that human beings could be in that hell. Clouds of grey smoke were pouring from inside her, and in places her very hull seemed to glow with a red heat. Once more she fired, a last wild shot, and then utter silence as the *Tiger* ceased fire.'[29]

It had been the first battle between capital ships of the Dreadnought era. Beatty was bitterly disappointed at the outcome and blamed Rear Admiral Sir Archibald Moore who had taken over command while Beatty was stranded in the *Lion*. The *Princess Royal* and *New Zealand* were quite unscathed, and though the *Tiger* had received seven hits, her ability to fight was not impaired. On the German side the *Seydlitz* had suffered badly. A 13.5-inch shell had started a cordite fire which rapidly spread, killing the entire crews of two turrets and might have destroyed the ship, had not her magazines been flooded. She had 159 men killed and thirty-three wounded. But a very valuable lesson about the danger of cordite fires had been learnt. Preventive measures were taken in all the German ships. The British had yet to learn. Indeed Beatty believed that the German 'guns are good, calibration too close, gunlaying excellent, but the projectile no good, and I am sure we can stand a lot of it'.[30] This belief was the more remarkable, since, according to Beatty's flag captain, Chatfield, the first 13.5-inch shell to hit the ship entered through the 5-inch armour near X turret magazine and would have blown the ship up, had it not failed to explode.

The British press could claim a victory, though not a decisive one, and pictures of the *Blücher* on her beam ends filled their pages. Nearly 880 of her men had died and the remaining 234 were prisoners. By contrast, the *Lion* had surprisingly suffered only two men killed and eight wounded, though she had had to be towed home for repair (a difficult task – one five inch diameter hawser had parted as she took the strain.) The other British casualties were ten dead and eleven wounded in the *Tiger*. In terms of men killed, 12 to 950 was a good ratio. The *Formidable* had been avenged, but the press could not know how well warned the British fleet was and how it might have turned out. Even so, Beatty, ever optimistic, was probably overdoing it when he wrote, 'I had made up my mind that we were going to get four, the lot, and four we ought to have got'.[31]

This time it was the *Admiralstab* who were looking for scapegoats. Von Ingenohl was replaced as C.-in-C. of the High Seas Fleet by von Pohl, who had been Chief of Staff. There was great puzzlement over the uncanny ability of the Royal Navy to appear out of the blue, whenever major forces of the *Kaiserliche Marine* put to sea. Was it the new direction-finding radio receivers along the English coast or spies or trawlers, which were passing the information? But if there was doubt on that score, one factor was becoming clearer. The attempt to whittle away the superiority in numbers enjoyed by the British Navy was not progressing fast enough. There was no hope of breaking the blockade with these tactics. In fact the surface fleet of the Royal Navy was stronger than it had been at the beginning of the war, as a result of the commissioning of new Dreadnoughts and Fisher's programme of building many more destroyers and light cruisers.

Nor was mining impeding British trade to anything like the extent that the British blockade was curtailing German trade. The United Kingdom suffered some losses of ships and cargoes, but the German Empire faced a complete interdiction of trade anywhere in the world outside the Baltic and her North Sea coast. Berlin therefore decided that the production of U-boats, which had been so successful against warships, should be stepped up and they should be used in another direction, against merchant shipping, to establish their own blockade.

This would raise questions of international law, but then the British were widely held to be breaking the law by the way they used their sea power.

Notes

1. Hurd, op. cit. Vol. I, p.254. In fact that was not quite true. In 1913 Lord Fisher had prepared a memorandum, in which he prophesied submarine war on commerce. However both Churchill and Prince Louis of Battenburg considered his paper 'marred by this suggestion'. (See Gibson, R.H. and Prendergast, Maurice, *The German Submarine War 1914–1918*, Constable, 1921, p.24)
2. Müller quoted in Fischer, Fritz, *Germany's Aims in the First World War*, Chatto & Windus, 1967, p.281
3. Wood, Walter, *Fishermen in War Time*, Samson Low, Marston, 1918, p.24
4. Memorandum for the Army Council prepared in November 1910, quoted in Hurd, op. cit. Vol. I, p.222
5. Hurd, op. cit. p.257
6. ibid. p.267
7. Wood, op. cit. p.21
8. The War Area ran off the Scottish coast down the line of longitude 1 degree east – about seventy-five miles into the sea at Whitby; south of Whitby it ran further east, along the line of 2 degrees 30', which is only thirty miles from the eastern tip of the Norfolk coast, and at its southern end hits the Franco-Belgian border.
9. *The Times Documentary History of the War*, Vol. III – Naval, Part 1, p.70
10. ibid. pp.74–5
11. Marder, Arthur J., *From Dreadnought to Scapa Flow* (5vols) Oxford University Press, 1961–70, Vol.3, p.44. Hipper was well served by his Chief of Staff, *Kapitänleutnant* Erich Raeder, who later took command of Hitler's navy.
12. *The Times History of the War*, (illustrated series in 21 Vols.), 1914–1919, Vol.II, p.361
13. The Hague Convention declared that unfortified towns should be exempt 'from bombardment or attack by any means whatsoever'. Convention IX of 1907, Regulation 25.
14. Other reports give eighty-six killed and 424 wounded. Hartlepool could fairly be described as a 'defended town' because it had three 6-inch guns in its fort. These, manned largely by Territorials and

commanded by a local businessman, had replied gamely, but its guns could not match those of a capital ship. If a town was a legitimate target, the Hague Regulations did not expect the attackers to be able to discriminate between residential and military areas, though they did expect churches, colleges and hospitals to be spared if they were marked.

15. Room 40 had been started by Sir Alfred Ewing, formerly Professor of Mechanical Engineering at Cambridge, who was invited by Jackie Fisher in 1902 to be the first Director of Naval Education.

16. Corbett and Churchill give the Admiralty credit for the choice of rendezvous. Marder says that it was Jellicoe's decision.

17. Churchill, op. cit. p.418

18. Young, Filson, *With the Battle Cruisers*, Cassell, 1921, p.94. 'That terrible fellow Filson Young', as Beatty once described him, was a journalist who wangled his way onto the Vice Admiral's staff through his contact with Fisher. He wrote an interesting account of his time with the battlecruisers, and a very divisive account of Jutland.

19. Both quotations are from Bulow, Prince von, *Memoirs*, Putnam, 1932, Vol.3, p.177

20. *Tagliche Rundschau*

21. *Berliner Tageblatt*

22. Samuel Storey, see *The Times History of the War*, Vol.II, p393

23. ibid.

24. Another ship was saved thanks to the extraordinary gallantry of a minesweeping trawler. The SS *Gallier* was showing no lights, but on a dark night Skipper Trendall searched and found her. To persist in that task in a gale in the middle of a minefield was an act of heroism for which he won the Distinguished Service Cross.

25. Chatfield, Admiral of the Fleet Lord, *The Navy and Defence*, William Heinemann, 1942, p.132

26. Each side fired over a thousand rounds of their heaviest guns, the four German ships loosing off as many as the five British. Chatfield admitted that the range was continually being lost owing to their lack of practice at those high speeds and distances. The *Seydlitz* managed to fire 390 shells. In the running fight between the six leading ships the Germans scored more hits, although even then less than two per cent of their shells struck the target. The luck of the engagement is shown by the fact that the three hits on the *Seydlitz* caused nearly 200 casualties, while the three hits on the *Derfflinger* injured no one.

27. King-Hall, Lieutenant S. 'Etienne', *A Naval Lieutenant 1914–1918*, Methuen & Co., 1919, p.78

28. Hurd, op. cit. Vol.I, p.359

29. King-Hall, op. cit. p.81

30. Marder, op. cit. Vol.2, p.165. Was this misplaced confidence crucial in affecting Beatty's judgement in the early stages at Jutland?

31.Roskill, Stephen, *Admiral of the Fleet Earl Beatty*, Atheneum, New York, 1981, p.114

CHAPTER FIVE

The Law and the Neutrals

The major problem for the British Admiralty in the first two and a half years of the Great War was how to make the blockade both secure and 'legal'. At this distance in time after the Second World War, in which almost all the rules of law and humanity were abandoned, it seems strange that the confines of international law should have been of such concern with regard to the blockade. However, for the first two and a half years of the First World War there were always three sides to any blockade – Britain and the Entente powers, Germany, leading the Central powers and thirdly the neutrals – because one neutral nation, the United States, was powerful enough to constrain the belligerents by an embargo on supplies or credit, or by the threat of armed intervention, if either side damaged neutral interests too severely by breaking the rules of warfare at sea.

And looking back after two World Wars in which the Americans fought decisively on the Franco-British side, when the Anglo-Saxon alliance had been such a cornerstone of victory, it is hard to envisage the circumstances which might have made the US enter the war on Germany's side. However, in 1812 the mutual maritime blockades of Great Britain and Napoleonic France had brought the exasperated United States into the conflict against Britain. There were lessons to be learnt, because the circumstances were not so dissimilar.

The Royal Navy had angered neutrals during the Napoleonic wars by stopping and examining vessels of every nationality in a blockade too widespread to comply with international law. James Madison, when US Secretary of State in 1804, wrote that 'The fictitious blockades proclaimed by Great Britain and made the pretext for violating the commerce of neutral nations have been one of the greatest abuses ever committed on the high seas'.[1] On the other hand Bonaparte's abuses could not be ignored either. He had the vain hope that he could bring Britain, his one constant foe, to terms by closing off her markets on the Continent. This, he expected, would hurt the 'nation of shop-keepers'[2] where it felt most painful. During this 'reverse blockade', even though French fleets rarely had control of the sea, their privateers took a toll not only of British ships, but American vessels too, and by decrees of 1808 and 1810 Napoleon ordered the capture and then confiscation of all US shipping in French ports. So it was questionable on which side the young United States would fight. Madison, by then President, demanded that the French withdraw their decrees and the British rescind their Orders in Council, which barred all neutral shipping from French ports. Napoleon announced that he would comply, while the British, although they in fact abandoned the blockade, did nothing about the Orders in Council. So war was declared on the UK by the United States in September 1812. (There were other irritants too: US ships were searched for British fugitives from the press-gangs and some American sailors had been pressed into the Royal Navy.) In the sharp conflict lasting two and a half years Toronto was burnt by the Americans and (more memorably) Washington by the British. In 1914 British relations with the US were of course much closer, but repeated infringements of the rights of US citizens to conduct peaceful trade while Europe was fighting could be disastrous again. Consequently, for over two years the results of the diplomatic démarches in Washington were no less important than the battles on the Western Front.

Blockading from far off was not 'legal'. Until 1914 a blockade had been thought of as a close ring of ships in the offing round a specified port; the Declaration of London was only restating the generally recognized principles of International Law in its first Articles:

1. A blockade must not extend beyond the ports or coasts belonging to or occupied by the enemy; and
2. A blockade in order to be binding must be effective.[3]

This meant that the investing fleet must not bar entry to free neutral ports, but at the same time must be able to stop *all* vessels from entering the blockaded ports. Clearly a fleet based at Scapa Flow blanketed the neutral Scandinavian ports, yet could not stop coastal traffic from passing from Scandinavia or the Netherlands into German North Sea harbours, and so at first the British Government did not use the word 'blockade'. The Royal Navy merely claimed to be exercising a belligerent's rights to capture enemy shipping and to stop and search neutral ships in order to ensure that there was no contraband passing to the foe.

It was accepted that one belligerent might legally prevent neutral nations from supplying contraband of war to any of its enemies. If found, contraband goods might be taken as 'prize'.[4] Unfortunately what was contraband to a belligerent was often fair trade to a neutral. The question for the government in wartime always is, what can safely be claimed to be contraband without driving the neutrals to hostility? Any contraband list will include arms and ammunition, uniforms and military stores. On the other hand articles which can only be used for peaceful purposes can never be seized, unless they are supplied in violation of a siege on land or the blockade of a port. (When a blockade is in force all goods can be stopped from passing through.) By treaties made in peacetime countries agreed with each other what should be included in the list of military stores, but any definition inevitably aroused disputes as soon as a conflict erupted. The everchanging technology of war ensured increasing dissatisfaction with any pre-war agreement. The dominant naval power engaged in the war always wanted the broadest definition of contraband and the weaker power wanted the narrowest. So too did the neutrals, who traded with the belligerents. During the Russo-Japanese war of 1904–5 the Russian government declared coal, provisions, cotton, railway materials and most ironwork to be contraband, and Russian cruisers asserted the right to seize or sink any collier in Far Eastern waters, whatever her destination. The British strongly protested then. Now it was they who wanted to extend the list of contraband goods.

Another difficulty was the distinction between absolute contraband, such as guns, which could always be captured, if on the way to the enemy even via a neutral port, and conditional contraband, comprising goods which might or might not be used for war, such as coal. Conditional contraband could be seized if destined for the enemy forces or government, but not if consigned to a neutral port; consequently goods, such as fuel, food and fodder had to be allowed through, if addressed to Rotterdam, even though for a known German agent there. Railways had made nonsense of the doctrine.

A further problem for the British authorities was that the judges of prize courts were independently minded, sometimes finding a seizure unjustified and ordering the British Government to pay compensation.

The judges saw themselves as applying not just the prize rules of English law but 'International Law, which originates in the practice and usage long observed by civilised nations in their relations with each other or in express international agreement'.[5] However, international law is not codified, so where is it found? With regard to interference with trade the law might seem to have been simplified by the International Conventions signed at Paris, the Hague and London in the preceding sixty years of peace. But none of those conventions had been ratified by all the belligerents without qualification, and no state is bound to acquiesce in a change of international law, however many others may have agreed it. In fact the Declaration of London, which attempted to codify the rules of contraband in 1909 was so impractical that it had been signed only by the United States, which was neutral in 1914. (The House of Lords had rejected it after vigorous agitation in the British press.) For example the limited list of contraband mentioned in the Declaration of London meant that:

Guns were contraband, but not iron ore for the steel which made them.

Explosives were, but not nitrates, cotton or silk, which were essential for some types.

Similarly ships, but not the oil fuel to power them.

Clearly these rules would not stand the test of war. 'The Declaration of London', wrote one publicist, 'had to mask an irreconcilable conflict of interests. It had to be built not on the rock of an enduring international purpose, but the shifting sand of ever-changing calculations of national advantage in a legalised game of war . . . and it crumbled, not because the combatants became maddened by passion, but because of the inherent impossibilities of the task of making rules for the orderly conduct of the supreme disorder, war.'[6] The British Government clarified its position by an Order in Council of 20 August 1914 stating that Britain would act on the Declaration of London, as if it had been ratified, but subject to certain additions to the list. Also conditional contraband would be liable to capture even though consigned to a neutral port. France followed suit. Germany said that she would apply the Declaration in its entirety, but she had little to lose, although her cruisers were still at large at the time.

Then from September 1914 Britain declared iron ore, copper, lead, glycerine and rubber to be conditional contraband. The US protested to Britain, and talks between the Foreign Secretary, Sir Edward Grey, and Ambassador Page resulted in a deal embodied in a new Order in Council on 29 October 1914, enlarging the list of materials 'essential for the making of munitions of war', which were absolute contraband, but limiting the right to stop conditional contraband.

It was also questionable whether Britain was bound by the Declaration of Paris, which had been signed in April 1856, a month after the Treaty ending the Crimean War. The British signatories had authority to sign the Treaty, but not the Declaration which was quite separate and had been neither ratified nor repudiated, just ignored. Among other things the Declaration of Paris forbade the seizure of any goods (other than contraband) belonging to the enemy or its citizens, if carried in neutral ships. When war came, the damage to Allied interests by this provision was clear. On the land which German forces controlled nothing protected Belgian and French goods, iron ore and coal from seizure, but on the sea that British and French forces controlled Germany had only to have its imports and exports shipped in neutral bottoms to make them immune. For the first eight months of the war German export trade suffered little in spite of the blockading squadrons, because the Declaration of Paris was initially observed by the Allies.

The work of interception, whether by the Northern Patrol or the Dover Patrol, was controlled by the Contraband Committee of the Foreign Office. Those gentlemen decided whether a ship should be sent before a prize court, but there often seemed to the boarding officers to be no guiding rules. For political reasons a neutral ship obviously carrying contraband might be set free and what appeared to be a harmless vessel might be detained in port. Those who had to examine and send ships into port in the often appalling conditions of the northern seas, saw themselves as 'pig in the middle', and Jellicoe at times wanted to withdraw the squadron for more useful work.

The boarding officer of a naval ship had no easy task. He was issued with a copy of the prize rules and a list of what goods were contraband, but he might not have been used to commercial documents and the enemy was cunning too. Goods were disguised to avoid capture, false flags flown and false papers produced. Consequently intercepted ships came to be sent into port, where they were boarded by ex-merchant navy officers, familiar both with mercantile documentation and the places where contraband could be stowed. This, however, caused delay for the neutral freighters and more complaints from their governments.

In fact the Navy's activities placed a continual strain on Britain's relations with neutral countries. Lloyd George was hardly sympathetic, 'When a war is in progress neutral countries are often placed in an embarrassing position. Themselves at peace with all the world, they naturally seek to maintain their normal commercial relations with both the belligerent parties. In addition they endeavour to improve the shining hour by doing an increased and more profitable business, by supplying the additional demands created by the war at the inflated prices made possible by the war's restriction of supplies. But while they thus earn greater profits, they are subject to greater hazards and less consideration. Nations fighting for their lives cannot always pause to observe punctilios.'[7]

The desecration of Belgium and the invasion of France had initially ranged the great majority of Americans on the side of the Allies. The destruction of the ancient town of Louvain and its library, rich in manuscripts and comparable to the Bodleian in Oxford, had shocked the world. So too had the accounts of villages destroyed because of shots fired by un-uniformed civilians, who, if caught, were executed as *francs-tireurs*. German public relations had not been helped by an exculpatory broadcast from Berlin: 'The only means of preventing surprise attacks from the civil population has been to interfere with unrelenting severity, and to create examples which by their frightfulness would be a warning to the whole country.'[8] German 'frightfulness' became a byword. But gradually stories of the war faded from the front pages of American newspapers. After all, 'Belgium was thousands of miles away from Illinois. German destroyers and submarines at Ostend were not within a few steam hours of New York.'[9]

Meanwhile the Royal Navy's interception of American ships on their way to Europe, and the widening interpretation by the UK government of the word 'contraband' caused growing friction. Protests from the White House resulted in temporary relaxation of the enforcement of the blockade, but then another incident would arise and the protest would become more insistent. The US government in the Civil War with the Confederate States had pushed the rights of a belligerent to the extreme, but now the boot was on the other foot and the United States claimed to protect the rights of neutrals. To shelter under the eagle's wing many German ships were registered in the US, and others just flew the Stars and Stripes.

In its attempt to be even-handed the US government balanced their protest against indiscriminate mining by the Germans with a note to Britain about the blockade. The Americans pointed out that, unless a blockade had been both declared and made effective, the sole right of a belligerent in dealing with neutral shipping on the high seas was to visit and search. Consequently it was not permissible to force ships to deviate nor to take them into port. The British government was on the horns of a dilemma. The blockade had still not been formally declared because of its questionable legality, and the US government insisted that in that case Britain could not capture non-contraband goods, such as cotton, in neutral ships heading for neutral ports. But cotton was a vital war material. (Lint and bandages might be let through on humanitarian grounds, but the long fibres of cotton are used in tyres, asbestos and military clothing, amongst other things, while the short fibres round the seed are an ingredient of the smokeless explosive, gun-cotton.) Before the war Germany had taken nearly all her needs from the Southern states, and it was only because cotton was so important to the US, that it had not been put on the contraband list. It was necessary to help pay for those German exports which were essential to US businesses. In November 1914 Ambassador Gerard was writing from Berlin, 'I have been especially engaged in getting cotton in and chemicals and dye-stuffs out. We have to have cyanide to keep our mines going and dye-stuffs to keep endless industries, and the Germans know this and want to use this as a club to force us to send cotton and wool in. So they only let us have about a month's supply at a time. Also they fear lest we should resell to the English . . . .'[10]

Copper was another US product, which was essential to the belligerents and had a strong commercial lobby. Britain eventually got her way through the length of her purse as much as the strength of her Navy. An attempt to buy up all the US copper exports failed, but European neutrals were persuaded to prohibit the re-export of copper in return for agreement on the amount which would be let through for their own needs. American copper producers were then reminded that Britain could refuse to buy any copper from them, and could hold up their shipments to Germany and Austria. This brought all the major producers, bar one, into line. Finally the Guggenheim group signed an agreement with the Admiralty, when it was announced in Parliament that the names of the compliant companies would be published so that orders could be placed with them. In this way ninety-five per cent of the exportable copper of the USA was channelled to Allied uses by the beginning of March 1915.

The most important reason, why the blockade was slow to take effect, even though few ships steamed into Germany's North Sea ports, was that she could easily satisfy her needs at home or elsewhere. Industry ran on coal and the basic raw materials of war were still iron and steel.

Not only did Germany have her own iron and enough coal and potash to export, but her forces had overrun the mining regions of Belgium, Luxembourg and northern France in the first weeks of the conflict. Besides that, high grade Swedish ore was never denied them and the Central Powers had oil in Galicia on the Austro-Polish border. Then, although direct imports from the USA to Germany had almost ceased, Germany and Austria at first simply ordered supplies through the neighbouring neutrals, Holland, Denmark, Norway, Sweden and Switzerland, whose entrepôt trade in all foodstuffs and raw materials boomed. For example, the imports of cotton by the Netherlands and Scandinavia jumped fifteen-fold in the first year of the war, copper five-fold. The overall figures for imports by the neutrals from the USA in December 1914 and January 1915 by comparison with twelve months before tell the clearest story:

	Dec '13 & Jan '14	*Dec '14 & Jan '15*[11]
	($000)	($000)
Holland	19,300	26,800
Sweden	2,200	17,700
Norway	1,500	7,200
Denmark	3,000	14,500

The problem of transhipment through neutral countries had been recognized from the outset. Before the war the Committee of Imperial Defence, when debating trade with the enemy, had believed that it would not be possible for either Belgium or the Netherlands to remain neutral. That was convenient because, for the British blockade to be effective, it was not desirable that they should be. The Committee concluded: 'In order to bring the greatest possible economic pressure upon Germany it is essential that the Netherlands and Belgium should either be entirely friendly to this country, in which case we should limit their overseas trade, or that they should be definitely hostile, in which case we should extend the blockade to their ports.'[12] But now, though Belgium was on the Allied side, there was no sign that the Netherlands would be involved, and trade flowed through her ports at a greater rate than ever. The logical answer, as Lloyd George had foreseen at that pre-war meeting, was that 'our policy should be to allow the Netherlands and Belgium to import what they required for their own consumption on the average, with a reasonable margin added. It was not essential to treat them as hostile. But they should only be allowed to import enough to go on with.'[13] Asquith had objected that this would damage the transit trade on which the Dutch were dependent, and that they should be compensated by a subsidy. Also there was no precedent for this 'rationing' of neutrals and no statistics on which it could be based, so it was a long time before it was introduced.

All the European neutrals found themselves getting rich but in a delicate predicament, as both sides vied for their favours with mercenary affection. The Dutch and Danish were open to invasion from Germany. The Norwegians, whose mercantile tonnage was fourth in the world, were dependent on shipping and fishing at a time when merchantmen were being sunk indiscriminately. Sweden, with a long history of close commercial ties with Germany, was in effect blockaded too. Switzerland landlocked between both Germany and France, was controllable by both.

The Dutch and Scandinavians depended on the import of coal, which was Britain's major export, and a range of other commodities which could be intercepted. So the UK government, using these levers, negotiated undertakings that the neutral importers would not re-export goods to the enemy. Alternatively, friendly concerns or newly established companies in the neutral country would be given importation monopolies for certain commodities, subject to a financially backed guarantee not to re-export. Goods might be intercepted and paid for by the British and then resold to the tame importer. These stratagems were effective, but not everywhere. The Swedes who had always taken half their coal from Germany, now took it all from there, and the Swedish government at first prohibited their merchants from undertaking not to re-export goods. The phosphorus-free Swedish iron ore, now especially valuable, was even convoyed across the Baltic under the guns of the Swedish navy. (When the Swedes did prohibit the re-export of certain goods, they hit back by refusing to allow the Entente powers to transport rubber, or any other of the listed items, to Russia via their trains.)

Slowly the blockade did take effect. The results showed themselves first in occupied France. 'Everything had come to stand still,' wrote one French citizen. 'The factories were shut down because the Germans were short of war material and the first thing they had done was to strip the factories and take all the copper parts from the machines, right down to the smallest components. Even if they could have run the machines without them there were no raw materials to work with and all the workers of military age had been mobilised and were fighting on the other side of the line.'[14]

Stopping foodstuffs was always a delicate issue. Supplies of flour to an army were as warlike as ammunition and could be intercepted. But how could it be known where the food went, and what of supplies to munition workers? When the SS *Wilhelmina*, carrying food for the civil population of Hamburg, was captured on the grounds that Hamburg was 'a base for the armed forces of the enemy', the US objected, but their criticism was blunted by releasing the food for sale to the Belgian Relief Commission. Fortunately for the British authorities the German Government decreed on 25 January 1915 that all grain and flour would pass under government control, and this gave the excuse for blocking all food.

The blockade of wheat or meat should have had little serious effect for some time, because, thanks to fertilizers and fodder, Germany produced eighty-five to ninety per cent of her *essential* food (though a great many varieties of foodstuffs had been imported). However, she had to look abroad for concentrated fodder and the nitrates for the fertilizer on which her agriculture depended. The shortage of these would tell later. Meanwhile confident of a short war, the General Staff, in all the perfection of its military preparations, had not thought to stockpile grain before war began, problems were exacerbated by government policy and for a time food supply went into a downward spiral. Because animals convert grain into meat inefficiently, a third of Germany's pigs were slaughtered early in 1915 so the price of meat and fat soared. Livestock became so profitable that farmers fed their animals on grain, potatoes and other foodstuffs which humans could have eaten. Then since price controls were introduced locally rather than nationally, produce was moved to uncontrolled areas and the shortages worsened in the controlled areas. Flour began to be mixed with turnips and potatoes to make 'war bread'. Soon a doctor was noting in his diary, 'Slowly but surely we are slipping into a, now still well organised, famine'.[15] In fact Germany was a long way from that and over the next four years the quantity of food available would fluctuate with the fortunes of her armies. After six months of war, 'She was still breathing normally but was haunted by the fears of suffocation; she beheld herself as it were in a fortress, already beset, a state of mind which was itself becoming an obsession.'[16] The supply of arms to her enemies from America heightened this obsession, but it was the interception of food by Britain which was the excuse for Germany to impose its own long-distance blockade, using submarines as they had never been used before.

Notes

1. Madison, writing to the US Minister in England, quoted in Parmelee, Maurice, *Blockade and Sea Power*, Hutchinson, 1924, p.56. (A really fictitious blockade, you might say, was the one declared by Napoleon against the British on 21 November 1806, barely a year after Trafalgar!)
2. Adam Smith's phrase originally, not Napoleon's.
3. *The Times Documentary History of the War*, Vol. III – Naval, Part 3, p.434
4. 'Prize', in its legal sense, 'is the term applied to a ship or goods captured by the maritime force of a belligerent at sea or seized in port'. (See Halsbury's Laws of England (Third edition) Vol.37 para. 1301, 1305.) By derivation the word is an anglicized pronunciation of the French word 'pris' (past tense of the verb to take). Goods captured by land forces are 'booty'.
5. Halsbury's Laws of England (Third Edition) Vol.37 para.1306. In applying this law the judges are bound by UK Acts of Parliament, but not by Government proclamations or Orders-in-Council, unless they were issued in accordance with an Act, or else were in accordance with International Law, or were in favour of the enemy or neutrals. As to International Law itself, many lawyers believe that, 'It is a matter of dispute whether it may properly be described as law in the sense generally accepted in jurisprudence'. (See Lauterpacht, H., *International Law*, Cambridge University Press, 1970, p.9)
6. Arnold-Forster, W., *The Blockade 1914–1919*, Clarendon Press, 1939, p.9
7. Lloyd George, David, *War Memoirs*, Odhams New Edition, 1938, p.393
8. *Times*, 28 August 28 1914.
9. Lloyd George, op. cit. p.395
10. House, Colonel E.M., *Intimate Papers*, Four volumes arranged by Charles Seymour, Ernest Benn, 1926, Vol.1, p.343
11. Table from Guichard, Lieutenant Louis, *The Naval Blockade 1914–1918*, Philip Allen, 1930, p.43
12. CID meeting, 6 December 1912, in PRO CAB 2/3. Niall Ferguson in *The Pity of War*, Allen Lane, 1998, p.67, claims that this means that 'if Germany had not violated Belgian neutrality in 1914, Britain would have', a statement which is repeated twice in the book, as though it were an established fact. However, it surely only meant that Belgium would have been treated in the same way as the neutral Dutch were in

1914 – which is rather different from marching an army through the country.

13. ibid. p.8

14. M. Pierre Dewavrin, quoted in *1915, the Death of Innocence* by Lyn MacDonald, Headline Book Publishing, 1993.

15. Alfred Grotjahn, quoted by Peter Loewenberg in Cecil, Hugh and Liddle, Peter H., *Facing Armageddon*, Leo Cooper, 1996, p.554

16. Guichard, op. cit. p.45

CHAPTER SIX

The First U-Boat Campaign

U-boat attacks on merchant shipping began almost by accident. Two and a half months after the war had begun, on 20 October 1914, an old, slow British steamship, the *Glitra*, was waiting for a pilot some distance from the Norwegian coast when her master observed a long submarine about three miles away approaching her. The Norwegian pilot boat turned away as did the *Glitra*. They sensed trouble, although no merchant ship had been attacked by a submarine before. The submarine, the *U17*, was five knots faster than the old ship and soon overtook her and circled round. A gun was fired and the *Glitra* stopped. A German boarding party then went up to the bridge and the master, with a pistol at his neck, was told that he had ten minutes to get his crew away in the ship's boats before she was sunk. The men were not allowed to collect their clothes and belongings, but the Germans took their charts and compasses, 'without a word of apology for such acts of theft'.[1] An engineer from the U-boat opened the ship's valves and she soon began to settle in the water. The submarine towed the boats towards the coast for a quarter of an hour and then cast them off. The crew were later picked up by the pilot boat.

The sinking of the *Glitra* was the first occasion in history, when a merchant ship had been sunk by a submarine. The event was considered by the British authorities to be an 'outrage of despicable character'.[2] They hoped that it would be an isolated incident, but were soon to realize that the rules of war, with which surface ships could easily comply, were to be debased, step by step, by the new weapon. Six days later the world was shocked by the sinking of a French steamer, the

Amiral Ganteaume. Belgian refugees were crowded on board and forty died. The loss of such a passenger ship from a mine would have been shocking enough in those early days of the war, but a fragment of a German torpedo was found lodged in one of the lifeboats. It was clear that she had been deliberately sunk without warning. (Schneider, the U-boat commander, said he thought that she was a troop ship.) As a result of the horror expressed by the world's press no more merchant ships were sunk by U-boats for a month, but the seed had been planted.

When *Kapitänleutnant* Feldkirchner returned to Wilhelmshaven in the *U17* after sinking the *Glitra*, 'he put into port a badly worried man'.[3] He was unsure whether he would get a medal or a court martial. Though he had taken some care for the safety of the crew, he had not been instructed to sink a merchant vessel, and he was by no means sure how the unprecedented action would be received by his superiors.

However, Feldkirchner was not reprimanded and while both sides pondered this development, the British on 2 November designated the whole North Sea a military area. The increased pressure on the German economy roused the *Admiralstab* and trials were run to see if submarines could damage enemy trade in the way that surface cruisers had been expected to do.

At the end of November Otto Hersing, who had distinguished himself by torpedoing the destroyer, *Pathfinder,* was dispatched with orders to sink freighters. Off the Normandy coast he held up two small ships, the *Malachite* and the collier *Primo,* averaging 1,000 tons displacement. After rather apologetically ordering the crews into their boats, he fired on the vessels – not very effectively in the case of the *Primo,* which did not sink, and was eventually sent to the bottom by a French torpedo boat, because the collier, abandoned and ablaze, was a hazard to shipping.

Both sides were learning the capabilities of submarines. Tirpitz admitted in an interview for the *New York Sun*[4] that they had thought that U-boat crews would be exhausted after three days away from their bases. In fact, by resting the boat on the bottom overnight in shallow waters, where the crew could sleep, it was possible for the larger ones to remain at sea for a couple of weeks. In that time they could circumnavigate Britain. Unlike battleships, which required destroyer escorts to protect them from torpedoes, and destroyers which needed battleships to protect them from the guns of cruisers, the submarine was self-sufficient. Indeed, Admiral Scheer considered that for endurance and independence 'the U-boat was superior to all surface ships'.[5]

In January 1915 the *U19, U20* and *U21* set out on a more determined effort to prove what could be done. On the 21st *Oberleutnant* Kolbe in *U19* struck the first blow, humanely, and, from the German point of view, economically. He chased the *Durward*, a small steamer of 1,301 tons, as she plied her way across the North Sea to Rotterdam. The U-boat was flying no colours but hoisted the flag which meant 'Stop immediately'. The master of the *Durward*, Captain Wood, ignored this unexpected signal, and, relying on his twelve knot speed, steamed on. After half an hour Kolbe caught up with him and now flew the signal 'Stop or I fire'. Wood had no choice and was instructed to send a boat over with the ship's papers. This being done, some German sailors got into the boat and rowed back to the merchant ship with two bombs, which they placed against the ship's side. The rest of the British crew were ordered in good English to get into their boats. After twenty minutes the bombs exploded and the ship began to settle. The U-boat then towed the two sea boats for more than half an hour, and then cast them off near a lightship off the Dutch coast. They were eventually taken to shore by a Dutch pilot vessel. It was clear that Kolbe was 'anxious to do what he could for members of the same great brotherhood of the sea while conforming to the orders he had received from his superiors'.[6]

Ten days later no less than six ships were sunk on one day by the two other U-boats. Hersing in the *U21* had again taken his boat through the minefields of the English Channel. He passed round Cornwall, turned north and waited outside Liverpool. By 2 p.m. he had sunk one steamer of 3,000 tons and two much smaller vessels. In each case the procedure was the same. The ships were stopped by a shot across the bows, and Hersing, this time not risking indecisive gunfire, had time bombs put on board while the crews clambered into their boats. The men of the first two ships were directed towards nearby trawlers, one crew even being given cigars and cigarettes for their journey. To save the crew of the last one, the *Kilcoan* (456 tons), Hersing went so far as to chase a steamer which was crossing to the Isle of Man, and when he had caught up with her, instead of planting bombs on board, he directed her to pick up the *Kilcoan*'s men.

On the same day, 31 January, *Kapitänleutnant* Droescher lay in wait off Le Havre, where he accounted for three ships, totalling nearly 12,000 tons. His methods were also uniform – but the opposite of Hersing's. In each case Droescher loosed off a torpedo without warning, waited at periscope depth to see the result and then disappeared. The crews of the first two ships were saved, but of the third, the *Oriole*, nothing was ever found except for two lifebuoys washed up on the

Sussex shore, and a beer bottle found on Guernsey with a paper inside announcing simply, '*Oriole* torpedoed – sinking'. The grief-stricken widow of the ship's carpenter identified her husband's handwriting from a photo in the newspaper. Seeing how easily Hersing could save lives, Droescher's was then an atrocity without excuse.

The trial had shown that an all-out submarine campaign might have dramatic results. It had first been discussed when von Ingenohl was the Commander-in-Chief of the High Seas Fleet. He had not been in favour, considering it uncivilized. Von Pohl, then Chief of Naval Staff, had at first also been unenthusiastic, deeming it not yet justified by Britain's breaches of international law, but now, appointed C.-in-C. after the Battle of Dogger Bank, he changed his mind. The launching of an unrestricted submarine campaign had become a political issue. Because the neutral countries would object strongly, the opponents of the U-boat campaign in Germany cajoled Tirpitz and Bachmann, the new Chief of Naval Staff, to put their names to a document, saying that they were 'convinced that Great Britain will end the blockade six weeks after the new commercial war begins'.[7] It was a rash estimate, born of a great leap of faith.[8] Germany had at the time only twenty-four overseas U-boats and another four for coastal defence. They generally carried only six torpedoes and some had no deck gun. Seven submarines had been lost since the beginning of the war and only three or four completed. But orders had been placed for twenty large U-boats and thirty-three small coastal and minelaying submarines, which could now operate from the captured Flanders ports of Bruges, Zeebrugge and Ostend. Moreover, theorists believed that Britain's food stocks would only last six weeks. With cereals, milk and flour beginning to be rationed in Germany, the Kaiser was persuaded to agree.

On 4 February 1915 the German government issued a memorandum denouncing the British blockade and declaring a war zone round Britain and Ireland. 'Since the commencement of the present war Great Britain's conduct of commercial warfare against Germany has been a mockery of all the principles of the law of nations,' the memorandum began, and it went on to enumerate their sins. They had repudiated the Declaration of London in the most essential points. They had 'placed a number of articles on the contraband list, which are not at all or only very indirectly capable of use in warfare . . . obliterated the distinction between absolute and conditional contraband . . . captured on neutral ships German property which was not contraband of war . . . and caused numerous German subjects capable of bearing arms to be taken from neutral ships and made prisoners of war. Finally, they have declared the North Sea in its whole extent to be a seat of war, . . . so that they have in a way established a blockade of neutral coasts and ports, which is contrary to the elementary principles of generally accepted international law. Clearly all these measures are part of a plan to strike not only at the German military operations, but also at the economic system of Germany, and in the end to deliver the whole German people to reduction by famine, by intercepting legitimate neutral commerce by methods contrary to international law.' It regretted that the neutral powers had to a certain extent contributed to this by prohibiting the export and transit of goods destined for peaceful purposes in Germany and looked 'with indulgence upon all these violations of neutrality to the detriment of Germany . . . admitting the vital interests of a belligerent as a sufficient excuse for methods of waging war of whatever description. The time has now come,' it concluded, 'for Germany to invoke such vital interests.'[9]

On the same day von Pohl issued a proclamation as follows:

1. The waters surrounding Great Britain and Ireland, including the whole English Channel are hereby declared to be a War Zone. On and after February 18th, 1915 every enemy merchant ship found in the said war zone will be destroyed without it being always possible to avert the dangers threatening the crews and passengers on that account.
2. Even neutral ships are exposed to danger in the war zone, as in view of the misuse of neutral flags ordered on January 31st by the British Government, and of the accidents of naval war, it cannot always be avoided to strike even neutral ships in attacks that are directed on enemy ships.[10]

The War Zone left a corridor down the Norwegian, Danish and Dutch coasts, so besides the embargo on all trade with Britain and Ireland, this was a direct challenge to all ships sailing for north Europe. The British were directing them to pass through the Channel and the Germans threatened to sink them unless they went to the north of Scotland and down the coast of Norway.

On 10 February the United States Government protested to the Wilhelmstrasse against the submarine war zone policy, but also protested on the same day to Whitehall against the use of the American flag by British ships.

The British replied forcefully on 1 March to the German declaration of the unrestricted U-boat campaign. They called it, 'a claim to torpedo at sight, without regard to the safety of the crew or passengers, any merchant vessel under any flag'. Since the enemy could not keep ships in the area, they would have to use submarines, which would be bound to involve loss of life of civilians and neutrals. 'The German declaration substitutes indiscriminate destruction for regulated capture', the statement continued, playing the starvation card as well; 'Germany is adopting these methods against peaceful traders and non-combatant crews with the avowed object of preventing commodities of all kinds (including food for the civil population) from reaching the British Isles or Northern France.' As the Germans escalated, the British retaliated. The 'Reprisals Order in Council' was issued on 11 March 1915. The Royal Navy would now 'prevent commodities of any kind from reaching or leaving Germany,' but, having command of the surface waters, the British could promise that their actions would be 'without risk to neutral ships or to neutral or non-combatant life, and in strict observance of the dictates of humanity . . .'.[11] Since Britain also claimed that the actions of the Navy did not extend the principle of confiscating property as prize, she only claimed the right to detain, not confiscate, all goods of enemy destination, origin or ownership. (The war was still not expected to last long.) The Order in Council made it clear that Britain did not consider herself bound by the 1856 Declaration of Paris, but it was not called a 'blockade'. To the shocked world, which doubted whether these actions were still legal the Prime Minister announced in the House of Commons, 'We are not going to allow our efforts to be strangled in a network of juridical niceties . . . Under existing conditions there is no form of economic pressure to which we do not consider ourselves entitled to resort.'[12]

Germany's 'new commercial war', the first U-boat campaign, started slowly. There were in truth too few U-boats. Even with new launchings there were never more than twenty-five available in the North Sea ports during the first couple of months of the campaign, and with mainte-nance, repairs, refuelling, rearming, training and rest for the crews, only about seven could be on patrol at one time round the whole British Isles. Further, on 23 January 1915 the Royal Naval Air Service had begun bombing the submarines moored at Zeebrugge, and just as the campaign was starting *U-41* was seriously damaged in a raid. This persuaded the *Admiralstab* to withdraw their U-boats from Belgium until they had organized anti-aircraft defences. Consequently for a time 250 miles was added to the distance which the boats had to travel before they could begin their attacks and, with their limited endurance, only one third of their patrol time could be spent on station.

The same effect could be obtained by closing the Straits of Dover to submarines, and during the war the Dover Patrol tried one technique after another to achieve this. The first barrage, laid from Folkestone to Cap Gris-Nez in January 1915, consisted of massive wooden floats connected by wire hawsers, which supported nets. The floats were moored by chains to heavy anchors, but it was found that after a few weeks of chafing in the gales and strong tides of the Channel, iron rings even three inches thick would be worn through. The barrage was never completed and its rescued sections were removed to the Firth of Forth. Still, from April 1915 the larger U-boats took the Scottish route from the German ports until the end of 1916, though the smaller submarines operating from Flanders still wormed their way round or over whatever obstructions were put in their way. Later rows of mines were laid too near the surface and, with the tide rising and falling fifteen feet, they were visible from shortly before low water to a little after. To a skilled and daring submariner like von Spiegel, the aristocratic author of a book on U-boat exploits, it was easy to skirt between the shoals, where mines could not be laid, or even slip through the gaps between the mines at low tide, when he could see 'the infernal black globes, surrounded by snow white foam from the breaking sea'.[13]

Once through the Straits the U-boats found numerous targets. There was a constant stream of traffic heading to or from London and the southern ports. On any night in 1915 there would be about 120 ships sheltering in the Downs, protected by the Goodwin Sands and the Dover Patrol,[14] while daylight offered a further swarm of transports crossing the Channel with munitions, coal, stores and men for the front in France. Troopships and the more valuable cargoes of munitions were convoyed, but there were plenty of unescorted steamers to pick off. The most profitable hunting ground was the southern end of the Irish Sea. Ships passed there on their way to Liverpool, south Wales and the Bristol Channel ports. The third area was on the east coast of England where U-boats could attack coastal trade, colliers taking coal from Newcastle, and freighters sailing or steaming to Scandinavia. (However, so much of the burgeoning trade to those neutral countries found its way to Germany in the early months of the conflict that the U-boats must often have been harming their own war effort.)

In spite of the efficient British direction finding system, which from May 1915 enabled the Admiralty to track U-boats as they crossed the North Sea, countermeasures were still largely ineffective, unless the submarine happened to be caught on the surface, where it could be shelled or rammed. The most widely used technique was for two trawlers to drag between them a hawser with an attached explosive charge, which could be fired electrically, and hope to catch the U-boat with it. Sometimes success attended their patience, as when a destroyer division sighted a periscope in March 1915. 'The *Viking* fired her explosive sweep over the spot where it had appeared. Beyond another glimpse of the periscope, nothing happened for a further hour. Then the destroyer *Maori* saw the periscope again, this time further down the Channel. Thereupon the *Ghurka* towed her sweep across the track the submarine appeared to be taking and at 5 p.m. it exploded with dramatic result. The stern of the *U-8* shot up to the surface almost vertically, and she was greeted by rapid fire from the *Ghurka* and *Maori*. Finding escape impossible, the submarine's crew of four officers and thirty-five men emerged from their sinking craft and surrendered.'[15]

Trawlers, however, were not fast, and the submarine, even with its slow underwater speed, could usually move out of the way before the pursuit arrived. Above all, these varied craft were hunting blind. The Cambridge Professor William Bragg and Commander C.P. Ryan were working on the hydrophone, which could detect the beat of a submarine's propeller, but trials had only begun in early 1915. It took two years to develop, and its first versions gave no indication of the direction of the sound. Also, to hear a submarine, the crew had to stop engines, at which point the hunter might easily become the prey. There were no depth charges until July 1915 and few for many months then. So, although the number of small armed craft patrolling the coasts had increased dramatically, successes were rare.

Among U-boat commanders the techniques of attack tried out by Hersing and Kolbe were practised and perfected. On sighting a freighter the submarine would fire a shot across the bows. A tramp steamer might try to evade the pursuer, but would more often be overhauled and after a round or two had landed on board would haul up the flag signalling, 'I have stopped'. As the U-boat approached, her captain would command by flags or voice, 'Abandon ship at once,' and the master of the merchantman would row across with the ship's papers. So far, the procedure was the same as with the surface raiders, but there the similarity ended. A considerate U-boat commander would tow the sea boat towards the shore or a lightship. Others would just give the crew a few minutes to get into their boats before the ship was sunk. And about twenty per cent of the victims were torpedoed without warning during 1915 and 1916.

For the steamer, flight was usually the best and only defence: few were yet defensively armed. A merchant ship, radioing desperately for help, could sometimes outrun a U-boat, but there were few cargo vessels capable of more than the fourteen knots which most German submarines, with their blast-injection diesel engines, could manage on the surface. (The first U-boats and the minelayers were slower.) Nonetheless only half the attacks led to sinkings. Often the merchant ship had enough start to get clear away, but not without risk. Captain William Propert, the master of the *Laertes*, was awarded the Distinguished Service Cross for his action in turning his ship away from a U-boat, and zig-zagging as fast as the ship could go under a hail of ineffectual machine-gun fire. (He was flying the Dutch flag and had obscured the name of the port of registration.) The SS *Vosges* steaming from Bordeaux to Liverpool, tried the same but narrowly failed. When the U-boat appeared, the master of the *Vosges*, Captain John R. Green, asked the five consular passengers he was carrying to help the firemen maintain steam pressure. A furious chase ensued. While the submarine tried to get to the side of the fleeing ship to torpedo her, her master kept turning her stern towards the pursuer. Shells were landing on the *Vosges*; the chief engineer was killed and others of the crew wounded, but she kept on. Eventually her pursuer gave up the chase, but water was gaining on the pumps and the steamer did not make Milford Haven before there was an explosion and she sank. 'Gentlemen, I did not give her away,'[16] Captain Green reported to the owners.

U-boats had no hope of overtaking their prey if forced to dive. Driving under water on their electric motors, none during the First World War were able to attain ten knots, and so one tactic was to make them submerge. The merchant ship could then escape while a destroyer, sloop or trawler, with more patience than optimism, tried to harry the U-boat until it used up its batteries and was forced to the surface. Any small gun could usually make a U-boat dive, or, if the submarine was close enough on the bow, a turn of the helm towards it would also do the trick.

This tactic had an unfortunate consequence in the case of Captain Charles A. Fryatt, a master mariner who had twice acquired fame by escaping from U-boats. On both occasions he had turned his ship away and fled under the shells of his pursuer – once after a forty mile pursuit into Dutch waters. Then in March 1915, when on his way to Rotterdam in command of the packet boat SS *Brussels*, he was once more signalled to stop by a submarine. This time instead of fleeing Fryatt altered course to ram. (The Admiralty had not only advised masters that if they turned towards the attacking U-boat, it would be forced to submerge, but had offered a reward for sinking one.) The submarine dived and escaped, but the German authorities claimed that Fryatt's action was a hostile act committed by a civilian against German forces. Three months later the *Brussels* was stopped by German torpedo boats off Zeebrugge and taken into port. Fryatt was tried at Bruges, condemned as a *franc-tireur* and shot the same day, just as many Belgians had been executed when caught with guns. As with Nurse Edith Cavell, who was shot later that year for helping Allied soldiers to escape, this heavy-handed action made a martyr out of Captain Fryatt. It was not logical that U-boats could kill civilians, but civilians could not kill U-boats. The 'vials of wrath' were simmering.

They boiled over when on 27 March *Kapitänleutnant Freiherr* (Baron) von Forstner in *U-28*, after sinking the *Aguila*, fired on the passengers and crew, and next day sank the 5,000 ton liner, *Falaba*, in a despicable fashion according to survivors. First he shot a torpedo into her while the boats were still being filled. Then, it was alleged, as the men, women and children were thrown into the water, the Baron and his crew jeered at them from the safety of the submarine's deck. The *Falaba* would not be forgotten; 104 passengers and crew lost their lives, including one American.[17]

But such atrocities were not frequent and when Winston Churchill in his capacity as First Lord of the Admiralty described the U-boat crews as pirates, who were outside the law, and should be treated as such, only a small minority in the Royal Navy agreed. 'Expressions such as this one are left to civilians,' one naval author wrote. 'When Mr Churchill announced that the officers and crews of captured U-boats would be treated differently from those taken in surface ships, the Navy strongly disapproved ... To retaliate upon subordinate officers and men for the crimes of their political chiefs seemed cowardly.'[18] (The practice of separating U-boat crews was discontinued when the Germans retaliated by throwing thirty-seven British prisoners from prominent families into solitary confinement.) That U-boat atrocities were not more frequent is perhaps surprising in the light of the campaign of hatred of the English – as distinct from the French or Russians – which was stirred up from platform, pulpit and press early in the war. Some German shops had had their windows broken in Britain, but in Germany hate had become a duty and an art form. *Gott strafe England* was a drinking toast and a greeting in the street. There were even sticky labels affixed to the backs of envelopes like charity stickers, while the rollicking *Hymn of Hate* by Ernst Lissauer was distributed throughout the army.

> French and Russian they matter not,
> A blow for a blow and a shot for a shot:
> We love them not, we hate them not . . .
> We have one foe, and one alone
>
> Hate by water and hate by land
> Hate of the head and hate of the hand . . .
> We love as one, we hate as one,
> We have one foe and one alone – ENGLAND!

One submarine captain who was respected by his enemies was Otto Weddigen, who had sunk the three Cressy-class armoured cruisers off the Dutch coast. One day in March 1915, he accounted for three freighters, ignoring the fire from a patrol vessel, while he ran on the surface to overhaul and torpedo his third victim. Weddigen's time was coming to an end, however. He was returning round the north of Scotland, when he stumbled into the path of the Grand Fleet. Relishing his good fortune, he fired a torpedo at the battleship, HMS *Neptune*, the last ship of the First Battle Squadron, and missed her. Then somehow he failed to observe the Fourth Battle Squadron approaching immediately on his beam. HMS *Dreadnought* had only to alter course one point and her stern sliced through the U-boat's hull. As she went down, the U-boat's bows rose in the air showing the number 'U29'. (That was the only vessel sunk by the great ship after which all subsequent battleships were called.) Weddigen's humane conduct, 'undimmed by any dishonour . . . had won for him, from his victims off the Scillies, the half-rueful and half-jesting sobriquet of the "polite pirate"'.[19] In Germany the death of the U-boat ace was as greatly mourned as the shooting down of the famous 'Red Baron' von Richthofen later in the war. Jellicoe had ordered that no information about the sinking of submarines should be released, and so his compatriots could only speculate why their hero failed to return. All kinds of lurid treachery were imagined to have secured his demise.

Besides courage, the U-boats demanded fortitude from their crews. Leading Seaman Schlichting described the conditions coming down off watch in a storm: 'Before I lay down I swallowed a little tea, and glanced into the engine-room; an appalling burst of heat flung me backwards; the thermometer stood at nearly 45 degrees Celsius. The men were standing over their engines in the bare minimum of clothing, their drawn, gaunt faces, smeared with oil and filth, looked like skulls. The air was unbelievable; the thudding combustion-engines exhausted such fresh air as could be pumped through the ventilators, and what remained of it was not enough to lighten the prevailing atmosphere. Hot whirling eddies of vapour hovered over the engines and drifted into other parts of the ship; the men were continually mopping their foreheads, and now and again one of them would moisten his lips with a drop of repulsive lukewarm tea, which, like all the food and drink on the boat, tasted strongly of oil.'[20]

Most of the U-boat commanders viewed their torpedoes as a luxury which had to be used sparingly. Gunfire, bombs or even sprinkled petrol would do the trick as well, and more economically. (In one of the most remarkable patrols of the war in August 1915 the first among the U-boat aces, *Korvettenkapitän* Max Valentiner, used his gun to sink twenty-two steamships, three sailing ships and five fishing boats.) Surface attacks could very often be made without any great danger to their own safety. If the horizon was clear, the U-boat crew knew that they had from half an hour to an hour from the time when smoke on the skyline would warn them of an approaching vessel to the moment when they had to dive. So, before the advent of regular aircraft patrols, after a night resting on the bottom, reading, listening to the gramophone or singing patriotic songs – 'no other evening's rest can be compared with it'[21] – an *Unterseeboot* would frequently surface in one of the main shipping routes and await events. Patrol boats churned up and down these routes, but they had to make smoke so they rarely saw a periscope. (By contrast the diesels of the U-boats when running surfaced or charging batteries gave off relatively little exhaust.) When dived, a submarine could also hear the engines or propellers of a vessel approaching close, unless it was directly behind, in which case there was a danger of surfacing right into the path of a hunter.

Consequently the toll of merchant ships steadily rose: twenty-nine in March 1915, thirty-three in April and then fifty-three in May. It was worrying, but still not disastrous. As shipbuilding expanded with world trade in the previous half century, British yards had led the world by a clear margin. In the twenty years before 1914 two thirds of the world's steam tonnage had been built in the UK, and at the outbreak of the war 'the British Mercantile Marine was the largest, most up to date, and the most efficient of all the merchant navies of the world . . . and was four times as large as its nearest and most formidable rival – the German Mercantile Marine'.[22] Its pre-eminence is shown by a table of the tonnage of seagoing steamships of the world in June 1914:[23]

		Tons net	Per cent
British Empire	United Kingdom	11,538,000	44.4
	Dominions and Colonies	902,000	3.5
	total	12,440,000	47.9
Germany		3,096,000	11.9
United States		1,195,000	4.6
Norway		1,153,000	4.4
France		1,098,000	4.2
Japan		1,048,000	4.0
Netherlands		910,000	3.5
Italy		871,000	3.4
Others		4,179,000	16.1
	Total	25,990,000	100.0

As to numbers, the newer ships tended to be larger and therefore fewer, but Great Britain still had over 12,000 steamships at her disposal. Of these 3,700 were over 1,000 tons and suitable for ocean trade. Sailing ships had declined steeply over the previous twenty-five years, but the remaining 850,000 tons at sea in 1913 were still economic.

These large numbers seemed comforting and safe (less than two per cent of the 12,000,000 gross tons of shipping possessed by the British Empire had been lost to cruisers, submarines and mines by the end of March 1915, when the six weeks promised by Tirpitz was up.) The Admiralty policy therefore continued to rely on the multitude of Royal Navy craft patrolling the danger areas, and to inform and direct ships into safe routes, but otherwise to leave their safety to the good sense and experience of their masters. On the other side, a more serious concern for the Navy was that U-boat losses since the war began had been only about one a month, and these were now quickly made good by the German yards. In August 1914 there had been seventeen at various stages of construction. They were hurried on and six more, being built for Norway and Germany's ally Austria-Hungary, were taken over by the Imperial Navy. So the U-boat fleet was stronger after six months of the war in spite of its losses.

The Royal Navy was more powerful too; five new dreadnoughts had been added since the war began. But it had very soon become apparent that the glorious Grand Fleet with its 70,000 men, was only half what was required to wage the new type of war. Though the Battle Squadrons could expect to deal with any other surface fleet that might be ranged against them, they could not defend Britain's widespread mercantile marine. Lord Fisher had built great ships, but to some extent at the expense of smaller, cheaper, and in the event more necessary, vessels. A host of smaller craft was needed to deal with the enemy submarines. The trawlers and drifters made excellent minesweepers, but the slow craft were not so effective in hunting U-boats, and the Navy had too few destroyers outside the Grand Fleet, though Fisher now ordered a hundred. (There were five at Milford Haven for instance, but none in south-west Ireland.) A large auxiliary fleet of sloops, private yachts, paddle steamers, and sundry other craft were pressed into service. A new design of small destroyer with guns but no torpedoes was introduced for anti-submarine patrols and dubbed 'P' boats, but there were still not enough.[24] The best protection for merchant shipping at this time was the ever present threat of US intervention.

Predictably, the unrestricted submarine campaign caused friction with all the neutral countries. Besides the British and French, the Norwegians, Swedes, Dutch and Greeks all had ships sunk without warning in the first months of the campaign. The United States' protest soon after the campaign was declared, resulted in a watering down of the instructions to U-boat commanders. Neutral shipping was not to be harmed provided that it was recognized as such. As British ships often flew neutral flags, this required the submarine captains to surface and inspect the ship's papers before opening fire. While this was in accordance with the Hague Convention, it put the U-boat at the mercy of any armed freighter, however small its gun, and it was not what Tirpitz, von Pohl and Scheer had in mind. Vice Admiral Bachmann at the *Admiralstab* was ready to call off the campaign, but it continued nonetheless, and the instructions were often flouted. On two occasions American lives had been lost – one when the *Falaba* went down, three when the US tanker *Gulflight* was torpedoed.

But all this was as nothing by comparison with the catastrophe which took place on 7 May 1915. *U-20* was on the surface in the bright morning after fog had cleared, when the lookout saw a large four-funnelled ship in the distance. It appeared that she was too far away to be attacked, but *Kapitänleutnant* Walther Schwieger dived in case she should alter course towards him. After about a quarter of an hour he was pleasantly surprised to see the great steamer duly turn on a course which made an attack possible. He put on all speed and crouched at the periscope. After rapid calculations of the course and adjustment of the angle of his submarine, Schwieger gave the order to fire one of his last torpedoes. By now it was clear to him that he had a huge liner in his sights. He dictated for the log; '3.10 pm Torpedo shot at distance of 700 metres, going three metres below the surface.' That close he could not miss a target 240 metres long. The torpedo struck just behind the bridge and he recorded, 'Unusually great detonation with large cloud of smoke and debris shot above the funnels. In addition to torpedo a second explosion must have taken place.'[25] He turned away from the periscope and the navigator, taking his place, exclaimed, 'My God, it's the *Lusitania!*'[26]

The great liner, which Cunard advertised as the 'Fastest and Largest Steamer now in Atlantic Service,' was soon listing to starboard and down by the bows. Her captain had been warned by Admiralty radio signals of the presence of U-boats off the south of Ireland as he approached the area, and had already swung the twenty-two lifeboats out as a precaution. Without that there would have been even greater loss of life. As it was, by the time the ship had slowed enough to make it safe to lower the boats, the *Lusitania* was listing so sharply that the ones on the port side were dangling above the boat deck. Five of them slithered into each other along the deck, mowing down the passengers, and not one boat on that side reached the water full of people. On the starboard side, with the angle of the ship constantly changing as she went down by the bows and listed still further to starboard, it became very difficult to climb into the boats and nigh impossible to lower them evenly. Several fell, bow or stern first, tipping their passengers into the water and some were eventually pushed under by their own davits. Only six lifeboats arrived ashore. The sea was just 255 feet deep, so as the ship plunged down and hit the bottom, her stern was briefly left pointing up out of the water, while passengers and crew frantically tried to save themselves. Then the stern slid under the waves, dragging hundreds down with it. Some 1,200 people died, including ninety-four babies and children. Only 764 survived.

A submarine could not rescue the hundreds in the water, and to have sunk such a huge passenger ship without warning, the U-boat commander being quite careless of whether soldiers or civilians were on board, was unheard of. To the British this was cold-blooded murder, and the public were all the more incensed by the way that the young German submarine commander was treated as a hero. The US Consul in Brussels reacted typically when a friend asked him, whether it was true that the *Lusitania* has been torpedoed and sunk? 'I had heard nothing of the kind,' he wrote, 'and did not, could not, believe it. . . . The *Lusitania*? Sunk? Impossible!' It was 'a hideous deed that one would have thought so short a time before no living being could be found low and dastard enough to commit.'[27] There were 128 US citizens among the dead, including such personalities as the wealthy sportsman, Alfred G. Vanderbilt, who was last seen helping children into their lifejackets. The clamour in the USA at the killing of their innocent citizens was loud and incessant, while the German press, claiming correctly that the ship was carrying munitions and incorrectly that the ship was armed, pleaded, 'But must we not, we whose throat the enemy is seeking to cut, we whose *defeat by hunger* and by lack of war material nearly every one would witness complacently as an unavoidable fate, *must* we not defend ourselves . . . ?'[28] Rifle cartridges, fuses and shrapnel were admitted in the manifest but almost certainly other explosive materials were carried and Canadian soldiers were among the passengers. The Germans asserted that the US was permitting her citizens to be used as a shield for contraband, and pointed out that they had warned the US public by advertisements against sailing through the dangerous waters. However, to the Americans announcing that you might commit a crime did not excuse the act, and they had accepted that goods which might be contraband, and even munitions, could be carried in liners.[29] Ex-President Theodore Roosevelt, who had always supported the Allies, was vehement in demanding reprisals and indemnities. 'For many months,' he thundered, 'our Government has preserved between right and wrong a neutrality which would have excited the emulous admiration of Pontius Pilate, the arch-typical neutral of all time.' Like many of his fellow citizens he was not impressed when Wilson told a great audience in Philadelphia that there was 'such a thing as a man being too proud to fight'.[30]

But the US as a whole was not ready for involvement in a European war. Besides, most Americans did not see Germany alone as being guilty of breaches of international law. Only two months before the sinking of the *Lusitania* the Reprisals Order in Council had proclaimed that Britain would put a stop to all enemy commerce, but the government had still not acknowledged that the blockade commenced on that date. At the same time the Royal Navy was insisting on bringing ships into port for inspection – arresting them in fact – because, when stopped at sea, they were sitting targets for U-boats, and rough weather often made the legitimate practice of inspection at sea impracticable. Waves would pour into the opened hatches, and on one occasion the seas forced HMS *Royal Arthur* into a Swedish freighter, which sank while a boarding party was trying to inspect her. As a result, when intercepted north of

Scotland, a suspect ship would be ordered to steam ahead of an auxiliary cruiser at half speed to Kirkwall, the capital of the Orkneys, or else a prize crew would be put on board to bring her in. After a while, under the threat of losing bunkering facilities, some lines voluntarily called in at Kirkwall, but, like the ships required to anchor in the Downs for inspection, they were delayed by doing so. Sometimes while the ships were thus detained the interception of cablegrams or wireless traffic or the censorship of mails would provide the Navy with evidence of the destination of the cargo. All this eased the problems of the Tenth Cruiser Squadron, especially in winter weather, but it was not popular with the neutrals.

These measures had from the start been an extension of the accepted precepts of the law and America was becoming impatient. 'We have been very meek and mild under their use of the ocean as a toll road,'[31] wrote Secretary Lane. The new Secretary of State, Robert M. Lansing, went further. There had in his opinion been 'many and flagrant'[32] violations of neutral rights on the High Seas. British actions constituted a blockade in all but name and hindered US trade with neutral countries; they were carried out far from the enemy coast, stopped non-contraband goods and prevented neutrals from purchasing German exports.[33] President Wilson was so angered that he threatened to cut off all war supplies to the Allies. As Wilson's biographer wrote, 'Throughout the entire period of our neutrality, if controversy with one belligerent died down, it was sure to flare up with another. If the Germans momentarily ceased to shock us by the bloody violence of their submarine attacks or their warfare in Belgium, the British and French straightway infuriated us with attacks upon our trade rights, or the pinprick seizures of our mails. There was no rest for the neutral!'[34]

Therefore after the sinking of the *Lusitania*, Woodrow Wilson sent Berlin only a strongly worded note of protest, demanding that the Germans should disavow the sinking, make reparations and take steps to prevent a recurrence. The reply was unsatisfactory and for some months, while notes flew back and forth, relations were cool between the USA and Germany, but Wilson was not to be budged from his position of neutrality, which so many Americans supported. Nonetheless, after the sinking of the *Lusitania*, as Winston Churchill wrote, 'the friends of the Allies in the United States were armed with a weapon against which German influence was powerless, and before which after a lamentable interval cold-hearted policy was destined to succumb'.[35]

Notes

1. Hurd, op. cit. Vol. I, p.270
2. ibid.
3. Thomas, E. Lowell, *Raiders of the Deep*, William Heinemann, 1929, p.34
4. 22 December 1914.
5. Scheer, Admiral, *Germany's High Sea Fleet in the World War*, Cassell & Co., 1920, p.36
6. Hurd, op. cit. Vol.I, p.276
7. See Gray, Edwin A., *The U-boat War*, Leo Cooper, 1994, p.84
8. Though U-boats had enjoyed some triumphs against warships, they had sunk only ten British merchant ships of 20,000 tons in total and one non-British, while mines had accounted for fourteen of 37,000 tons in all and cruisers had destroyed fifty-one vessels aggregating 215,000 tons.
9. Hurd, op. cit. Vol.I, pp.280–3
10. ibid. p.284
11. ibid. pp.284–5
12. 1 March 1915, *Hansard* 5th Ser. LXX, 600, quoted in Kenworthy, Lieutenant Commander the Hon. J.M. and Young, George, *Freedom of the Seas*, Hutchinson, 1928, p.27
13. Spiegel, Adolf von, *The Adventures of U-202*, Century Company, New York, 1917, p.80. His accounts may not always have been of his own experiences, and a little 'artistic licence' is evident. He recounts how his boat survived several patrols, though caught in heavy steel nets, dragging the floats behind them like a marker and chased by trawlers. They could outrun and outgun one trawler, but two or three made it too risky.
14. Bacon, op. cit. p.68
15. Gibson and Prendergast, op. cit. p.3
16. Hurd, op. cit. Vol.I, p.306. Green received the Distinguished Service Order and the crew were given a gratuity.
17. Reports differ. According to Simpson, Colin, *Lusitania*, Longman 1972, p.83, the *Falaba* had explosives on board, Forstner extended the time for abandoning ship and only fired his torpedo when an armed trawler appeared.
18. Copplestone, op. cit. p.45
19. Gibson and Prendergast, op. cit. p.35
20. Neureuther, Karl and Bergen, Claus (ed.) *U-Boat Stories*, Constable & Co., 1931 p.99

21. von Spiegel, op. cit. p.64

22. Hurd, op. cit. Vol. I, p.85

23. From table prepared for the Departmental Committee on Shipping and Shipbuilding, Cmd. 9092. The US merchant fleet is more than doubled if you count the 1,693,000 tons plying the Great Lakes.

24. Early in 1915 a British naval delegation contracted with US companies for the construction of submarine chasers and submarines. The boats were completed in Canada, because the American rules of neutrality required that they should not be wholly built in the USA. See Granville, Wilfred and Kelly, Robin P., *Inshore Heroes*, W.H. Allen, 1961, p.18

25. Gray, op. cit. p.18

26. Thomas, op. cit. p.87. On his return Schwieger told a friend that it was the most terrible sight he had ever seen, but that had not stopped him from offering the periscope to the crew.

27. Whitlock, Brand, *Belgium under German Occupation*, William Heinemann, 1919, p.400–1

28. *Frankfurter Zeitung*, 9 May 1915, quoted in Lauriat, Charles E., *The Lusitania's Last Voyage*, Houghton Mifflin Company, 1915, p.105. The *Lusitania* had mountings for guns, but did not carry them. (See Rintelen, op. cit. p.117.) Her loss, one of the climactic events of the war, was controversial, because of the second explosion. Only one torpedo was fired, but the British Public Enquiry, whitewashing Cunard and the Admiralty, found that the liner was sunk by two. The British and American governments kept the full truth about the cargo secret – the British, because there were almost certainly more explosives, and the Americans because they gave clearance for sailing on the basis of an incomplete manifest. The explosives, absence of an escort, inadequate lifeboat drill, collapsible boats not provided with oars and the subsequent attempt by the Admiralty to blame the Master for the disaster make up one of the greatest scandals of the twentieth century – even if explosions of coal dust or of the boilers in fact caused the second detonation. (See Simpson, op. cit. for a damning indictment.)

29. Woodrow Wilson's biographer noted, 'On almost all questions of neutrality – sale of munitions and their carriage on passenger ships, loans and shipments of food – rulings were to Germany's disadvantage'. (See Baker, Ray Stannard, *Woodrow Wilson, Life and Letters*, William Heinemann, 1938, Vol.6, p.121)

30. Baker, op. cit. Vol.6, p.8

31. House, op. cit. Vol.1, p.462

32. Lansing, Robert, *War Memoirs*, Rich & Cowan, 1935, p.27.

(Lansing had replaced Secretary William Jennings Bryan, who refused to sign the third note sent by the US government to Germany about the *Lusitania*, because he did not believe that the US had 'enforced its statutes with scrupulous vigilance', as it claimed.)

33. Preventing exports was a natural step, because it damaged German credit. The British action was not unprecedented. In the American Civil War the North had blocked the Confederate South's exports of cotton, to the annoyance of the Lancashire textile industry.

34. Baker, op. cit. Vol.6, p.312

35. Churchill, op. cit. p.771

CHAPTER SEVEN

The Legacy of the *Lusitania*

With the *Lusitania* the last hope of a negotiated peace died. It had been only a faint heartbeat, but it had been borne in the breasts of Woodrow Wilson and one of the most unusual and influential men who ever advised a US President. Colonel Edward M. House, Wilson's 'special representative' was known to few people outside the inner circles of politics in America and Europe, and yet no one except for the President had a greater influence on their government at home and embassies abroad. Colonel House never gave public speeches, nor even appeared beside politicians on the platform; when abroad he avoided government offices, generally managed to keep his name out of the papers and, on the rare occasions when he felt the need to hold a press conference, gave nothing away.

Edward House had breathed politics since his school days, but his health was poor and he resolved never to run for office. Instead he became a campaign manager for the Democrats in his home state, Texas. In alternate years through the 1890s the candidates that House backed, often from a minority position, were always elected Governor. The Colonel, as he became universally known, then felt ready to tackle national politics and sought for the 1912 Presidential election a Democrat who was clean, available and electable. He finally turned to the fifty-five year old Woodrow Wilson, who had been elevated from president of Princeton University to governor of New Jersey. In two years as governor Wilson had courageously introduced reforms, which showed him in House's eyes to be 'the only man in the East who in every way measured up to the office for which he was the candidate.'[1] The two men took to each other at once. Both were idealistic reformers, both had been brought up in the South and both remembered the bitter months of chaos after defeat in the Civil War. Wilson, the first Democrat president in twenty years, devoted himself immediately to internal reforms, but he was politically inexperienced and did not mix easily. House, shrewd and vastly experienced, had an easy way with all men, friend and foe alike, and assisted the President in building a Cabinet, drafting a programme and choosing ambassadors. When asked if House represented him accurately, Wilson once replied, 'Mr House is my second personality. He is my independent self. His thoughts and mine are one.'[2]

This alter ego of the President had evolved and shared with Woodrow Wilson an idealistic vision of a world at peace, in which the wealthy nations joined in improving the backward tropical countries and used their overflowing energies to civilize rather than destroy. His first proselytizing mission in the summer of 1914 on what he called 'The Great Adventure' had been frustrated by the outbreak of war. Then in February 1915 he sailed to Europe seeking some common ground which might start talks between the belligerents and lead to a permanent peace based on disarmament and joint action against future aggressors. But after meeting the leading men in Britain, France and Germany he reluctantly concluded that he was too late.[3] Both sides felt confident of success and so would settle only on a victor's terms. Britain wanted the evacuation of Belgium and compensation for her destruction, while South Africa and Australia wanted to keep the German colonies they had taken; France wanted Alsace-Lorraine; Germany wanted to keep Belgium and would pay no indemnity, because 'their campaign in that country cost the German nation such infinite sacrifices of human lives'.[4] Each of the nations, gorged with its own propaganda and anticipating victory, refused to 'throw across the chasm the first thread'.[5]

Then had come the sinking of the *Lusitania* with all its bitterness, and Colonel House considered war against Germany inevitable for the United States sooner or later. However, in a last effort to salvage something from his mission House proposed a deal which would save the US from its constant conflict with one or other of the warring nations. He suggested that the Imperial Navy should cease the U-boat campaign, if the United Kingdom would allow food supplies through to Germany via neutral ports. Though he was encouraged by Sir Edward Grey's first response, House found neither government prepared to accept the bargain. Food was not enough for the German army, and the British did not realize how dangerous the submarine would become, while they overstated the effect of their own blockade.[6]

German triumph over the *Lusitania* was soon seen to be an error. When a medal was privately issued in Germany celebrating the sinking, Captain Reginald Hall had thousands of copies of the tasteless item made and distributed worldwide in a neat box containing a caustic leaflet on the 'German Naval Victory'. In the face of the propaganda disaster the Kaiser ordered on 6 June 1915 that passenger liners should not be sunk, whatever flag they were flying. Though Tirpitz in anger tried again to resign, the order had little effect on the campaign, since the great majority of vessels in the waters round the British Isles were cargo liners and tramp steamers. Some might be let by, when a patrol was passing, but there were enough slow vessels on the seas for the submarines to be able to stop them at leisure, and sink them by gunfire, bombs or torpedoes. Still, the only real hope that the Germans had of bringing the war to a close by the U-boat campaign lay in so frightening the seamen or ship owners, British and neutral, that for the safety of their lives or hulls they would not risk putting to sea. This they could not achieve. Leaving aside the courage of the merchant navy crews, which were not deterred whatever their losses, there were just not enough submarines at the disposal of the *Admiralstab* within that first year of the war to break the nation's will. The few U-boats could not stem, and rarely interrupted, the flow of ships along the coasts of Britain.

But the waters round the British Isles were not the only area where U-boats could attack shipping. They were increasingly active in the Mediterranean Sea too. Traffic from the eastern parts of the British Empire had always passed through the Mediterranean, and now there was growing military traffic as the campaigns in Gallipoli and the Middle East developed. A submarine base had been established in the splendid, safe harbour at Cattaro (now Kotor in Montenegro) at the southern tip of the Austro-Hungarian Empire. It menaced the Allied supply lines for the duration of the war, and the threat of enemy submarines in the eastern Mediterranean affected the naval blockades by encompassing dramatic changes at the Admiralty and hastening the fall of the British government.[7]

The great strategic plan of forcing warships through the Dardanelles, the straits which separate Asia Minor from Europe, and exposing Constantinople to bombardment by a Franco-British fleet had been calculated to knock the Ottoman Empire out of the war. This in turn would reopen a supply line to Russia and remove the threat to the

114

Suez Canal. However, premature bombardment of the forts in the Straits alerted the Turks to the danger, while dilatory preparations gave them time to prepare. Mobile howitzers were especially effective in driving back the British minesweepers, which had civilian crews, and in March 1915 two old battleships were sunk by mines. The Navy now held off until the army could clear the peninsula. Troops were landed on 25 April 1915, but the Turks were by then well prepared, supplied and led, and there followed the disastrously mismanaged Gallipoli campaign. The continued drain on military and naval resources and the strain of these setbacks inevitably told on the men at the head of the Admiralty.

When the thirty-six year old Winston Churchill had been appointed First Lord of the Admiralty in 1911, he had viewed Lord Fisher, then aged seventy and retired, with almost filial respect. He had tried at the time to have the old Admiral reappointed First Sea Lord. On the resignation of Prince Louis of Battenberg, Fisher could hold that post again and his relationship with his First Lord was at first as cordial as it was dynamic and fruitful. But in times of such tension as the stalemate in Gallipoli provoked, it was inevitable that relations between two such titanic characters, the grand old Admiral and his young political master, would deteriorate. The limits of authority of the political First Lord and the First Sea Lord were not precisely defined as in a job specification, and Churchill, who believed he knew better than the naval experts, even in technical matters, encroached regularly on the executive functions of the Sea Lords. Fisher, growing ever more irascible and obstinate, even childishly so, complained that Churchill was always circumventing him.

Matters came to a head over the reinforcements required for the Dardanelles. Churchill, keen to push the campaign to a victorious conclusion, wanted to send more ships than Fisher considered could be spared from home waters, the main theatre of war. There were no modern battleships in the eastern Mediterranean, except for the new super-dreadnought, *Queen Elizabeth*, but after the old battleship *Goliath* had been sunk, Lord Fisher wanted even her sent home – in spite of Lord Kitchener's plea that it would look as though the Navy was deserting the Army. The two great chiefs of the services were for a while at loggerheads. Finally, Lord Fisher stated flatly that 'either the *Queen Elizabeth* left the Dardanelles that afternoon or he left the Admiralty that night.'[8]

Fisher got his way, and the *Queen Elizabeth* was replaced by two old battleships and two monitors. But two days later at a gloomy meeting of the War Council, Kitchener was still not reconciled and more reinforcements were considered. Churchill and Fisher reached an agreement in the evening, but then their very different hours of working, as much as anything else, caused a rupture. While Fisher started at dawn and left work hours before his colleague, Churchill began late and worked at the Admiralty till well after midnight. So it was that Fisher received at about five in the morning of 15 May four memoranda written by the First Lord the previous night. In the fourth one Churchill appeared to be going back on his word. More reinforcements than had been agreed, including two of the latest E class submarines, were proposed to be sent out. 'They were for Fisher the last straw, as he realised that any concessions would only be followed by fresh demands.'[9] He resigned and, even though the High Seas Fleet was thought to be coming out just at that time, refused the Premier's demand in the King's name that he should stay at his post. Instead he skulked in the Charing Cross Hotel, so as not to meet Churchill, whose eloquence the petulant old sailor feared he might be unable to resist.

The resignation of a First Sea Lord does not generally give rise to a political crisis, but that of Admiral of the Fleet Lord Fisher, so long the embodiment of the strength of the Royal Navy, coinciding as it did with the revelation of the country's scandalous lack of shells, now brought the government to its knees. A coalition government was formed with Asquith still Prime Minister. There was a press campaign not to let Fisher go, but he scuppered any chance there was by demanding six megalomaniac conditions for his retention of office. Churchill should not be in the Cabinet; Sir Arthur Wilson and the entire Board of Admiralty should be replaced; Fisher should have absolute control of all ships, construction and dockyards, and of the appointment of all officers of every rank while the First Lord of the Admiralty should be restricted to policy and Parliamentary procedure. In a post script he added:

> P.S. – The 60 per cent of my time and energy which I have exhausted on nine First Lords in the past I wish in the future to devote on the successful prosecution of the war. That is the sole reason for these six conditions. These six conditions must be published verbatim so that the Fleet may know my position.[10]

As Fisher's loyal biographer, Admiral Reginald Bacon, conceded, 'Prime Ministers are not accustomed to submit to such dictation, nor to be told whom they are to exclude from their Cabinets.'[11] Asquith accepted Fisher's resignation on 22 May 1915. Churchill, who had struggled to retain his place in the turmoil, had resigned with dignity the day before. Finding no real employment in the government, he left for the trenches as a Lieutenant Colonel. His departure from the Admiralty was met with widespread approval among both the press, who blamed him for the Gallipoli fiasco, and the admirals, who scorned his layman's intrusion into matters in which he was not an expert. Beatty, forgetting the First Lord's great contribution to the fleet, confided to his wife, 'The Navy breathes freer now it is rid of the succubus Churchill.'[12]

The new First Lord of the Admiralty was to be Arthur James Balfour, who had been Conservative Prime Minister from 1902–5. He had a brilliant mind and, aged sixty-seven with his ambitions behind him, made a more amenable colleague. The First Sea Lord was Sir Henry Jackson, a former Chief of the Admiralty staff and a clever scientific inventor, whose wireless experiments once kept pace with Marconi's. Jackson might have been expected to push on the development of new weapons to tackle the U-boats, but he could not delegate and the new naval administration did not have the drive of its predecessor.

Balfour did, however, have the good sense to summon Vice Admiral Sir Lewis Bayly from Greenwich, where he had been languishing as President of the Royal Naval College since the torpedoing of the battleship *Formidable* while under his command. 'Luigi' Bayly promised that he would check the U-boat campaign from Queenstown (Cobh) in south-west Ireland, if given adequate powers. He took a chart and pencilled off the vast area of which he must have command – from Mull in the Inner Hebrides, round the west coast of Ireland and down to Ushant off the western tip of Brittany. All this, except for the waters off Liverpool, were given to him, and Bayly set about the task. He was above all a hard working man. On his torpedo course at Greenwich he had won the £80 prize by working a minimum of eleven hours a day, six days a week, broken only by an evening walk in the park and an hour for tennis on summer mornings. On Sundays he relaxed – by walking at least twenty miles. Bayly became 'a hard, tough, independent man, a stern disciplinarian and a most redoubtable autocrat'.[13] As captain of a battleship in the Mediterranean, he forbade the band from playing when the ship entered harbour, and when appointed to command the Third Battle Squadron he stopped all bands playing tunes after the National Anthem at colours in the morning. At Cobh, to prevent leaks through gossip, he announced that there would be no social events at Admiralty

House. He never married, and such entertaining of officers as took place was organized by his niece, Violet Voysey, his companion for thirty-one years.

The Admiral quickly abolished red tape, stopping the weekly meeting of the Queenstown dockyard officers and the submission of defect lists by ships' captains on entering harbour. When returning from patrol a ship merely signalled any serious defects and the dockyard sent the required workmen on board as she came alongside. Coal-fired sloops of 1,200 tons were beginning to arrive as he took up his post, and he worked the dozen ships, their crews and young commanders hard, five days at sea and two in harbour. Ships were coaled on Sundays, if necessary, in spite of the opposition of priests. In all Bayly was an effective commander at a time when all his men were pushed to the limit, but he lacked the right ships and weapons.

Without the focused energies of Fisher and Churchill to develop new weapons the Royal Navy did its best with the tools at its disposal. A novel submarine trap was tried in June 1915. So frequent had the attacks on fishing fleets been, (fifty-eight were sunk in that month alone) that it was planned to snare the U-boats by putting a sting in the tail of a trawler. After several weeks of practice Lieutenant Taylor in command of submarine C24 was towed submerged behind a decoy trawler, the Taranaki, which lay on the fishing grounds, seemingly pursuing its trade. The trawler was connected to the submarine by telephone, and when a U-boat surfaced and fired a shot across her bows, the Taranaki phoned the enemy's position to Taylor, waiting patiently in his submerged submarine. However, things then went wrong. First the tow rope could not be slipped from the C24. It had jammed and the only recourse was for the Taranaki to let go of her end. The weight of 600 feet of thick wire hawser on the C24's bows caused her to dip down. She was now blind, slowly diving below periscope depth. Luckily though, the U-boat had not observed anything unusual. Taylor managed to control his boat, rise to peer through the periscope, manoeuvre to aim and fire a torpedo. It hit the U-40 amidships and only the captain and a petty officer survived.

One more U-boat, the U-23, was sunk in this way, and there were to be no more U-boat attacks on the fishing fleets for over a year. But the story of the end of the U-23 leaked out. The British authorities responsible for German prisoners were also ignorant of the secret and housed the U-boats's surviving seamen with some civilians who were shortly to be repatriated to Germany. Thereafter U-boats shelled trawlers from a distance, but the Royal Navy soon ceased the practice anyhow, when

1. The Grand Fleet putting to sea in 1914 - Jellicoe's flagship HMS *Iron Duke* leading followed by HMS *Marlborough*. *(Author's collection)*

2. First Sea Lord, Admiral of the Fleet Lord Fisher of Kilverstone. *(Photos of the Great War Archive - www.ku.edu/~kansite/ww one/photos)*

3. Secretary of State for the Imperial Navy, Grand Admiral Alfred von Tirpitz. *(Photos of the Great War Archive - www.ku.edu/~kansite/ww one/photos)*

4. Vice Admiral Graf Maximilian von Spee, victor of Coronel, who was killed in the Battle of the Falkland Islands.
(Photos of the Great War Archive - www.ku.edu/~kansite/ww one/photos)

5. Rear Admiral Sir Christopher Cradock, Commander of the British Squadron at Coronel.
(Photos of the Great War Archive - www.ku.edu/~kansite/ww one/photos)

6. Vice Admiral Sir F.C. Doveton Sturdee, victor of the Battle of the Falkland Islands.
(Photos of the Great War Archive - www.ku.edu/~kansite/ww one/photos)

7. Fregattenkapitän Karl von Muller, Captain of the *Emden*.
(Photos of the Great War Archive - www.ku.edu/~kansite/ww one/photos)

8. The ill-fated armoured cruiser HMS *Good Hope*, flagship of Rear Admiral Sir Christopher Cradock, leaving Portsmouth Harbour. *(Courtesy of Mike Allen)*

9. The *Emden*, shattered and beached on Keeling Island. *(Author's collection)*

10. The end of the *Blücher* in the Battle of Dogger Bank.   *(Author's collection)*

11. The British Blockade in action: questioning the crew of a neutral ship. *(Author's collection)*

12. The Lusitania medal with its box: one of thousands copied and distributed by order of Captain Reginald Hall, Director of Naval Intelligence. *(Author's collection)*

13. The British view of US neutrality - Dame Wilson to PC Fisher, 'Oh, Constable! Don't hurt him. I'm sure he won't murder anyone else!'
(London Opinion)

14. Vice Admiral Sir David Beatty.
*(Photos of the Great War Archive -
www.ku.edu/~kansite/ww one/photos)*

15. Admiral Sir John Jellicoe.
*(Photos of the Great War Archive -
www.ku.edu/~kansite/ww one/photos)*

16. Rear Admiral Franz Hipper in command
of the German Scouting Group.
*(Photos of the Great War Archive -
www.ku.edu/~kansite/ww one/photos)*

17. Vice Admiral Reinhard Scheer,
Commander-in-Chief, High Seas Fleet
*(Photos of the Great War Archive -
www.ku.edu/~kansite/ww one/photos)*

18. Ships of the High Seas Fleet under the watchful
    eye of a Zeppelin.
    (Photos of the Great War Archive -
    www.ku.edu/~kansite/ww one/photos)

"morning,
J.O.!"

19. A caricature of Sir Reginald
    Hall, Director of Naval
    Intelligence.
    (Public Record Office)

20. The German battlecruiser *Seydlitz* after the Battle of Jutland.
    (Photos of the Great War Archive – www.ku.edu/~kansite/ww one/photos)

21. Naval airship watching for U-boats. *(Author's collection)*

22. 'How the Americans arrive in France.' 7 men each minute; 420 each hour; 10,080 each day; 300,000 each month. Cartoon from a propaganda newspaper dropped by balloon. *(Author's collection)*

a trawler dragged a submarine into a mine with fatal consequences.[14]

Though losses of merchant vessels were rising, few U-boats were sunk, because few were seen, except by their victims. This fact gave rise to the development of another scheme which adapted an old 'ruse de guerre' and took it to extreme lengths. It had always been accepted that merchant ships could be converted into warships and that a warship could fly other colours, so long as it hoisted the flag of its own nation before firing at an enemy (as the German cruisers on the outer oceans had often done.) The Royal Navy now armed harmless looking tramp steamers, and sometimes even sailing ships, and sent them out to loiter on the trade routes. Their guns were hidden or camouflaged in such a way that they could be revealed at a moment's notice, if and when a U-boat got close enough for the crew to have a good chance of sinking it. The White Ensign would be run up a split second before the guns opened fire. These decoys, known as Q-ships, enjoyed some success, and were used until the end of the war. They demanded the greatest patience, discipline and courage from their crews.

The first Q-ship had been commissioned as early as November 1914. She never sighted a U-boat and was paid off after six weeks. The next was prepared with greater care, and two experienced submarine officers Lieutenant Commander Godfrey Herbert, (whose submarine, *D5*, had been blown up at the time of the Yarmouth raid) and Sub Lieutenant G.C. Steele, RNR, were chosen as Captain and First Lieutenant, on the grounds that they could anticipate the actions of an attacking U-boat. Twelve Royal Marines were added to the crew. After another fruitless cruise[15] these officers and men were then transferred to the *Baralong*, which became notorious. This ship was chosen because she looked nondescript. She was given a 12-pounder gun disguised under what looked like a sheep pen, and her holds were filled with watertight casks to give her greater buoyancy, if she should be holed. They set off on their cruise in April 1915, seeing the wreckage of U-boat victims but never sighting one. In May they picked up the *Lusitania*'s call for help, but arrived too late. 'This unspeakable outrage inflamed the minds of the *Baralong*'s crew,' said Steele. 'It just required the sight of those silent figures of drowned children from the *Lusitania* as they were laid out on the front at Queenstown in a temporary mortuary, to rouse the deepest hatred in the *Baralong*'s crew. A meeting was held . . . and it was agreed to give no quarter to German submarine crews.'[16]

Nothing occurred for another three months, and then on 19 August the White Star liner *Arabic* with 180 passengers on board was torpedoed. This happened fifty miles south of Kinsale, near where the *Lusitania* was sunk, and about twenty-five miles from the *Baralong*. The Q-ship steamed to the position indicated in the *Arabic*'s signal and found nothing. The liner had gone down as suddenly as the *Lusitania*.[17] Then a white feather of escaping steam was seen on the horizon, and the *Baralong* made her way fast towards it. There she found the SS *Nicosian*, under fire from a U-boat. When the *Baralong* appeared, flying the US colours and with the Stars and Stripes painted on boards down her sides, the U-boat approached to inspect her and then resumed shelling the *Nicosian*, whose boats were already in the water. The *Baralong* passed close behind the *Nicosian* signalling that she would pick up her crew. In the half minute that the Q-ship was sheltered from the U-boat's sight the order was given, 'Clear away guns!' The gun covers fell over the ship's side and the American flag was replaced by the White Ensign, while the boards with the Stars and Stripes fell into the sea. The submarine coming into view round the bows of the *Nicosian* was met by rapid gunfire and a hail of bullets. In one minute thirty-four shells had been fired, and the *U-27* was sunk, but some of her crew escaped and made for the rope ladder hanging down from the abandoned steamer.

The *Nicosian* had a gun at the stern (a dummy as it turned out) and it was thought that the German seamen could capture her and turn the tables with the help of the gun and rifles in the chart room. So Herbert put his ship alongside the *Nicosian* and ordered the marines to board her. 'They spread out,' according to Steele, 'took occasional cover and, seeing here and there some German figure crouching behind hatches, winches or anything else, opened fire. The Germans scattered and fled . . . Our boarding party, with cries of "*Lusitania!*" shot four remaining Germans at fairly long range.' The U-boat's captain, Wegener, hid in a cabin and jumped into the sea as the door was battered down. A corporal shot him in the head as he swam. What happened to the four others who retreated into the engine rooms is not known. None came out alive. 'Anyhow they were pirates and treated as such,'[18] Steele concluded. But the story did not end there. The *Nicosian* was carrying munitions and mules from America, and some of the muleteers told the press of the incident. Tales were lurid. By one account the sailors were shot; by another they were thrown into the furnaces. Germany was incensed and believed the worst.

The Admiralty rejected the claims, awarded several medals and gave £1,000 to be divided among the crew of the *Baralong*. It was pointed out that on the same day as the *Baralong* incident, German sailors had acted no better by killing fourteen men from the submarine *E13*, when it became stranded on a Danish island. Clearly the 'Brotherhood of the Sea' was being replaced by a new savagery. German wrath intensified when the *Baralong* sank the *U-41* in September, using the same disguise. Only two survived from the submarine and the German press referred to it as murder. One captain of the *Kaiserliche Marine* required his officers to refer to the Royal Navy as 'Baralongers' from then on.

The Germans had a few of their own mystery ships. The minelayer *Meteor* was one. She emerged into the North Sea in August 1915, flying the Russian flag, and was intercepted by the *Ramsay*, an armed boarding steamer, which lowered a boat to examine her. The *Meteor* then unmasked her guns and torpedo tubes and opened a deadly fire at point-blank range. The *Ramsay* sank in a few minutes, and her captain and crew were taken on board the *Meteor*, which proceeded to lay a large minefield off the Moray Firth before turning home. However, there were British cruisers between her and safety. When warned of these by a Zeppelin, the *Meteor* was scuttled. (Jellicoe kept the mines in place as a defence against U-boats.)

Although the *Baralong* incident went some way to counterbalance examples of Teutonic 'frightfulness', problems with neutrals, primarily the US and Netherlands, became a crisis for the German government in the autumn of 1915. First it had been the *Lusitania*, now the *Arabic*, which had been outward bound and so could not have been carrying contraband. Forty lives had been lost, including three Americans. What was to be done to stop the killing of neutral citizens? If the German methods of warfare could not be conducted without loss of neutral lives, the White House argued, the methods should be changed. The excuse of retaliation was not enough. The President's roving ambassador, Colonel House, had pressed Wilson to break off relations even at the risk of war. In the face of American protests Ambassador von Bernstorff gave Secretary of State Robert Lansing a letter dated 1 September 1915, stating, 'Liners will not be sunk by our submarines without warning and without safety of the lives of non-combatants, provided that the liners do not try to escape or offer resistance,'[19] and on the 6th Bachmann, who had objected to the Kaiser's appeasement of neutral feeling, was replaced as head of the *Admiralstab* after only seven months in office. (Yet on the same day *Kapitänleutnant* Walther Schwieger, the man who had destroyed the *Lusitania*, torpedoed and sank the 10,000 ton liner *Hesperian* without warning.)

The German submarine fleet was then six months into a campaign which Tirpitz had declared would bring Britain to its knees within six weeks. Nor, though British losses had risen, especially in August, was there any indication that the U-boats would ever accomplish that end. Less than five per cent of the British mercantile marine had been destroyed, and this was more than replaced by new construction or ships captured from the enemy.[20] Every ship and cargo sunk was a drain on the United Kingdom's resources, but the state reinsurance of shipping risks had ensured that insurance premiums were not so high as to deter shippers. The country would fight on.

On the other hand the danger to Germany of the United States' entering the war on the side of the Allies had definitely increased. Besides the horror at warfare which many, like Lansing, considered was 'illegal and utterly unworthy of a civilized nation',[21] there had been several pinpricks of a different kind. An attempt had been made, under orders ultimately traced to the German military attaché, Captain Franz von Papen, to blow up the bridge at Vanceboro on the border between Maine and New Brunswick; the German Naval Attaché, Captain Karl Boy-Ed, had been caught trying to involve Mexico and the US in a dispute through a plot to bring back the ousted President Huerta; then Dr. Heinrich Albert, the financial adviser to the German Embassy, left his briefcase unattended for a moment on the train and it had been stolen, the contents disclosing the work of various agents and attempts by the Embassy to control the American press. Finally, in August it had been the turn of the Austrian Ambassador, Dr Dumba, to be exposed. Commodore Guy Gaunt, the energetic British Naval Attaché in Washington, had planted Czech agents in the Austrian Consulate in New York, and one of them had obtained a copy of documents in which Dumba had proposed inducing Hungarian employees in US munition factories to organize strikes. He wrote, 'We can disorganise and hold up for months, if not entirely prevent, the manufacture of munitions, which in the opinion of the German Naval Attaché, is of great importance, and amply outweighs the small expenditure of money involved.'[22] Dumba had used an American journalist, James Archibald, to carry these dispatches to Central Europe, and as the liner was directed to put in to Falmouth, Captain Hall at the centre of the web of Naval Intelligence had Archibald's belongings searched. Soon he held the original of Dumba's letter, which was forwarded to Washington. When summoned by the Secretary of State, the Ambassador fluently defended his actions with regard to the strikes, but was silenced when Lansing changed tack and asked whether he thought it proper to employ a US citizen to carry dispatches through the lines of the enemy. For once Dumba seemed taken by surprise. His eyes became watery and his lips trembled. He stammered that he was not prepared to answer, as he had not thought about it. Lansing replied, 'You should have thought of it, sir, before you employed Archibald, as you have cast suspicion on every American going to Germany'.[23] Within an hour the request for Dumba's recall was being prepared. The German military and naval attachés, von Papen and Boy-Ed, were sent home too.

In the summer of 1915 some ships carrying munitions to Europe had mysteriously caught fire at sea. This was the work of Lieutenant Commander Franz von Rintelen, who had smuggled himself into the USA under orders to buy up as much of the US production of explosives and other war material as he could to stop it going to the Entente. Von Rintelen personally did not consider this quite legitimate activity to be enough. If America was unpopular in Britain for her ineffective protests against German U-boat actions – a dud shell was nicknamed a 'Wilson' – she was doubly so in Germany for selling arms to the Allies, while, because of the British blockade, the Central Powers could not buy them. So von Rintelen adopted the motto, 'I buy up what I can, and blow up what I can't',[24] telling his ambassador in Washington, that he 'cared nothing for America's so-called neutrality', that the whole of Germany thought as he did, and considered America as 'the unseen enemy'.[25] Operating out of a German merchantman stranded in New York docks, he used German sailors and Irish dockers to plant clever chemical detonators on munition ships and commit other acts of sabotage.

'My chief puzzle is to determine where patience ceases to be a virtue,'[26] Wilson complained to Colonel House. Both were now definitely anti-German. The President would not consider an embargo on sending munitions to the Allies, seeing them as 'standing with their backs to the wall, fighting wild beasts'.[27] To prevent further antagonizing the US, the new head of the German Naval Staff, Admiral Henning von Holtzendorff, on 18 September 1915 ordered his submarines to avoid the Channel and the west coast of Britain altogether, so far as merchant shipping was concerned. Sinkings in the North Sea were permitted but only in accordance with the prize rules. This was the end of the 'unrestricted' submarine campaign round the British Isles and in the Atlantic. (Little restraint was shown, however, in the Mediterranean, where U-boats continued to reap a plentiful harvest of vessels without fear of antagonizing the United States.) As though to seal the deal on 5 October, Bernstorff, the German ambassador in Washington, was authorized to send a formal letter disavowing the sinking of the *Arabic* (but not the *Lusitania*). Colonel House credited the envoy with this, writing that, 'If it had not been for his patience, good sense and untiring effort we would now be at war with Germany'.[28]

The war had now lasted over a year; the Grand Fleet still unchallenged, controlled the entrance to the North Sea, and the U-boat threat had been contained. True, damage had been done to the United Kingdom, but, the Chief of the German General Staff recognized 'there had so far been, no perceptible influence on the enemy's warlike operations'.[29] Indeed, it seemed to the Royal Navy that they might review the past twelve months with some relief and satisfaction. Mr A.J. Balfour, the new First Lord of the Admiralty, felt confident enough to say in a speech at the Opera House, 'Picture to yourself, if you will, what the condition of Western Europe and the Mediterranean would have been if the German Fleet had ridden triumphant in the North Sea, in the Atlantic and the Mediterranean, when war broke out and afterwards. I do not believe the struggle would have been possible for our Allies . . . I ask you only to consider how we should have been situated if France had been cut off from England on the north, from her colonies on the south, if no overseas trade could have reached her shores, if she could not have brought in the raw materials of her manufacture of munitions . . . It would have been fatal in the long run to us, but it would have been fatal immediately and within a few months to those to whom we are now proud to call our Allies.' Balfour went on to congratulate 'that great body of the merchant marine upon whom we depend for our daily bread . . . One of the miscalculations of our opponents was that by a system of piracy they would not merely destroy but would frighten. (*Ironic laughter*) They have not destroyed as much as they hoped, and they have not frightened at all. (*Cheers*) But the fact that they have not frightened is not due to any forbearance on their part; it is due to the inherent spirit of gallantry and endurance which makes our mercantile marine go out upon its daily avocations as indifferent to the chances of life and death as if they belonged to one of the great military services of the country.'[30] (*Cheers*)

The other lately recognized heroes of the time were the men of the fishing fleets. Their harvests were vital, as fish still constituted a third of the country's meat supply, and now they had a multitude of other tasks. The Great War had brought the fisherman into the forefront of Britain's maritime power. 'It saved him from the obscurity and gave him that honoured place in public life from which for many generations he had been unjustly kept.'[31] The men in the trawlers and drifters had been in the front line of the naval war, unarmed or with inadequate weapons, 'outranged by the submarines they have engaged with, with few comforts on board and the knowledge that they have no watertight compartments to keep them afloat'.[32] Those who were on war service had joined up as surely as the volunteers of Kitchener's army, and were generally proud of it. 'The grim Skipper who had sported a battered bowler, an immensely fishy dopper and enormous clumpers, and had gravitated, when travelling, to the third class smoker, turned gold-braided, blue-clad Chief Skipper, with a place in the navy list and the Gazette, and a first class pass when travelling by train.'[33] Their places in the fishing fleets were often filled by men, who, like their boats, had been taken out of retirement.

When the unrestricted U-boat campaign came to an end, the merchant shipping losses declined sharply in the seas round the British Isles, but they did not cease. Towards the end of 1914 orders had been placed for two new types of small U-boats, the UB coastal submarines and the UC minelayers. These types took only four months to build, and the first were delivered as the U-boat campaign gathered momentum. They were prefabricated in three sections, which could be lifted by crane onto rail trucks, assembled in Belgium and launched into the canals. In the middle of 1915 the first UCs emerged from Zeebrugge harbour, carrying a clutch of twelve mines (later eighteen). The initial model was underpowered, scarcely able to make headway against the eight or ten knot currents in the Straits of Dover, but their small size and shallow draught enabled them to lay mines in the shoaled waters of the Thames estuary and the coasts of England, even off the harbour mouths of Folkestone and Boulogne, and later types benefited from experience. These minelaying craft destroyed ninety-four vessels in the summer and autumn of 1915 off the east and south coasts of England.

Overall shipping losses continued to decline as the winter weather developed. The British blockade on the other hand continued with increasing efficiency. Neutral shipping lines became reluctant to accept contraband cargoes, because nothing could get past Dover without being investigated, and only a small percentage of the vessels taking the stormy route round Scotland managed to avoid the patrols. In 1915 the Tenth Cruiser Squadron under Admiral de Chair intercepted over 3,000 ships, sending 743 of them into port with a prize crew or under escort. However, 'Blockade was a form of paralysis creeping slowly over the body economic, and it would be many a long day before the German "will to victory" was numbed by such a malady.'[34]

For some time the Central Powers could make use of their 'invisible stocks' of raw materials. Kitchen pots were requisitioned for their copper, organ pipes for their tin. Old copper mines were reopened, and Hungarian aluminium was widely used instead of copper, brass and tin-foil. Margarine replaced butter; ersatz coffee was drunk. In finding substitutes for commodities formerly supplied from abroad the Reich relied heavily on its outstanding chemical industry, without which it could not have continued fighting. Thanks to the researches of Fritz Haber and Karl Bosch, Germany was kept supplied with nitrates for explosives and agriculture, when the Chilean supplies were cut off. Without them the guns would have stopped firing and famine would have come closer. (However, producing the nitrates took time, phosphates could never be synthesized for fertilizers, and potash, which was plentiful, was a poor substitute, so agricultural output still declined.) The lack of cotton, which was made absolute contraband in August 1915, exercised the chemists' skills to the limit. Germany had imported 430,000 tons before the war; now she needed 300,000 just for explosives, but by 1916 the army's problem had been solved, even if the textile shortage was not, because nitrocellulose obtained from the purest Swedish wood pulp was found to be almost as efficient as nitrocotton. When the army ran out of lead, they fired steel bullets coated with a glazing compound, which took the grooves of the rifling, but did not damage it, as hard steel would have done.

The blockade was never perfect either. Determined to get the mail through, fast liners frequently managed to avoid interception as they ran north of Scotland.[35] Also, contraband was smuggled through with increasing ingenuity. Double bottoms or double decks or bulkheads would conceal guns or ammunition. Cotton was found hidden in flour barrels and rubber was disguised as coffee beans or even as rubber onions. Hollow masts could hold a variety of wares. However, these ruses met with increasing awareness from the inspection teams of ex-merchant navy officers. Sailing ships were required to unfurl their sails and were made to heel over in case their keels were made out of solid copper or thick copper plates were nailed onto their bottoms. Ship's manifests were not to be trusted either. In some cases boarding officers were amused to have both false and true manifests produced, when the skipper knew that the game was up. Not only goods were smuggled; a boarding party once saw the head of a man in a tank, up to his neck in oil. The captain denied that there were any more in there, but when the naval officer threatened to shoot into the tank, three more appeared. All were German officers trying to return home.

The food situation in Germany had been eased in July 1915 when Romania, following the Russian defeats and the adhesion of her neighbour Bulgaria to the Central Powers, agreed to let grain be exported. This, in Falkenhayn's opinion, 'warded off severe famine in Germany, and especially Turkey'.[36] Just as important, however, to Germany or Austria were the large quantities of vital products of all kinds which were still being imported by neutral countries for onward transmission to them. To prevent this, Britain began to ration the northern European neutral countries – that is to detain goods, whether contraband or not, in excess of the normal pre-war usage of the country concerned. This was not at first implemented, because there was no legal authority for condemning goods on statistical grounds, and had there been any such ruling, there were no reliable statistics to show how much of any particular product the neutral countries had imported before the war for their own use. However, the legal position eased in September 1915, when four ships were condemned as prize in the 'Kim' judgement because they had been carrying enough lard to Denmark to meet the country's normal imports for thirteen years, and this was accepted as evidence of enemy destination.

The embargoes had exceptions too. No restriction was imposed on the import of fodder and fertilizer to Denmark and Holland in the hope that the Danes and Dutch would continue to divide their food exports between Britain and Germany as before. Also, to avoid ruining Norwegian fishermen fifteen per cent of their catch was permitted to be sent to Germany.

Even so the new quota system was an extreme irritation to neutrals. When the U-boat commanders' actions were restricted after September 1915, there was no countervailing annoyance on Germany's part to draw America's wrath. In a note dated 21 October 1915 Secretary of State Robert Lansing wrote to Ambassador Page in London, 'I believe it has been conclusively shown that the methods employed by Great Britain to obtain evidence of enemy destination of cargoes bound for neutral ports and to impose a contraband character upon such cargoes are without justification: that the blockade upon which such methods are partly founded, is ineffective, illegal, and indefensible; that the judicial procedure . . . is inherently defective for the purpose; and that in many cases jurisdiction is asserted in violation of the law of nations.'[37] The United States unhesitatingly championed neutral rights, but still hoped for peace.

On 5 January 1916 Colonel House landed at Falmouth with a plan under which, if the Allies would give the word, the US Government would offer 'reasonable terms' to Germany, and if she would not accept them, America would come into the war on the Allied side and force her to. However, the Allies were again expecting victories in the summer and House saw that, 'peace discussion at this time would be about as popular in England as the coronation of the Kaiser in Westminster Abbey'.[38] In the Wilhelmstrasse he found that America would be a deeply unpopular arbitrator and the Germans would not consider giving up conquered territory.[39]

The US administration was beginning to swing behind the Entente powers. Though anger might be aroused in America because of the interference with her trade, and in the northern European neutrals because of the rationing of their imports, no lives were lost, no ships were sunk and confiscated goods, other than contraband, were paid for. Besides, if the USA lost its exports to Germany, the neutrals had in 1915 imported twice as much as before the war. Also Britain, France and Russia were the best customers of America's increasingly prosperous arms manufacturers, so much so that Ambassador Gerard reported to Colonel House from Berlin that the Kaiser had said that 'he would attend to America when this war was over,'[40] and House believed that if Germany won, it would be America's turn next. So Britain persisted in her blockade (now officially declared) and she did so with growing confidence and success. A Ministry of Blockade was created in February 1916, Lord Robert Cecil, third son of the Marquess of Salisbury, the great, late Victorian Prime Minister, being appointed the first Minister of Blockade. The choice was perhaps surprising because Lord Robert was a committed Christian. He held the belief, more common today in the east than in the west, that 'no healthy political or international system can be built except on a religious foundation,'[41] and, as his nephew Lord David Cecil wrote, 'to administer the blockade was a peculiarly distressing job for a Christian; it meant starving the German people out'.[42] But, holding that same belief which quietened the consciences of those who directed the U-boat campaign – that these measures were necessary to shorten the war and prevent further suffering – Lord Robert took a firm hand. He enforced the statutory Black List, prohibiting trade with named persons and firms, hostile and neutral, which were known to be working with the enemy, and, to encourage the friends of the Allies, from March 1916 issued letters of Assurance, or 'Navicerts', to approved skippers to enable them to pass the blockade without examination. In July he persuaded the French to join in formally abandoning the Declaration of London (a logical if empty formality).

The bunkering policy was effectively taming neutral shipping lines. They could only receive coaling and other facilities in British or Allied ports worldwide, so long as *all* their vessels complied with strict conditions and were on the 'White List'. So for these shipping companies British coal carried the additional price of a remarkable interference with their trade. Ultimately, no vessel was permitted to:

– be chartered to any subject of Germany or its allies or any person who might be notified to the shipping line; (i.e. firms on the Statutory Black List);

– trade with any port of Germany or her allies, nor carry any German subject or cargo;

– send wireless messages, which might be of service to Germany;

– carry coal or oil, except to approved consignees; or

– be bought, sold, chartered, or withdrawn from trade without British approval.

Returns were to be submitted each month to show the employment of all ships, and every shipping firm was to provide reasonable service in return for coal.[43]

'We ask no favours from neutrals,' Cecil roundly declared in reply to the protests of the Prime Minister of Sweden. 'But we do ask that they should not hinder our belligerent rights in a life and death struggle which we and our Allies are waging. It follows that the unrestricted import of goods which would release home products of a similar nature for exportation, cannot be agreed by us.'[44] His Majesty's Government demanded that the quantities imported to Sweden should be restricted to the known requirements of Swedish home consumption, that there should be prohibition of export and that the importer should afford effectual guarantees against re-export in any form. Cecil dismissed their difficulties. 'How these objects can best be secured without injury to genuine neutral trade is, no doubt a problem,'[45] he admitted, suggesting only that goods should be imported through central associations. That would steady prices, avoid delays and prevent speculation. Swedish exporters, he pointed out, had gained from the increase in prices for their goods.

The transit trade might be controllable, but none of the neutrals would shut off the supply of their own surplus produce from Germany altogether. To do so would have been unneutral – and very unwise in

129

view of the successes of the Imperial armies. The best that the Entente could hope for was to regulate by agreement the supplies, which they and the Central Powers would receive. So in August 1916 Norway agreed to send two thirds of its copper pyrites ore to the Entente and one third to Germany, (though the benefit to Germany was greatly reduced by the requirement that they should send back to Norway articles containing an equivalent amount of copper). The agreement with the Netherlands in November divided her surplus produce among Great Britain and Germany in proportion to their deliveries of coal. Since Germany provided about sixty per cent of the Dutch imports, Britain was only allowed between twenty-five per cent and fifty per cent of her produce. And not all that got across the water.

In the spring of 1916 the U-boat campaign had revived. In the first days of the year von Pohl, 'a clever man, but without much power of command'[46] and never the most aggressive of the Commanders-in-Chief of the High Seas Fleet, had died of cancer. He was replaced on 24 January, not by Grand Admiral Tirpitz, whose policy on the use of the fleet the Kaiser considered inconsistent, but by Vice Admiral Reinhard von Scheer. The new C.-in-C. was not content that his U-boats should be bound by the Hague Conventions when attacking commerce. The rules were not designed for submarines and exposed them to impossible risks. Under von Scheer's dispensation merchant ships within the war zone round the British Isles could be destroyed without more ado, but (in response to threats of resignation from the Chancellor and Foreign Minister) outside the zone they could only be torpedoed without notice, if armed.

The arming of merchantmen now became a critical issue. The Admiralty considered it essential. It had always been allowed to protect them from pirates and privateers. The Germans, however, claimed that the submarine was a new weapon which changed the rules, and a freighter with any gun was equivalent to an auxiliary cruiser. A 'defensive' gun on its stern could sink a U-boat surfacing to visit and search a merchant vessel just as well as an 'offensive' gun in the bows. Lansing, the US Secretary of State, came to agree and on 18 January 1916 he presented an informal note to the Allied ambassadors, pointing out that 'pirates and sea rovers have been swept from the main trade channels of the seas and privateers have been abolished,' and concluding, 'Any armament, therefore, on a merchant vessel would seem to have the character of an offensive armament'.[47] From Berlin Ambassador Gerard, who 'rather sympathised with the submarine on this,' pungently endorsed his view: 'A submarine is a recognised weapon of war as far as the English go, because they use it themselves, and it seems to me an absurd proposition that a submarine must come to the surface, give warning, offer to put passengers and crew in safety, and constitute itself a target for merchant ships, that not only make a practice of firing at submarines at sight, but have undoubtedly received orders to do so'.[48] Lansing proposed that all merchantmen should be disarmed in return for an undertaking that they should not be torpedoed without warning, nor shelled unless they fought or fled.

When the note was leaked in the press, the Allies claimed that it was designed to ease the settlement of the *Lusitania* dispute with Germany. The British were seriously worried. Not only were guns the most effective defence for a steamer, but it raised the greater issue of whether the US should intern all British vessels which were armed. The Germans then too hastily announced that armed merchant ships would be treated as warships from 29 February. This appeared to be an attempt to force Wilson's hand and, to immense relief in Whitehall, he reacted by dropping Lansing's proposals.

Meanwhile worldwide shipping losses rose sharply to 117,500 tons in February 1916, 167,000 tons in March and a record 191,600 in April – two and a half times the rate of the previous spring. (U-boats were so successful in the Mediterranean that in March 1916 merchant shipping was ordered to avoid it and take the long voyage round the Cape.) However, included among the victims was a cross-Channel passenger boat, the SS *Sussex*, torpedoed without warning on 24 March 1916. Fifty passengers had been killed and several were American. A sharper note from the US Government warned that 'unless the Imperial Government should now immediately declare and effect an abandonment of its present methods of warfare against passenger and freight carrying vessels this government can have no choice but to sever diplomatic relations with the Government of the German Empire altogether'.[49] In response, on 26 April the *Admiralstab* was ordered to ensure that its submarines observed the prize rules or 'cruiser rules'. That meant examining papers and not sinking the ship until the crew and any passengers were safe, unless they tried to escape or resist. Woodrow Wilson accepted this, ignoring the condition that Great Britain would cease her trade restrictions. Admiral Scheer could not accept it, however. 'You do not demand of an aeroplane that it should attack the enemy on its wheels. . . . As war waged according to Prize Law by U-boats in the waters around England could not possibly have any success, but, on the contrary, must expose the boats to the greatest dangers,' he wrote, 'I recalled all the U-boats by wireless, and announced that the U-boat campaign against British commerce had ceased.'[50]

This concluded the first U-boat campaign. It had never been life-threatening to the United Kingdom, but it must be admitted that it was American protests, rather than any action by the Royal Navy, that had raised the German blockade. However the submarines, withdrawn from the commercial war, would not be allowed to rust and their numbers were growing rapidly. (In the first five months of 1916 only seven had been sunk, while thirty-four had been completed.) Scheer had plans to employ them in combination with the High Seas Fleet in an attack on its main foe, which chafed at anchor in Scapa Flow. Only by weakening the Grand Fleet could the *Kaiserliche Marine* in its turn relieve the pressure of the British blockade.

Notes

1. House, op. cit. Vol.1, p.44. Once Wilson had won the hard fought nomination, he was sure to win because Theodore Roosevelt and Taft split the Republican vote.
2. ibid. p.118
3. Since, as House admitted, 'this plan would involve the shutting down of Krupps', Armstrong's and other manufacturers', (House, op. cit. Vol.1, p.392) it could hardly have expected a smooth passage at any time.
4. Letter to House dated 4 February 1915. (ibid. p.377)
5. In Deputy Foreign Secretary Zimmerman's words (ibid. p.414)
6. The British Cabinet did not even discuss the proposal and they would not have accepted it anyway, in Lloyd-George's view. (See Lloyd George, op. cit. Vol.I, p.401) There was for the British one unfortunate outcome. The idea that merchantmen, whether of neutrals or the belligerents, should be able to sail the seas freely in peace and war became a plank of US diplomacy, under the slogan 'the Freedom of the Seas'. House believed that only implements of war, not raw materials, should be contraband. All the rest should be allowed through to any port that was not effectively (i.e. closely) blockaded. He thought Britain would gain as much as Germany, or more, from this.
7. It was in the Mediterranean that the supreme U-boat ace, Lothar von Arnaud de la Periere, who sank 400,000 tons in ten patrols, mainly operated. The work of British submariners does not often concern our story, but they too were successful in Turkish waters, sinking in 1915 a

Turkish battleship, a destroyer, five gunboats, over fifty transports, store ships or ammunition ships and other steamers, as well as at least 150 sailing vessels.

8. Bacon, op. cit. Vol.II, p.242. The torpedoing of a mock *Queen Elizabeth* two weeks later justified Fisher's fears, as did the sinking in the Dardanelles of the battleships *Triumph* on 25 May and *Majestic* on 27 May, a unique feat by Otto Hersing who had brought his *U-21* from the North Sea.

9. Marder, op. cit. Vol.2, p.278

10. Bacon, op. cit. Vol.II, p.269. The demands were not made public. Churchill did not know of them until Asquith was writing his memoirs after the war.

11. ibid. p.268. Bacon puts the blame for Fisher's resignation squarely on Churchill, 'the youngest and, politically the most inexperienced of any First Lord who had held office' in a hundred years.

12. Marder, op. cit. Vol. 2, p.288. Succubus, a female spirit, which has sex with men while they sleep, is an unexpected epithet. Perhaps the admiral meant 'incubus', a nightmare, or male spirit with similar heterosexual habits. (The incubus was recognized by the law in the Middle Ages, but does not feature in the current edition of Halsbury's Laws of England.)

13. ibid. p.12

14. See Edwards, op. cit. Chapter V.

15. A few other decoy ships were fitted out in 1915 but it was not until 24 July that the first U-boat was sunk by one, a converted collier, the *Prince Charles*.

16. Chatterton, E. Keble, *Gallant Gentlemen*, Hurst & Blackett, 1931, p.164

17. The culprit was Schneider, who had committed 'the first atrocity of the German submarine warfare' by sinking the *Amiral Ganteaume* when full of Belgian refugees. He was later washed overboard and drowned.

18. Chatterton, op. cit. p.173. It is an interesting comment on the passions of the time that, writing as late as 1931, Chatterton headed his chapter, 'The Gallant Baralong'.

19. Lansing, op. cit. p.48

20. To September 1915 total losses were 1,294,000 tons, while 1,233,000 tons had been built and 682,000 tons captured. (Halpern, Paul G., *A Naval History of World War I*, UCL Press, 1994, p.303)

21. Lansing, op. cit. p.48

22. James, Admiral Sir William, *The Eyes of the Navy*, Methuen, 1955 p.97

23. Lansing, op. cit. p.65

24. Rintelen, op. cit. p.74

25. ibid. p.83–4. British naval intelligence knew all about von Rintelen and plucked him off a liner at Falmouth, when returning to Germany. Von Papen became Chancellor of Germany in 1932.

26. House, op. cit. Vol.2, p.48

27. ibid. p.49

28. House to Ambassador Gerard on 6 October 1915 (ibid. Vol.2, p44)

29. Falkenhayn, General von, *General Headquarters and its Critical Decisions 1914–16*, Hutchinson & Co., 1919, p.156

30. Speech delivered by the Right Hon. A.J. Balfour at the London Opera House, 4 August 1915.

31. Wood, op. cit. p.11

32. Bayly, Admiral Sir Lewis, *Pull Together!*, George G. Harrap, 1939, p.187

33. Wood, op. cit. p.17

34. Gibson and Prendergast, op. cit. p.84

35. In twenty-three crossings of the Atlantic the SS *Bergensfiord* was intercepted only thirteen times and the *Kristianaford*, steaming rapidly without lights, was apprehended only nine times in the same number of crossings, but when the British Government threatened to withhold coal from their owners, the Norwegian-American Line, the ships voluntarily went in for inspection.

36. Falkenhayn, op. cit. p.206

37. Parmelee, op. cit. p.67

38. House, op. cit. Vol.2, p.184

39. The terms included not only the restoration of Belgium and Serbia but the return of Alsace-Lorraine to France, for which Germany would be compensated by colonies. Italy was to take from Austria the southern slopes of the Alps, now Trentino and Alto Adige, as she had been promised by secret treaty. The Austrians were not to be compensated for this loss of their South Tyrol.

40. House, op. cit. Vol.2, p.102. Ambassador Gerard believed that Tirpitz wanted a ruthless submarine campaign to beat Britain, after which her Grand Fleet could be used to impose terms on the US.

41. Cecil, David, *The Cecils of Hatfield House*, Constable, 1973, p.296

42. ibid. p.295

43. See Appendix II of *The Economic Blockade* in PRO ADM 186/603

44. Cecil, Lord Robert, Interview in reply to PM of Sweden, 1916.

45. ibid. p.7

46. Goodenough, op. cit. p.87

47. House, op. cit. Vol.2, p.210
48. ibid.
49. Seymour, Charles, *Woodrow Wilson and the World War*, Yale Univ. Press, 1921, p.59
50. Scheer, op. cit. pp. 228 and 242

CHAPTER EIGHT

The Fleets Engage

Throughout 1915 and 1916 the British continued their blockade without let-up, and the Tenth Cruiser Squadron, battling the northern seas in its incessant watch for blockade runners, had little time for relaxation. The experience of HMS *Changuinola*, a former banana boat of just under 6,000 tons gross of the Elders and Fyffes Line, was typical. She spent 260 days and nights at sea in 1915. During this time her boarding parties – four to eight men usually led by a teenaged midshipman, who was hung about with a sword to show his authority – inspected 159 ships and thirty-one fishing craft, sending another fifty into Kirkwall.[1] They might well envy the rest of the Grand Fleet which for much of the time exercised its power by swinging at its anchors. Now that Scapa Flow had been protected by booms and blockships, the fleet did not have to be kept at such constant readiness to sail, and the submarine scares were almost unknown in harbour. The problem for the captains of the battleships and cruisers was to keep the crews busy and avoid the morale-sapping tedium and frustration which could have ruined the fighting qualities of the fleet. For the officers there were bracing walks, golf and shooting parties, while for the men interest was maintained by football matches, ship's concerts, film shows and runs ashore. However, the bare sexless beauty of the Orkadian landscape held few attractions for the seamen and marines, and the canteen on Flotta was so unalluring that some did not bother to go ashore for weeks or months. But even that short trip could be dangerous. 'I remember the ratings from a battleship coming ashore in a pinnace for a game of football,' one old sailor recalled. 'The inward run was all right, but on returning the weather turned foul and all the twenty-odd men were drowned.'[2]

And of course there was coaling for all but the latest oil powered ships.

> Coaling, coaling, coaling,
> Always —— —— coaling,

sung to the tune of the hymn, *Holy, holy holy*, and with each man's preferred expletive added. A ship would be coaled as soon as she came back into harbour. It might be every five days or even every other day for some ships. 'Of all exhausting, prolonged, filthy, noisy, abominable jobs, this is surely the very worst,' wrote one officer. 'No one in the ship is exempt from taking part in the irksome but necessary duty, which is not seldom extended through all hours of the night. Finally it takes at least two days hard work thoroughly to clean the ship from the coal-dust that penetrates everywhere.'[3] Men were often injured coaling too. The trouble was that around the turn of the century 'coal ship' had become an 'evolution'. 'Ships' Commanders now made or marred their reputation on the coaling-performance of their ship, because good coaling was only possible when the men responded whole-heartedly to good leadership, when the organisation was very thorough and when the many whips and guys and derricks were rigged by a good seaman.'[4] But at any time an accident might happen as the coal bags were swung inboard, rushed in a trolley to a chute and dumped below for the tired stokers to trim the bunkers. A stoker in HMS *Bristol* was killed when a large piece of coal hit him on the head. Another fainted and was smothered under a black avalanche.

Men had to be ready to coal anywhere in the world, but was the system really necessary in the main harbours? If any of the engineers had been set making coaling less arduous, dirty and dangerous, no doubt they would have found a solution. (It needed someone like 'Blinker' Hall to take coaling in hand. When Captain of the battlecruiser *Queen Mary*, he had observed that it took his 120 stokers up to an hour to get a hot wash when they came off watch. Hall had the time reduced to fifteen minutes by telling the Engineer Commander, who was at a loss for an answer, that he would be replaced if one was not found. Within ten days a multiple tap system was providing plentiful hot water in the washrooms.)[5]

For the Commander-in-Chief these months sequestered in the inhospitable northern waters gave an opportunity to draw up and revise the Grand Fleet Battle Orders (GFBOs), which contained the distilled views of himself and his senior officers on the tactics to be adopted by the squadrons and flotillas. In preparing instructions for the great battle which had been so confidently expected from the outset of the war, Jellicoe had to work largely from scratch. 'The art of tactics had stagnated in the century after 1815.'[6] Anyhow the technology of naval warfare, on which tactics inevitably depend, had changed so fundamentally and was continuing to change so rapidly, that even if Jellicoe had fought a battle, say in the Boer War which ended in 1901, his experience would not have been of much help in the Great War. The changes in the previous fifteen years were as revolutionary in their time as the introduction half a century later of nuclear propulsion, guided missiles and satellite communications. Since the beginning of the century the range of guns had increased five times and that of torpedoes fifteen times. Wireless had come into general use and submarines could go anywhere. Mines had been perfected and could be dropped behind a retiring squadron. Jellicoe expected that the Germans would try to entice him onto mines and have submarines operating in concert with their fleet. But how would they use their airships and would wireless be a boon or a bane? With all these novelties the Royal Navy could only guess at the form which the battle would take. The confidence of the British in their mighty fleet was balanced by uncertainty about the new weapon technology. It was hard to gain any real experience of modern battle in the peacetime manoeuvres, and none of the Western European powers had taken part in the only recent battle between two large fleets at Tsushima, where the Japanese had annihilated the Russian fleet. That encounter, only a decade before the Great War, was still instructive.

When the Russo-Japanese war broke out in 1904, the Japanese had begun by launching a torpedo boat attack on the Russian fleet in harbour, before hostilities had been declared. The Russians therefore sent their Baltic fleet of seven battleships, supported by cruisers, destroyers and transports, to sail round Africa and Asia to join up with their diminished eastern fleet at Vladivostok. The Baltic Fleet had only just emerged into the North Sea in October 1904, when they came across a host of small ships at night. In the dark the Russians took them for more Japanese torpedo boats and opened fire, sinking several of the vessels with inevitable loss of life. Unfortunately the boats they had sunk were part of a fleet of British trawlers fishing off the Dogger Bank. When the 'attack' was successfully beaten off, the Russians realized their error. The British public was aghast and the Cabinet was seriously debating war with Russia, when Admiral Sir John Fisher roused himself from bed, where he had been nursing flu, and confronted the ministers. Using all the force of his personality and prestige as First Sea Lord, he persuaded them that such a mistake could innocently be made by inexperienced officers. The Russians apologized and paid a considerable sum to atone for their blunder.[7]

Such an event did not bode well for their fleet when the Russians eventually met the Japanese. Vladivostok, Russia's most southerly port on the Pacific side of their great land mass, is ringed by the Japanese islands. To reach it the Russian fleet had little choice but to go through the straits between South Korea and the most southerly Japanese island of Kyushu. In the middle of this lies Tsushima Island, where Admiral Togo waited. Admiral Rozhdestvensky arrived there on 27 May 1905, seven months after leaving the Baltic ports.[8] The battle started in the afternoon, when several Russian ships were sunk and others severely mauled with little damage done to Togo's fleet. Forty minutes had decided the issue. During the night the main Japanese fleet retired, leaving their destroyers and torpedo boats to attack. Their flotillas scattered the defeated Russian fleet and the following morning the main Japanese capital ships and cruisers picked off the survivors. Admiral Togo had won one of the most decisive victories of naval history. Out of more than thirty Russian ships only two destroyers and a light cruiser reached their destination.

At Tsushima wireless transmission was first used in naval warfare with critical effect. Both sides employed W/T extensively, but both understood that its use could give away the position of the ship transmitting the signal. The Russians maintained wireless silence throughout the battle and did not even use it to rally their ships in the morning. The Japanese on the other hand used radio to give them warning of the approaching fleet's position, course and speed before the battle, and to give the position of the four surviving groups of Russian ships next morning. The new facility should help the dominant fleet, but would the signals be rendered indecipherable by jamming?

At first sight the British might take comfort from Tsushima in the thought that the big guns of a well handled fleet, much of it built in British yards, could totally destroy a weaker foe. But it also showed that a newly built navy might beat one with long experience.

Against this background Jellicoe produced his Grand Fleet Battle Orders. The previous C.-in-C., Admiral Sir George Callaghan, had written very little on the subject, preferring, as Nelson had done, to rely on discussions with his senior officers, when he stressed the need for initiative. By contrast Jellicoe's orders extended to seventy pages by mid-1916, and even then did not include his last instructions concerning destroyers. That most understanding of critics, the US Professor Arthur Marder, has described them as 'excessively detailed'.[9] This fault would have been less important had the GFBOs not been set in concrete. Once they had been promulgated, after lengthy discussions at conferences with the admirals of his squadrons and the captains of his ships, there was no scope for further argument. Jellicoe considered that unless there was time for the Fleet to practise alternative tactics, they should not be discussed, because it would undermine confidence in the GFBOs. This accentuated the fault which some critics believed to be found in too many of his ships' captains – lack of initiative.[10]

The prime object of the GFBOs was to ensure that at the critical moment all the great battleships would deploy into one long battle line and, trading salvo for salvo, crush the enemy with the weight of their broadsides. In 1916 the British could happily fight a battle of attrition; they had the ships and the heavier guns – and all but two of their dreadnoughts had Captain Percy Scott's revolutionary Director Firing System, which fired a broadside of all the main armament at the push of a single button.[11] However, in order to destroy the enemy fleet totally it was necessary to keep the heavy ships in touch with them. That would require some flexibility and it is doubtful if Jellicoe had really worked out in his mind what Scheer would do, and what his own response should be, if the Grand Fleet succeeded in achieving the most desirable position, crossing the enemy's 'T'. This required steaming across the head of the enemy's line, so that all your ships could fire their full broadsides, while the enemy was only able to bring his forward guns to bear, and the guns of his rear ships would be masked by his own leading ships. What was more, as the foremost ships took punishment, they would bunch up and slow down, bringing chaos to their own line and making easy targets of themselves.

However perfect the battle orders, the Grand Fleet first had to make contact with the High Seas Fleet. During the winter of 1915–16 several senior officers of the Fleet worked out detailed proposals for luring the German Fleet out of its bases or attacking it where it lay. Beatty suggested bombarding Heligoland with four old battleships; other officers added submarines to ambush the pursuing enemy, or a dawn attack on Shillig Roads at the mouth of the Jade, where part of the High Seas Fleet was lying. All these were turned down under closer scrutiny because of the risks of mines, shore batteries or U-boats. Jellicoe would not be drawn. All the tasks of the Grand Fleet were satisfied while the enemy fleet was confined to its harbours. 'Although of course the destruction of the High Seas Fleet gives a greater sense of security,' the C.-in-C. wrote, 'it is not in my opinion, wise to risk unduly the heavy ships of the Grand Fleet to hasten the end of the High Sea fleet.'[12] To attack them in their ports was out of the question, because, as Marder observed, 'They were so strongly protected by nature and man that an attempt to force these defences would assuredly, as Jellicoe viewed the matter, involve losses out of all proportion to any success that might be achieved'.[13]

Though the newspapers from time to time called for more action and the Fleet fretted, none of his subordinates accused Jellicoe of pusillanimity. They were only too conscious that on the outcome of the battle would depend the fate not only of the United Kingdom but of the Allies. The Commander-in-Chief's responsibilities were, as Churchill recognized, 'on a different scale from all others. It might fall to him as to no other man – Sovereign, Statesman, Admiral or General – to issue orders which in the space of *two or three hours* might nakedly decide who won the war. The destruction of the British Battle Fleet would be final. Jellicoe was the only man on either side who could lose the war in an afternoon.'[14] Captain W.W. Fisher had absolute faith in him: 'I see the C-in-C quite often and am struck every time with his marvellous alertness and precision. Rather commonplace description of him – but it's correct. No unsound however attractive proposal has a rabbit's chance when he runs his searchlight brain on it – it's riddled by a dry fact or two that he knows but that no one else seems to.'[15]

When Jellicoe did try to lure his enemy out, he used offensive methods which have understandably been described as 'feeble'.[16] Bombing raids on Zeppelin sheds by a few seaplanes seemed hardly likely to tempt the whole German fleet from its bases to sink the seaplane carriers. Nor were the attacks successful, loudly though the British press praised the daring of the aviators and the bombing of one shed. Yet the pinpricks were so nearly fruitful. In the first raid in March 1916 five sea planes were launched onto the water from HMS *Vindex* and flew off. Only two returned, but Hipper did come out and Beatty was only sixty miles away when the German Scouting Squadrons returned to base. On 4 May 1916 *Vindex* and another seaplane carrier, *Engadine*, supported by four cruisers and sixteen destroyers, launched a second raid with eleven seaplanes. This time only three planes managed to rise from the rough seas, and only one reached the target, and then its bombs missed, but Scheer was enticed from his base by this small tempting force. Unfortunately he did not do so until 3 p.m., an hour or so after Jellicoe, disappointed, but perhaps all along half-hearted, had turned for home.

Since dawn the Grand Fleet had loitered off the Skagerrak straits between Denmark and Norway, with Beatty's battlecruisers further south. Its destroyers were running too low in fuel for fighting, and the C.-in-C. had never liked the prospect of starting an action in those hostile waters with little daylight left.

Beatty empathized with his C.-in-C.'s problems, particularly the short time that the vital destroyer flotillas could go without refuelling: 'We cannot amble about the North Sea for two or three days and at the end be in a condition in which we can produce our whole force to fight to the finish the most decisive Battle of the War: to think it is possible is simply foolish and tends towards losing the Battle before we begin.'[17]

Destroying the enemy fleet is of course only a means to an end. It is often a prerequisite for the attainment of the prime objective, such as landing an army or defending maritime trade, but in the Great War both hostile navies could achieve their major objectives without fighting a battle. The prime naval purpose of the Grand Fleet, after protecting the country from invasion and ensuring the flow of food and supplies to the UK and the fighting fronts, was to maintain the stranglehold of its naval blockade. The Royal Navy could do that while their battleships waited in the Orkneys.

The High Seas Fleet on the other hand, having abandoned any hope of protecting its own worldwide seaborne trade, could cause Britain to haemorrhage money, and keep tens of thousands of trained seamen, gunners and engineers unprofitably employed, merely by remaining a 'Fleet in Being'. Its presence also safeguarded Germany's Baltic trade and protected the minesweepers in the Heligoland Bight, which in turn prevented the U-boats from being blocked in by British mines. Further, it halved the number of British destroyers, the U-boat's greatest enemies, which could be patrolling the coasts, because the Grand Fleet could not emerge without a shield of one hundred destroyers. And the High Seas Fleet could do all that without ever leaving the mouth of the Jade. Consequently the German Fleet was forbidden to offer battle more than 120 miles or so from its bases, so that their damaged ships would have a better chance of getting home (and the British ships correspondingly less chance). In that event, as the Grand Fleet would also not stray far from its bases, unless there was a definite prospect of battle, an engagement between the battleships of the two fleets could only take place through a miscalculation on one side or the other. That finally occurred on 31 May 1916 off the Jutland Bank in the mouth of the Skagerrak straits.

The miscalculation that brought about the battle was the German belief that their signals were not being read. Their station at Neumunster, south of Kiel, was intercepting some British signals, but the *Admiralstab* had no conception of the extent of the listening and decoding activities of their rivals in the Admiralty in Whitehall. The 'self-effacing industry and imaginative genius'[18] of Room 40, Old Building were then at the height of their efficiency and usefulness. Without Room 40's advance warnings or a piece of amazing luck, Britain might have watched helplessly while German battlecruisers regularly bombarded the English coast and escaped home, before the Grand Fleet could get at them. With Room 40's help, however, sooner or later, given Reinhard von Scheer's attacking spirit, the High Seas Fleet would be trapped.

Scheer had decided that, by using the increased numbers of under-water craft to weaken the Grand Fleet, he might be able to bring about an action on more level terms. In short he planned a resumption of the *Klein Krieg*, (which had been abandoned after the Battle of the Dogger Bank) but with the new factor of having dozens of U-boats at his disposal. His first two tentative moves half way across the North Sea, first north-west to the Dogger Bank in February 1916 and a month later due west to the Texel off the Dutch coast, produced meagre results, a sloop and two fishing smacks sunk, but no obvious reaction from the Royal Navy, (though the Grand Fleet, alerted by Room 40, had moved south on the second occasion.) So Scheer's third plan was to be bolder.

It happened that in early April the Irish Nationalists requested some German action in support of what became the Easter Rising. The General Staff in Berlin, after negotiating with the renegade Sir Roger Casement, resolved to help. A freighter, disguised as a Norwegian passed through the British patrols, rounded Scotland and arrived at her rendezvous off Tralee in south-west Ireland at the appointed time. In her holds, hidden under a cargo of timber, were 20,000 captured Russian rifles and ten German machine guns. However, there was no one to meet her. The ship loitered off the Kerry coast, until she was arrested by a British sloop, and while she was being taken into Cobh, her captain scuttled her. Casement's movements were meanwhile being closely followed by Captain Hall's Naval Intelligence Division; he was arrested before he landed and was ultimately shot, but the rising went ahead.

To coincide with the uprising, Scheer was instructed to make a demonstration to distract British forces. On 26 April he ordered Rear Admiral Friedrich Boedicker, Hipper being ill, to make a sortie with the battlecruisers. The *Seydlitz* soon struck a British mine and returned to harbour, but the remaining four ships, led by the new battlecruiser *Lützow*, carried on. Jellicoe now received a telegram, saying, 'Trouble has broken out in Dublin, and it is reported that the G.P.O. has been seized by the rebels. We have information that the German fleet will assist by demonstrating against the East coast, and this is confirmed by their making the usual preparations for coming out at night.' This was followed by a signal giving the position of the German Scouting Group, and ending 'We think the main fleet is out. Information scanty'.[19] The Grand Fleet raised steam, and Beatty rushed south.

Boedicker's battlecruisers arrived off the East Anglian port of Lowestoft, silencing the 6-inch batteries, and then, ten miles further north attacked Great Yarmouth, which had been bombarded in November 1914. A couple of hundred houses were damaged in the raid and a few citizens were killed. Tyrwhitt's force came out of Harwich and might have been crushed by the German battlecruisers, had not Boedicker backed away, fearful that Beatty might be over the horizon, though in fact they were seventy miles apart. All the German ships returned safely, and Balfour, First Lord of the Admiralty, promised to bring 'important forces' to the south. The Grand Fleet was to be moved to the Forth as soon as the Rosyth base was ready.

The powerful radio transmitters of the U-boats were a double-edged weapon. By May 1916 they could carry 770 miles and could report back from off the Orkneys, but they could also be picked up by the Admiralty's listening posts all along the coasts of Britain.[20] Suspicion of another impending German action was aroused when on 16 and 17 May nine U-boats were heard to have left their bases for the northern waters of the North Sea, and yet, strangely, no merchantmen were attacked there during the next ten days. Repairs to the *Seydlitz* delayed Scheer, but on 30 May another timely report from Captain Hall's staff gave Jellicoe sufficient warning of the movement of the High Seas Fleet for him to leave harbour half an hour before midnight – three hours in fact before Hipper's battlecruisers and the light cruisers forming the First and Second Scouting Groups led the way out of the Jade.

Much of the credibility of Room 40's decryption was destroyed next day, when Captain Thomas Jackson, the Director of the Operations Division, through which all Room 40's intelligence was disseminated, asked where the directional stations placed the German call sign DK. He was told, quite correctly, 'in Wilhelmshaven'. DK was the call sign of Scheer's flagship when in harbour but, as he always had done before, Scheer on putting to sea had transferred his harbour call sign to the wireless station ashore. Room 40 knew that and had the question been,

'Where do the directional stations place Scheer, or his flagship, the *Friedrich der Grosse*, now?' he would have received a different answer. Jackson, who 'displayed supreme contempt for the work of Room 40', according to a lieutenant who worked there, did not enquire further and was not given any more information.[21] Operations division, without showing the signal to Room 40, then informed Jellicoe and Beatty: 'At 12 noon our directional stations place the German fleet flagship in the Jade. Consider it probable that lack of reconnaissance may have delayed their start.'[22] In fact Scheer was already at sea.

Scheer's plan had originally been for Hipper to bombard Sunderland, a little further than his previous most northerly target, Hartlepool. The High Seas Fleet would follow behind to catch the avenging squadrons which were expected to hurry down to cut Hipper off. Because the weather was unsuitable for Zeppelin patrols Scheer decided not to cross the North Sea, but to attack British cruisers which were believed to be off the Danish coast. As Scheer followed Hipper's Scouting Group there was no intention in his mind of risking his squadrons in an action with the whole Grand Fleet. That would have been both contrary to common sense and strictly against the orders of his Supreme War Lord, the Kaiser. He knew that if the Grand Fleet emerged he would be out-numbered in a ratio of two against three, whether calculated from the hundred warships in his fleet, or in artillery, where approximately 200 German heavy guns were faced by 300 British.

The tally, if counted in torpedo tubes, would have been more level, for, besides the greater number carried by German ships, Scheer had disposed eighteen U-boats in the likely paths of the British fleet.[23] Seven lay off the Firth of Forth to catch Beatty's battlecruisers, which were the intended quarry, and another three south-east of Scapa Flow and the Moray Firth to warn him, if the Grand Fleet should emerge. Three more submarines were to lay mines in the same waters and others lay in wait further south. In the event, however, no British ships were tor-pedoed as they came out. (Von Spiegel got within 1,000 yards and fired two torpedoes at the leading light cruisers *Galatea* and *Phaeton*, without hitting. His periscope then jammed and he was forced to dive.) The only casualty at this stage was one of the U-boat minelayers, caught by an armed trawler. Nor did Scheer receive warning of the approach of Jellicoe's armada, though U-boats did report movements of individual ships and squadrons.

That night the Grand Fleet mustered 151 warships, two thirds steaming with Jellicoe from Scapa and the Moray Firth, the remainder under Beatty from the Firth of Forth. 'Rarely has a fleet so itched for action or had such confidence in the outcome,'[24] though they could not know what their admirals had been told, and the common belief was that they were only out to support seaplane carriers or minelayers in the Bight. At 10.00 p.m. the C.-in-C. ordered all ships in company to 'Cease W/T communication except on sighting the Enemy or replying to the Admiral. W/T guards may use auxiliary in case of necessity.'[25] From now on orders would be passed from the Senior Officers to their squadrons and divisions by flashing light or flags. Every ten minutes from 2.35 a.m. Jellicoe ordered the fleet to zigzag by turning two points (22.5 degrees) to port or starboard, but in the early dawn even these instructions could be by flags.

Once Jellicoe's main force of twenty-four battleships had assembled at noon the next day, 31 May, they steamed in six majestic columns surrounded in front and on both flanks by fifty destroyers and an outer ring of cruisers. About seventeen miles ahead was a broad line of scouting cruisers, thirty miles wide, spearheaded by the *Invincible*, *Inflexible* and *Indomitable* of the Third Battle Cruiser Squadron under Rear Admiral Horace Hood. Beatty's six battlecruisers were supported by four oil-fired Queen Elizabeth-class super-dreadnoughts, with their 15-inch guns and twenty-five knot speed under Vice Admiral Hugh Evan-Thomas, and were screened by twenty-four light cruisers and twenty-seven destroyers. He had been ordered to sail almost due east and then turn north as he approached the Danish coast to join the remainder of the Grand Fleet.

It was early in the afternoon that the hostile fleets made contact. A Danish merchant ship was being questioned by the advance guard of Hipper's light cruisers, when the *Galatea* and *Phaeton*, (on Beatty's right wing after his turn to the north) were detached for the same purpose. They opened fire on each other at 2.25 p.m.[26] and then both sides returned to report back to their admirals, the *Galatea* with a dud German shell inside her. Georg von Hase, Gunnery Officer in the battlecruiser *Derfflinger*, was enjoying a coffee in the wardroom, when 'the alarm bells rang through the ship, both drums beat for action, and the boatswains of the watch piped and shouted: "Clear for action!".'[27]

Hipper's five battlecruisers now turned west, while Beatty's six turned east towards the smoke and sound of guns, and nearly an hour and a half later the real battle started. Beatty's battlecruisers adopted line of battle and his light cruiser commanders, who 'knew exactly what Sir David expected of them'[28] took up stations ahead and astern of them without waiting for orders. Having sighted the enemy, Beatty closed rapidly. He wanted to get within the shorter range of the guns of *New Zealand* and *Indefatigable*. In so doing, to the Germans' grateful surprise, he threw away the advantage of the greater range of his other ships' guns. In fact it was the Germans who opened fire first at a range of over ten miles, guns flashing along the line of the five battlecruisers. Seconds later the *Lion* replied. In the haze both sides overestimated the distance between them. The British shot well over their targets at first, and the German official account smugly recorded, 'the development of rangefinders in the British ships had not kept pace with the increase in range of their guns'.[29] A few minutes more and the range was down sufficiently for the German ships to engage their secondary armament of 5.9-inch guns. Hipper's Scouting Group then turned according to plan to bring Beatty down towards Scheer's battleships fifty miles away to the south.

Beatty turned south too, hoping to cut the German ships off from their bases. He had no idea how dangerous that was. He had been warned that the High Seas Fleet was preparing to go out in force, but as a result of the blunder of that signal from Operations Division, he still believed that Scheer was in Wilhelmshaven. As Beatty saw it, he had twice been deprived by unfair fortune of the chance to destroy the rival battlecruisers. He was determined that they should not escape again. If he could get between them and their home ports, the 15-inch guns of the four Queen Elizabeths behind him would make doubly sure of the outcome. Unfortunately at the start of the encounter because of a signalling error, Evan-Thomas's four great ships were ten miles away. They had been steering in the opposite direction for eight minutes before HMS *Barham* led them back. Beatty did not wait for them. In the previous engagement between the battlecruiser squadrons the British had come off best, and no doubt he foresaw the same outcome now. Why should he not? As his friend Roger Keyes wrote, 'He had every reason to think at that time that his six ships were, ship for ship, superior to his five possible opponents, though he was soon to be disillusioned.'[30]

Whether or not Beatty was acting reasonably in not waiting for the Fifth Battle Squadron, there were two significant differences between the action off the Dogger Bank in January 1915 and the Jutland battle. The first was that at Jutland, since the battlecruiser action began at 3.48 p.m. and he was to the south-west of Hipper, the light was very much against him. Lieutenant Stephen King-Hall in the after control of the light cruiser, *Southampton*, noted, 'The Germans were almost entirely merged into a long smoky cloud on the eastern horizon . . .

and from this gloomy retreat a series of red flashes darting out in our direction indicated the presence of five German battle cruisers.'[31] But, while the British spotters had difficulty making out their opponents, their own ships were silhouetted against the afternoon glow. Thanks to the German stereoscopic rangefinders, the superior lenses of their optical industry and their method of ranging, Hipper's guns almost immediately found the range.[32]

The ships were running on parallel courses nine miles apart. Salvo after salvo crashed out in rapid succession on both sides. In the *Derfflinger*, with the big guns firing every twenty seconds and the secondary armament firing two rounds in the interval, a salvo left the battlecruiser every seven seconds. About fifteen minutes after firing commenced HMS *Indefatigable* at the rear of Beatty's line was struck by two shells (or was it three?) from one salvo of *von der Tann*. With their hardened steel heads and delayed-action fuses, they blasted into the after part of the battlecruiser. Seconds later, the *Indefatigable* appeared to be settling down by the stern, as she fell out of line. Almost immediately she was hit by two more heavy projectiles, this time near the bows. There was a massive explosion as a magazine blew up. Stephen King-Hall was aghast to see how, 'without any warning an immense column of grey smoke with a fiery base and a flaming top stood up on the sea, where *Indefatigable* should have been. It hung there for I don't know how many seconds, and then a hole appeared in this pillar of smoke, through which I caught a glimpse of the *Indefatigable* lying on its side; then there was a streak of flame and a fresh outpouring of smoke,'[33] The ship quickly turned over and disappeared beneath the waves, taking 800 men with her. German light cruisers passing the spot later found only two survivors.

For a few minutes after the disaster the five remaining ships on each side, continued to hammer each other as they rushed to the south towards the main fleet of Admiral Scheer. The gunnery officers of both sides had the unnerving experience of seeing groups of enemy shells coming towards them, like elongated black spots, or bluebottle flies. Gigantic spouts of water one or two hundred feet high, rose into the air around the ships, dwarfing them, as the huge shells plunged into the sea and exploded. Water and splinters rained onto the decks and the open bridges of the ships. The crash of gunfire was almost incessant. Then at 4.08 p.m. the balance tilted again in favour of the British, as Evan Thomas's battleships caught up and joined the fray at long range. As von Hase observed, Beatty's squadrons were firing well. 'I was trying to get in two (half) salvoes to the enemy's one. Several times I was unable

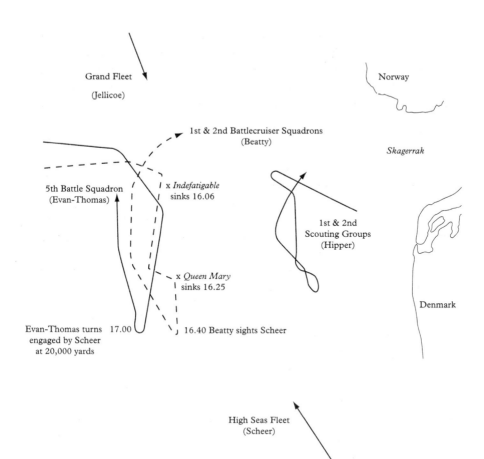

Grand Fleet

(Jellicoe)

Norway

1st & 2nd Battlecruiser Squadrons
(Beatty)

Skagerrak

5th Battle Squadron
(Evan-Thomas)

x *Indefatigable*
sinks 16.06

1st & 2nd
Scouting Groups
(Hipper)

x *Queen Mary*
sinks 16.25

Denmark

Evan-Thomas turns   17.00
engaged by Scheer
at 20,000 yards

16.40 Beatty sights Scheer

High Seas Fleet
(Scheer)

Jutland – Initial phases
The Battlecruisers run south and then north.
16.00–17.30

to attain this, as for full salvoes the enemy was firing with fabulous rapidity. I observed that the gunnery officer of the *Queen Mary* was firing the guns himself with central fire-control, using the famous Percy Scott "Firing-director", for all the guns fired and the shots fell absolutely simultaneously. The English gunnery officer was probably stationed in the fore-top, where he was above the smoke, and firing the guns electrically from there. The ability to do this gave the English a great advantage.'[34]

But the Germans still had the light in their favour. Beatty's ships frequently had no other target than the flashes of the enemy guns in the obscurity of the mist. Add to that the gentle breeze which blew their own smoke from funnel and gun in front of the British and it is not surprising that in this phase of the battle the German ships scored more hits. The battlecruiser *Queen Mary* was being engaged by both the *Seydlitz* and the *Derfflinger*. At 4.25 p.m. the *Derfflinger* caught her with a salvo which totally destroyed her in seconds, breaking the ship in half, sending a column of smoke a thousand feet into the air and killing all but twenty of her crew of 1,280 men. Close astern of the *Queen Mary*, the *Tiger* passed through the dense cloud of smoke caused by the explosion, and steel and woodwork fell on her decks, but otherwise the *Queen Mary* had completely vanished.

In the space of eight minutes two great battlecruisers had blown up, and against Hipper's five ships Beatty now had only four. 'There seems to be something wrong with our bloody ships today', was his famous comment to his flag captain, Chatfield – 'a remark which needed neither comment nor answer.'[35] That was the second difference from the fight off the Dogger Bank. Without the near-fatal experience which the *Seydlitz* had undergone at that battle, the British had not taken any special precautions against cordite fires in their turrets.[36] Beatty's own ship, the *Lion*, had narrowly avoided destruction just two minutes after the action began thanks to the courageous action of Major Francis J.W. Harvey, Royal Marines, in charge of the midships Q-turret. A shell had blown the top of his turret open and, though mortally wounded with his legs shot off, Harvey ordered the magazine to be flooded. Shortly afterwards smouldering material fell onto a cordite charge, and the ensuing explosion tore right down and through the turret in a great sheet of flame, killing all the magazine and shell room parties gathered at the bottom of the ammunition hoist. But for Harvey's 'sublime act of personal devotion'[37] the flames would have blown up the magazine.

Twelve British destroyers led by the *Nestor* (Commander the Hon.

Barry Bingham) were ordered to attack the German battlecruisers, and ran at their full speed of thirty-five knots to take up position to launch their torpedoes.[38] One struck the *Seydlitz*, buckling her plates and letting in water, but she was not sunk, maintained her speed and kept in line. Fifteen of the smaller German destroyers pitched in to defend their heavy ships, and a sharp, confused encounter took place at high speed and close range, while the shells of the two groups of capital ships roared overhead. Two of the German destroyers were sunk but as their flotillas withdrew a light cruiser came out from behind the German battle-cruisers and crippled the destroyers *Nomad* and *Nestor*. The two British destroyers now lay in the path of the approaching German battleships. The *Nomad* was the first to go, smothered by the secondary armament of the great ships under the eyes of the helpless *Nestor*. Soon her turn came, and in two or three minutes the *Nestor* was slowly settling by the stern. Bingham ordered 'Abandon ship' and watched with his First Lieutenant, Bethell, as the boats and rafts were filled up. The Captain then turned to his Lieutenant and asked, 'Now where shall we go?' The answer came, 'To heaven, I trust, sir!'[39] At that moment Bethell turned aside to attend to a mortally wounded signalman and was seen no more amidst a cloud of fumes from a bursting shell. Bingham was rescued from the water by German destroyers and taken prisoner with a con-siderable number of the crews of the two destroyers, as the German battle fleet passed by.

Hipper's ships had taken heavy punishment by now. He had fulfilled his orders bravely, bringing a significant part of the British fleet within range of Scheer's guns, and so he turned away.

Minutes later Commodore Goodenough in the *Southampton*, steaming ahead of Beatty, sighted sixteen battleships with destroyers on each bow. 'Look, sir,' said his First Lieutenant, Arthur Peters, 'this is the day of a light cruiser's lifetime. The whole of the High Seas Fleet is before you.' Scheer's arrival was quickly reported to Beatty and as Goodenough hung on for a few moments before confirming it, his Commander coolly said, 'If you're going to make that signal, you'd better make it now, sir. You may never make another.'[40] Courageously remaining within range for an hour as the large calibre shells plunged around his squadron, Goodenough kept the enemy in sight and sent reports (though not very accurate) of his position and Scheer's bearing and course. It was, to Beatty's surprise in view of the information received from the Admiralty, what the Grand Fleet had been praying for during twenty-two months of frustration. The greatest naval gun battle in history would take place, if he could lead the High Seas Fleet on towards Jellicoe's advancing armada without letting Hipper's Scouting Group see it.

As the German dreadnoughts approached, Beatty turned north at 4.40 p.m. to bring them within range of Jellicoe's overwhelming forces. Hipper's ships followed, saving their ammunition, 'We were filled with the proud joy of victory', von Hase wrote, 'and hoped to accomplish the destruction of the whole force opposed to us. We had acquired an absolute confidence in our ship. It seemed out of the question that our proud ship could be shattered in a few minutes like the *Queen Mary* and the *Indefatigable*. On the other hand, I had a feeling that we could blow up any English ship in no time, given a straight course for a time and not too long a range.'[41]

Scheer followed up fast, quite unaware of the trap. It appeared to him, as ignorant of the true state of affairs as Beatty had been, that there was at last a chance to reduce the preponderant power of the Royal Navy. Had the weather in the North Sea allowed the scouting Zeppelins to keep station and report the approach of the Grand Fleet, he must have turned back and there would never have been a Battle of Jutland. (Beatty too received little help from his seaplanes, which took nearly half an hour to be swung out onto the water, had limited endurance and were hampered by the poor visibility. Lieutenant Frederick Rutland[42] flew with an observer at 900 feet under the low cloud, and into a storm of shrapnel, to report the position of four enemy light cruisers – the first time that planes had been used in a naval battle – but other aircraft from the *Engadine* could not take off in the choppy water.)

The four super-dreadnoughts of the Fifth Battle Squadron were now getting into trouble. As Beatty began his run back to the north, Evan-Thomas was approaching in the opposite direction. Just before the flagships passed each other the *Lion* hoisted, 'Alter course in succession 16 points (180 degrees) to starboard'. Exactly when the flags were raised, and when they were lowered as the signal to execute the order, is not clear. (In view of the danger to the Battle Squadron which ensued, the post mortem reports were tampered with.) Suffice it to say that for twenty minutes Evan-Thomas continued his run south before he followed Beatty back. By then his four Queen Elizabeths were again on their own, but within range of the twenty advancing German battle-ships. In those circumstances the manoeuvre which Beatty ordered was extremely dangerous. It required each ship to turn at the same place one after the other. The enemy could and did concentrate their guns on that spot, so that the British ships passed it with volcanic eruptions exploding round them every seven to ten seconds. All four received hits – the

Malaya almost fatally – and 250 casualties were suffered, but fortunately in the eight critical minutes of turning, no ship was crippled. If any of them had had her steering put out of action or her engine room disabled, nothing could have saved her from destruction. A signalling confusion coupled with strict obedience to orders had for the second time caused Evan-Thomas to be out of place. But the Fifth Battle Squadron fired back effectively – when their spotters could see through the forest of splashes – and had at least given breathing space to Beatty's battlecruisers.

Jellicoe's Grand Fleet was only sixteen miles away, steaming intently south-east: 40,000 men at action stations; no zig-zagging now, and speed increased to twenty knots. He dispatched the *Invincible, Inflexible* and *Indomitable*, comprising the Third Battlecruiser Squadron under Rear Admiral Horace Hood, to race ahead and reinforce Beatty. This they did with good effect. Their 12-inch shells crippled the battlecruiser *Lützow*, damaged the light cruisers *Pillau* and *Frankfurt*, and nearly brought their sister ship, the *Wiesbaden*, to a halt.

However, Rear Admiral Sir Robert Arbuthnot then unwisely led his squadron of four obsolescent armoured cruisers between the battle lines to finish off the torpedoed *Wiesbaden*. In doing so he approached within 8,000 yards of the German battlecruisers in the patchy visibility. His flagship, the *Defence* was rapidly hit by two salvos, her magazines blew up and she broke in half. 'Black smoke and debris shot into the air, a flame enveloped the whole ship, and then she sank before our eyes,' von Hase noted.[43] The *Defence* was lost with all hands. For the third time a British ship had exploded into nothing. It was a terrible waste. Chatfield had previously warned him both of the dangers he would run and the problems which his smoke would cause to the fire control of the fleet, if he crossed in front of them. As Andrew Gordon writes, 'When all allowances have been made, cruisers had no business to be messing around in the killing ground between the fleets.'[44]

A similar fate might have overtaken her sister ship, *Warrior*, but for an accident in the new dreadnought *Warspite* of the Fifth Battle Squadron. Her steering jammed, and the *Warspite* had almost described two great circles to starboard before the defect was corrected and she rejoined the line. While helplessly circling towards the enemy ships she was subjected to their concentrated fire. There were, one officer recalled, 'four or five German dreadnoughts firing at us for about twenty minutes and hitting us about once a minute. Why we weren't sunk is a perfect mystery. Personally, after seeing the *Defence* go, I thought we should go any minute.'[45] But the heavily armoured battleship took the punishment and returned it with her own 15-inch guns, drawing the fire from the *Warrior*.

Beatty had lost ships but not his nerve. His battlecruisers were three knots faster than Hipper's, and as he pulled away he turned his squadron in a shallow arc to starboard, which put him across the bows of Hipper's ships and forced them to turn to eastwards too. Hipper therefore remained unaware of the approach of the Grand Fleet, and could not warn his Commander-in-Chief until it was too late for Scheer to avoid action between the battle fleets.[46]

For some while Jellicoe, peering ahead on the bridge of the *Iron Duke*, was not much better informed. The light cruiser *Chester* was sent to investigate and challenged a light cruiser with the British recognition signal. No answer was received and the ship disappeared. Two more light cruisers then appeared and opened fire on the *Chester*, which soon had three of her guns disabled. Many of the men in her guns' crews had their legs shorn off at the ankles as they stood behind the unturreted guns. An officer reported that 'in the central ammunition passage these wounded men – cheerful Cockneys, for she had a Chatham crew – sat, smoking cigarettes, the bloody stumps of their tourniqueted legs out in front. An hour or so later most of them were dead from shock.'[47]

Jellicoe could hear the great guns firing in the distance, but visibility was down to seven miles and too few reports were coming in. Admiral Burney in the *Marlborough* on the right wing could only answer, 'Gun flashes and heavy gun fire on the starboard bow',[48] but could not say where the enemy ships were. At last at 6.14 p.m. Beatty, in response to his C.-in-C.'s second enquiry, reported sighting the enemy battle fleet bearing south-south-west (but failed to give its course).

There was no time to lose. Deployment would take twenty minutes and, with the visibility so low, the reports meant that the enemy could not be more than a few miles away. Jellicoe must not have his dread-noughts bunched in cruising formation when they met the High Seas Fleet, and if they were caught still deploying from the right, the Germans would be able to concentrate on each division as it turned. After staring at the compass for twenty seconds he crisply ordered the signal to deploy on the left wing, which would give a little more time to deploy. The decision was exactly right and the fleet executed it with precision. The six columns of battleships formed into one great line six miles long and continued their south-easterly course. Their guns were trained on the spot where they expected the enemy to appear, and spare white ensigns sprouted from their masts in case one or more was shot away. The deployment brought them in front of the three squadrons of

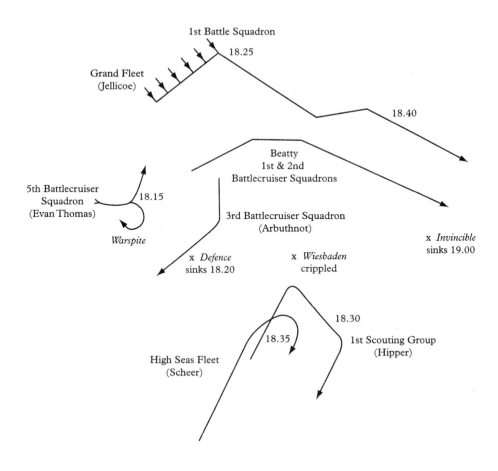

Jutland – The Grand Fleet Deploys
18.15–18.45

the High Seas Fleet, which had been cruising already in line ahead, flanked by destroyers. Jellicoe had succeeding in 'crossing the T' of Scheer's fleet. If the German Admiral continued his course he might push through the rear of the Grand Fleet's long line, but he would suffer terribly in the process, and many of his ships would risk being surrounded. That one decision of the British C.-in-C. gave him the advantage of position and light, which he retained for the remainder of the daylight battle.

Scheer was stupefied not only to find the Grand Fleet in front of him, but to find them expecting him too.[49] However, the Grand Fleet's advantage was greatly diminished by further deterioration in visibility. 'At this time', Jellicoe recorded, 'owing to smoke and mist, it was most difficult to distinguish friend from foe, and quite impossible to form an opinion on board the *Iron Duke*, in her position towards the centre of the line, as to the formation of the enemy's Fleet. The identity of the ships in sight on the starboard beam was not even sufficiently clear for me to permit fire to be opened.'[50] It was not until the leading German ships were only 12,000 yards away, that the *Iron Duke* opened fire and the Second and Fourth Battle Squadrons followed. At this stage of the battle those British ships which could see the enemy, fired well and effectively. In the *Iron Duke* Captain Dreyer, watching his ship's accurate firing at the *König* was heard to mutter, 'Beautiful, beautiful,' like a rose-grower at a show.[51] Spotting was not easy for either side as the smoke from guns and funnels further clouded the scene, but the British ships had the advantage of the sunlight and many hits were scored. It was the turn of the Germans to see only gun flashes in the gloom and to King-Hall, observing from the sidelines, the German shooting now 'was simply ludicrously bad'.[52] Scheer could not let this situation continue. His objective had always been to avoid meeting the assembled Grand Fleet and this was just what he found himself doing. However, the High Seas Fleet had practised the tactics which they would employ if they met a superior force in battle. Scheer ordered a 'Battle Turnaway'. His whole line reversed direction almost simultaneously; starting from the rear, each ship turned as soon as the one behind was seen to be turning – a difficult manoeuvre in battle conditions. At the same time his destroyers were ordered to run between the two fleets and lay a smokescreen. Without targets all the guns fell silent. Scheer had saved himself for the moment.

In fact it was the British again who suffered worst at this time. Another disaster struck. Aside from the main battle line Rear Admiral the Hon. Horace Hood's Third Battlecruiser Squadron, scarcely visible in the mist, was effectively pounding Hipper's battlecruisers, when his flagship, *Invincible*, emerged from the haze to become the only clear target for the *Lützow* and *Derfflinger*. They concentrated their fire on Hood's flagship and at 6.34 p.m. landed five projectiles on her at the same moment. As with the *Lion*, the roof was torn off the Q-turret amidships, but there was no time to flood the *Invincible*'s magazine. A series of tremendous explosions rent the ship. Black smoke and coal dust rose into the air, as flames enveloped her. She broke in two and her masts collapsed inwards and disappeared. All but six of the ship's complement perished, including the admirable Horace Hood, 'the perfect leader in any difficult situation'.[53]

The Royal Navy had now lost three capital ships and a heavy cruiser; 4,212 men had been killed in those four ships and only a handful had survived. No major ships of the enemy had been sunk. There were only a couple of hours of daylight left. Would the British be able to redress the balance? In football terms they were four goals down at half time.

Nevertheless, even if the German ships were not sinking, they were suffering terribly. As the Captain of the *Moltke* admitted, 'The enemy's salvos lie well and close; their salvos are fired in rapid succession, the fire discipline is excellent!'[54] The battlecruisers had fared worst. When Hipper's flagship, the *Lützow* was forced out of line listing heavily, he signalled to his squadron asking for reports on their ships. Of the four others only the *Moltke* was in a fit state for him to transfer his flag to her.

In response to Scheer's 180 degree turn Jellicoe altered course slightly to starboard and ran south. This again was the correct decision because it would enable his ships to form a line between the enemy and their base. Also if the German ships were found they would be silhouetted against the setting sun, while the British were almost invisible. A quarter of an hour later Scheer unwisely decided to turn back and in doing so blundered straight into the middle of Jellicoe's battle line, finding it again across the top of the 'T'. Once more the High Seas Fleet was in a desperate situation. In these last few minutes of daylight the British scored seventy hits with heavy guns against the Germans' twenty. The battleships in the van were taking the heaviest punishment, could not maintain their speed or station and caused the ships behind them to bunch up. For a short while it seemed possible that Jellicoe had the High Seas Fleet at his mercy, as their ships still came on and the range reduced to only five and a half miles. Those German officers who could see what was happening were under no illusions. 'Our fleet ended up

157

by butting into the very centre of the enemy's fleet, which was forming a semicircle around us; it would thus have been exposed to the murderous fire of the whole hostile fleet, and soon lost all power to manoeuvre'[55] – if their C.-in-C. had not responded with calm resolution.

Scheer first sent Hipper off on a desperate charge with a flag signal, which became famous in the German navy, 'Battlecruisers at the enemy! Give it everything!'[56] Once again he ordered his main fleet to execute a 'Battle Turnaway', covering it with a torpedo attack by his destroyers, which were to raise a smokescreen at the same time. Only a third of Scheer's flotillas were able to attack effectively and Jellicoe met them with his own destroyers, so another confused mêlée resulted. However, the German ships managed to fire some thirty-one torpedoes at the long line of British ships. Had the Grand Fleet maintained its course, broadside on to the torpedoes' paths, with only about two ships' lengths between each of the great vessels, each torpedo would have had a one in three chance of hitting. What should Jellicoe do? To turn towards the torpedoes would have kept his ships in touch with the German fleet, but the chance of being struck was greater; the enemy destroyers might have laid mines too. To turn away was safer, and, as Jellicoe had forewarned the Admiralty what he would do in these circumstances, he turned his ships to port. Every one of the torpedoes was avoided by a combination of sharp observation and good ship handling. But while taking avoiding action, Jellicoe did not see the German battleships turning about behind their smokescreen, and none of the captains, of other ships, who did see them, reported it. At the cost of great damage to his battlecruisers Scheer's objective had been attained: the Grand Fleet had lost contact. Scheer had withdrawn the High Seas Fleet 'in a very masterful fashion out of the closing jaws of Jellicoe'.[57]

The price of their 'death ride' had been the complete destruction of Hipper's battlecruisers as a fighting force. Though none had been sunk, they had few turrets between them still firing, and little ammunition left in those. Both of the after turrets of the *Derfflinger* had been penetrated. Huge tapering flames had leapt skywards and down, killing all but six of the 160 men serving the guns. In the cartridge chamber all the cases which had been removed from their protective packing were set alight – but the ship survived. The other ships of the squadron suffered similarly. *Seydlitz* had a struggle to keep afloat. On several ships much of the secondary armament and search-lights had been destroyed, which made their captains nervous about night fighting.

Was there yet time for Jellicoe to bring off a second Trafalgar, or rather a second Tsushima? He was still firmly between Scheer and the German bases, and, except for the battered *Warspite*, which he sent back to Rosyth because her speed was reduced to sixteen knots, and the *Marlborough*, which had been hit early on by a torpedo but could still fight, the dreadnought squadrons under his command were almost untouched. But night was falling. In the night action at Tsushima, Togo had the advantage that his enemy had no torpedo craft to launch at him. He could, without fear of reprisals, let his flotillas loose to scatter the dispirited Russians, who were 300 miles from safety, and still have time to mop up the survivors next day. At Jutland the situation was different. Once action had been broken off that night, neither side knew exactly where the other was, though at one time the leading battleships were only a few miles apart. What if Jellicoe had sent his destroyers out on an abortive search to find and attack the High Seas Fleet? His antagonist, far from dispirited, had well-handled destroyer flotillas, and Jellicoe might find his own squadrons subjected to a torpedo attack in the dark without their destroyer screen. What would the nation have said then? It was too dangerous, so he reformed his fleet into four columns a mile apart with his flotillas five miles behind. From there the destroyers could be brought forward to provide a protective screen if required, and would not run the risk of being mistaken for the enemy. The British C.-in-C. wanted to avoid fighting at all during darkness. Like the admirals in most navies he considered a night action between the battle fleets to be too much of a gamble, 'as there is little opportunity for skill on either side'.[58] Churchill spelt it out: 'The far ranging cruisers were blinded. The friendly destroyers became a danger to the ships they guarded. The great guns lost their range. Now, if ever, the reign of the torpedo would begin.' The capital ships would be haunted by the fear of destroyers, invisible or tardily identified, firing torpedoes, which would be seen too late to be avoided. (Perhaps also, even before the battle, Jellicoe did not feel confident that the training and equipment of the British light forces for night fighting was equal to his enemy's.)

But if there was to be no night attack on the High Seas Fleet, everything would depend on placing the Grand Fleet across the path of the High Seas Fleet at dawn next day. There would be no second chance. Scheer was only eighty miles from safety, if he risked crossing the Grand Fleet's path, or 150 miles from home by the safer route. By first light he could be close to the mined areas, where paths would be kept swept wide enough for his ships to enter, but too narrow for a fleet to manoeuvre and fight. If Jellicoe was not there, the Germans would get away: if he could block their way with a full day's fighting ahead, a crushing victory should follow. What he desperately needed to know was which of three possible routes home would Scheer take? It was an agonizing gamble.

In Old Building at the Admiralty in Whitehall they knew the answer. Scheer reported that he would steer a course towards the Horns Reef, a sandbank jutting out from the Danish coast. Near there was the northern entrance to a channel between the minefields, which the Germans kept swept for 120 miles right round to the River Jade. Room 40 received and decoded that signal and successive messages indicating that Scheer was keeping to that plan, and passed them on to Operations Division, who were responsible for keeping the Fleet informed. With plenty of time to spare the British Commander-in-Chief had the first decoded message in his hands. But then everything went wrong. First, Jellicoe did not believe the signal. He simply did not trust the Admiralty's information. Not only had he been told at the start of the battle that the High Seas Fleet was still in the Jade, when he found them out at sea, but a subsequent message had given a wrong position for some German ships, because the Germans themselves had wrongly reported their position. Now he was being told that Scheer was turning south-east, when his cruisers had reported them going due south. (He could not know that when the enemy were spotted they had turned south to avoid a torpedo attack, and had resumed their easterly course soon afterwards.) As more messages came in confirming Scheer's route, Operations Division, unaware of Jellicoe's doubts, did not bother to pass them on to the Fleet. In particular a signal from the German C.-in-C. urgently requesting air reconnaissance by Zeppelins early next morning off Horns Reef would have left Jellicoe in no doubt as to his intentions. Six other signals giving Scheer's position or course were passed on by Room 40, only half an hour on average after being received. Once again the Operations Division had ruined the work of decryption. Their frustration can only have been matched by that of the British Commander-in-Chief when he learnt the truth! Well might he say, 'It is impossible to understand this extraordinary omission on the part of the Admiralty Staff, but there can be no doubt whatever that the escape of the High Seas Fleet from being engaged at daylight off the Horn Reef was due to this neglect.'[59]

Jellicoe guessed that the German ships would head south for the mouths of the Rivers Jade or Ems to avoid crossing the Grand Fleet's path, and both he and Beatty turned in that direction (or a little east of south). But Scheer had already decided to take the shortest, most

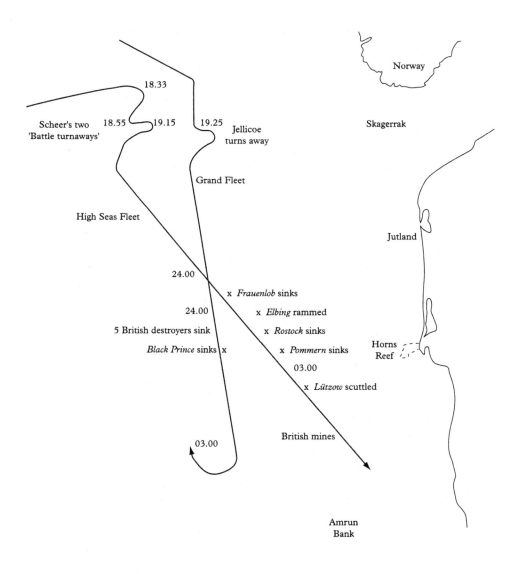

Jutland – The last of daylight and the night actions

northerly route to safety. To get there he rightly estimated that he would have to pass through some part of the Grand Fleet, but he formed his ships into two columns and ordered them to drive south-east in a dead straight line, and hold their course come what may.[60] This they succeeded in doing. In the darkness the lines taken by the two fleets converged in a narrow 'V'. At the intersection of their paths, making a cross of St Andrew, seven savage little battles with the British destroyer screen ensued and both sides lost ships. Jellicoe did not give any instructions to his light forces other than to keep station at the rear of his fleet. They fought on their own.

Scheer's battle fleet was far better prepared for fighting than the destroyers they met that night. For a start they expected they might crash into the British. When they did, their searchlights were a blinding weapon operated with paralysing effect, they had powerful binoculars which gave better night vision than the British ones and their surprisingly brilliant star shells could illuminate an enemy three miles away, while giving only the briefest indication of their own position. As Jellicoe recognized in his report, 'The German organisation at night is very good. Their system of recognition signals is excellent. Ours is practically nil . . . I am reluctantly compelled to the opinion that under night conditions we have a good deal to learn from them.'[61]

Another advantage which the Germans enjoyed was knowledge of the British recognition signal. When early in the afternoon the two-letter signal had been flashed at a light cruiser, it was immediately passed on to the rest of the High Seas Fleet. During the night British destroyers found looming towards them huge ships, which challenged them with the correct two letters. They had hardly time to flash back the reply, before a devastating fire was opened up on them from the 5.9-inch guns of the battleships. The British flotillas fought furiously, but by daybreak the destroyers were widely scattered.

In spite of their advantages, however, the Germans fared worse in the night. The battleship *Pommern*, succumbed to a torpedo and blew up and all her crew were lost as the High Seas Fleet pressed on in the night. Goodenough's squadron had suddenly found five German cruisers only 800 yards away on their beam. As they challenged, the Germans switched on coloured lights. Then both sides simultaneously blazed their searchlights and opened fire. 'The range was amazingly close . . . There could be no missing. A gun was fired and a hit obtained – the gun was loaded, it flamed, it roared, it leapt to the rear, it slid to the front – there was another hit.'[62] Within a couple of minutes three quarters of the men on the *Southampton*'s upper deck were casualties, and with most of the guns' crews mown down, the firing stopped. However, she had loosed off a torpedo at the light cruiser opposite, which broke in two. Only seven of the *Frauenlob*'s complement of 300 survived. Two more German light cruisers were sunk, the *Rostock* by gunfire, and the *Elbing* by being rammed by one of her own battleships. Another German destroyer was fatally torpedoed. Against this by the end of the night the British had lost five destroyers and a third armoured cruiser, the *Black Prince*, which was struck at close range by a devastating salvo from a battleship and drove on for a while, a blazing red torch in the night.

The actions of the British Fourth and Twelfth Flotillas were characterized, Jellicoe reported, by 'splendid dash, skill and gallantry'[63], but the fact remained that the High Seas Fleet had driven home through a screen of fifty-five British destroyers without great loss, and without being engaged by the battleships. The officers of the German dreadnoughts may have thought that they were being sought out and pluckily attacked by the British destroyers, but more often the flotillas were themselves surprised by hostile ships steering towards them out of the Stygian darkness.

An extraordinary aspect of the night fighting was that the destroyer actions were, with one exception, simply not reported to the Commander-in-Chief either by the destroyer captains, who may well have been too overwhelmed by the furious engagements as the German battle fleet steamed through, or by the rearmost squadron of his battleships, which were aware of the fighting behind them. The last destroyer attack as dawn approached was reported, but the weak wireless signal did not get through the German jamming, and it would by then have been too late for Jellicoe to intervene.

The German destroyers achieved nothing; they never found the British fleet. Yet, while being completely out of the action, Scheer's torpedo craft may, by their very existence, have saved two of his capital ships. In fear of a destroyer attack Jellicoe's battleships would do nothing which might give away their position. They would not open fire, even against a crippled enemy, unless fired upon first. 'In other words the security of the battle fleet was given a higher priority than that of making known the enemy's presence or attacking him.'[64] Typical was the Captain's report from HMS *Thunderer* (Second Battle Squadron): '(10) About 10.30 p.m. an enemy cruiser challenged three times, switching on and off 4 red lights horizontal above 4 green horizontal. Fire was not opened as it was considered inadvisable to show battlefleet unless obvious attack was intended.'[65] For the Royal Navy's reputation the most regrettable aspect of the hours of darkness had been the lost opportunities. Hipper's badly damaged battlecruisers had struggled through the night at the rear of the German squadrons without interference. Worst of all, the *Moltke* and *Seydlitz* had limped home on their own, when they had hardly a big gun in action between them. And both had been sighted by British ships. The *Seydlitz*, 'wandering drunkenly through the Grand Fleet,'[66] had passed between two divisions of battleships, less than a mile away from the nearest. Neither had been attacked because the Captains of the *Agincourt, Marlborough* and *Revenge* (First Battle Squadron) thought better of it. The captain of the *Revenge* reported: 'About 12.30 what was at first taken for destroyers approaching was observed and 6-inch guns turned on them and the order had been given to open fire, when it was seen that the object was a large ship. She was challenged and made the reply "PL" and rapidly disappeared astern. She had the appearance of a Battle Cruiser and resembled our own.'[67] Had the two German battlecruisers been sunk – and a salvo or two from the ships which observed them would have been enough – the score would have been levelled, and the world's verdict on Jutland would have been very different.

In the end all the German battlecruisers got home except for the *Lützow*, which was so down by the bows that her stern was right out of the water, and she had to be sunk by torpedo after her crew had been taken off. The *Seydlitz* grounded twice in the shallow waters of the Bight. She had 5,300 tons of water on board but in the semi-darkness of her stricken hull, her indomitable crew, working in the company of floating bodies, baled her out, until two pumping vessels could come alongside.

At three in the morning, just as dawn was breaking, Scheer was a few miles away from the swept channel and as good as home. Jellicoe surveyed the empty seas as far as the low cloud would allow. The Grand Fleet had steamed eighty-five miles since 10 p.m.. It was now thirty miles to the south-west of the German ships, and would be unable to catch them before they were safely behind their mine barriers. Nothing could now hold them back. The dreadnought *Ostfriesland* struck a mine, laid that night by HMS *Abdiel* off Horns Reef, but was not sunk, and though three British submarines had been sent to lie in wait for the enemy's return and had arrived on time, they had strangely been ordered not to surface until 2 June. By then the High Seas Fleet was safe in its bases.

Sick with disappointment, Jellicoe turned his ships home, deployed in a long line and prepared for fighting if an opportunity occurred.

However, the destroyers were not gathered until mid-morning, and so Jellicoe would not have welcomed action until then. All had arrived at Scapa Flow by noon next day. They coaled ship and next evening, to make a point, their Commander-in-Chief reported the Grand Fleet ready again for battle.

Notes

1. Notes of Captain H.C.R. Brocklebank, RN, in library of Greenwich Maritime Museum.
2. Brown, Malcolm and Meehan, Patricia, *Scapa Flow*, Allen Lane Penguin Press, 1968, p.86
3. Bingham, op. cit. p.41
4. James, Admiral Sir William, *Admiral Sir William Fisher*, Macmillan, 1943, p.48
5. Things could be different. Arriving just before the war at Tampico, Mexico, Leading Signalman Buchan in HMS *Bristol* was amazed to record, 'Passing through the American fleet, we...prepared for coaling. Soon the lighters, *Libertad* and *Independencia*, came alongside us, one each side, and coaling was carried out here by a method entirely new to us. Each of the lighters passed a big tube inboard, which was placed directly over the bunkers. The coal was then hoisted by means of an endless chain of buckets, which filled themselves with coal and emptied themselves down the tube, and so the coal was transferred direct from the lighter to the bunker, all done by machinery, and nobody had to worry at all, except the stokers, who were required to trim the coal.' The virtue for the Navy of 'coaling ship' was that it brought the whole ship's company together, officers and men. (German officers did not always join in coaling with the men, and they did not replace the drudgery either.)
6. Marder, op. cit. Vol.3, p.3
7. There was an international Court of Enquiry in Paris, when the Russians still claimed that hostile destroyers attacked them. However, the Naval Intelligence Division had intercepted and translated the Russian signals, sent *en clair*. The Court was satisfied that the shooting had started when the nervous Russians had mistaken their own cruisers for the enemy.
8. Having no coaling stations along the route, the Russian fleet was re-fuelled by eighty ships, owned or chartered by the Hamburg-Amerika line, which led the London *Times* to question whether Germany was being neutral.

9. Marder, op. cit. Vol.3, p.30

10. Probably the most forceful contemporary critic of the upbringing of naval officers was Commander (later Admiral) K.G.B. Dewar in his *The Navy from Within*. (See now Gordon, Andrew, *The Rules of the Game*, John Murray, 1996)

11. With Scott's system, as the ship's Gunnery Officer, high up in the mast, trained his periscope glasses round on the target, a pointer in each turret moved on a dial. A gunner in each turret then turned the handle to train the turret round until another needle was over the director pointer. All the guns could be fired at the same instant by the gunnery officer, giving a very closely bunched salvo. At trials in November 1912 HMS *Thunderer*, fitted with Scott's system, scored six times as many hits as HMS *Orion*, the best in the fleet with the old system of individual aiming. (A back up allowed the turret officer to operate duplicate dials independently.) However, director firing had not been introduced for all ships by 1916. The Germans had a similar system, but without centralized firing.

12. Memorandum to the Admiralty, 12 April 1916.

13. Marder, op. cit. Vol.2, p.416

14. Churchill, op. cit. p.1015

15. James, Admiral Sir William, *Admiral Sir William Fisher*, Macmillan, 1943, p64

16. Halpern, op. cit. p.311

17. 14 April 1916; Jellicoe MSS, quoted in Marder, op. cit. Vol.2, p.423

18. Churchill, op. cit. p.1020

19. See Naval Staff Monograph (Historical) XVI p.11

20. Captain Hall's organization was at the time the Admiralty's only long distance source of information. Until later in 1916 the weak radio transmitters of the British submarines could not reach England from the Heligoland Bight. Scheer, besides his U-boats, also received intelligence from Zeppelins, though not as much as might be expected.

21. Lieutenant W.F. Clarke quoted in Marder, op. cit. Vol.3, p.47

22. James, op. cit. p.117. Professor Marder and others claim that this wrong information caused Jellicoe to steam at a slower speed towards the rendezvous and so to arrive at the scene of battle two hours later than he would have done. However, Andrew Gordon disproves this, mainly because, even if Jellicoe had increased speed for two hours after he received the signal, the Grand Fleet would only have met Scheer, who would of course have been further away, about sixteen minutes earlier than it did. (Gordon, op. cit. p.415)

23. Against the three hundred and eighty-two British 21-inch and

seventy-five 18-inch tubes the Germans carried three hundred and sixty-two 19.7-inch and one hundred and seven 17.7-inch.

24. Marder, op. cit. Vol.2, p.436

25. Battle of Jutland Official Despatches p.408. Only the S.O. 2nd Battle Squadron broke wireless silence.

26. Greenwich Mean Time is used throughout the account, although, as the battle was fought off the Danish coast about six degrees east of Greenwich, darkness fell earlier than at the same hour by GMT in Britain. German accounts of the action using Continental time make it take place later in the day, which perhaps gives a better idea of the available light on that misty evening.

27. Von Hase, op. cit. p.135.

28. King-Hall, op. cit. p.130

29. *Der Krieg in der Nordsee*, Band V, p.226, quoted in Tarrant, V.E., *Jutland, The German Perspective*, Arms and Armour Press, 1995, p. 80

30. Keyes, Admiral of the Fleet Sir Roger, *Naval Memoirs*, Thornton Butterworth, 1934, Vol.2, p.39. Who was to blame for Evan Thomas's being so slow in turning? Was it just a signalling failure in the *Lion* – flags raised and then, as though forgotten, not hauled down to tell Evans Thomas when to execute the turn? And with all the problems of visibility, shouldn't it have been repeated by searchlight? Or was it Evan Thomas's lack of initiative – waiting for the signal to execute, when he knew that the enemy had been sighted? (See Gordon, op. cit. part III)

31. King-Hall, op. cit. p.130

32. See Marder, op. cit. Vol. 3, p.196 for the difference between the German stereoscopic rangefinders, which required operators with equal vision in both eyes, and the British coincidence type, which was easier to operate, but was not so accurate at long ranges. Perhaps though, rangefinders aside, the Germans would still have scored the first hits because of the way they fired their first salvos. The British ranged their guns by the 'bracket' system. When the spotters saw from the splashes that the shells were falling in front of the target, the elevation was raised until the shells fell over it, then lowered again until a salvo fell all round it, 'straddling' the target. The Germans used the 'ladder system' firing half a salvo, one gun from each turret, deliberately short, and while the projectiles were still in the air firing another a set distance further, and then another further still. The target was thus straddled remarkably quickly.

33. King-Hall, op. cit. p.131

34. Von Hase, op. cit. p.158

35. Chatfield, op. cit. p.143

36. Campbell, N.J.M., *Jutland, An Analysis of the Fighting*, Conway Maritime Press, 1998. Campbell points out that the Germans had not, as is often said, fitted flash doors, except in the *Lützow*, but they had drastically reduced the number of charges kept out of their magazine cases.

37. Churchill, op. cit. p.1028. Harvey was awarded a posthumous VC. It was the second time that good fortune had saved Beatty and his ship-mates from being been blown sky-high.

38. The Brown-Curtiss geared turbines of the *Nestor* and her class developed 25,000 horsepower, equal to that of the early dreadnoughts.

39. Bingham, op. cit. pp145-6

40. Goodenough, op. cit. p.95. The light cruisers literally dodged the 11-inch shells, any one of which could have sunk the lightly armoured ships, by turning away from the last fall of shot. If the battleships fired about every thirty seconds and there were from twenty-three to forty seconds between flash and splash, depending on the range, the light cruisers could move 300 to 400 yards between each salvo or while the shells were in flight. It was a nerve-racking game – and more frightening still, when more than one battleship was firing at the same cruiser! 'Damn how I hate this wet', said his navigating officer as the shells plunged around.

41. Von Hase, op. cit. p168

42. 'Rutland of Jutland' had a curious history. He was awarded a DSO for his services in the battle and a bar to his DSO in 1917. Between the wars he became a paid agent of the Japanese, intended to spy on the US Navy base at Pearl Harbour, so when he returned to the UK during the Second World War he was interned.

43. Von Hase, op. cit. p.179

44. Gordon, op. cit. p.445. The *Wiesbaden* succumbed later in the battle, with only one survivor.

45. Lieutenant Commander P.E. Vaux, personal record in IWM, P447.

46. Was it an inspired move by Beatty to mask the Grand Fleet, as many have claimed, or was it only intended to bring Hipper and then Scheer nearer to Jellicoe's centre, as Andrew Gordon believes?

47. Admiral Sir Frederic Dreyer quoted in Legg, Stuart, *Jutland*, Rupert Hart-Davis, 1966, p.85. At this time sixteen year old Jack Cornwell, Boy 1st Class, earned a posthumous VC and a place in schoolboy stories as he stood, wounded and alone by his gun, awaiting orders, when all his gun's crew were either dead or injured.

48. Jellicoe, op. cit. p.344

49. The secret of the encounter was well kept. As Georg von Hase wrote

long after the battle, 'That the entire English fleet was already at sea and bearing on the same point as ourselves, not a man in the German fleet suspected, not even the Commander-in-Chief. And in the same way, according to all published reports, no one in the English fleet knew that the German fleet had put to sea. (Hase, op. cit. p.127)

50. Jellicoe, op. cit. p.354
51. Legg, op. cit. p.97
52. King-Hall, op. cit. p.140
53. Marder, op. cit. Vol. 3, p.44
54. Quoted in Herwig, Holger H., *Luxury Fleet – The German Imperial Navy 1888–1918*, George Allen & Unwin, 1980 p.184
55. Von Hase, op. cit. p.98
56. Tarrant, op. cit. p.157
57. Bennet Copplestone, writing in *The Spectator*, 9 June 1917.
58. Jellicoe, op. cit. p.373
59. Jellicoe, op. cit. Naturally the Admiralty kept silent about their information, even while Jellicoe was lambasted for his failure to crush the foe.
60. The German wireless receiving stations had picked up Jellicoe's signal telling his destroyers to take station astern, and this had been promptly passed on to Scheer.
61. Battle of Jutland Official Despatches p.3.
62. King-Hall, op. cit. p.150
63. Jellicoe, op. cit. p.381
64. Marder, op. cit. Vol.3, p.183
65. Battle of Jutland Official Despatches p.376
66. Gordon, op. cit. p.490
67. Battle of Jutland Official Despatches p.86

CHAPTER NINE

The Aftermath of Jutland

No sooner had the guns fallen silent and the fleets returned to their bases, than the controversy started. What was the effect of the Battle of Jutland, and why were the results so disappointing for the Royal Navy? No sea battle except Trafalgar has been the subject of so much literature. In the propaganda war the Germans struck the first blow. Their announcement published 2 June about the Battle of the Skagerrak as they called it, was received in neutral countries at least twenty-four hours before any news issued from London. It was notable not so much for its exaggeration of British losses, since the number of capital ships sunk was correct – though it did claim to have destroyed 'the large battleship *Warspite*' and damaged 'a large number of British battleships' – as for what was omitted. The statement concluded, 'On our side the small cruiser *Wiesbaden* was sunk by hostile artillery fire during the day engagements, and the *Pommern* during the night by a torpedo. The fate of the *Frauenlob*, which is missing, and of some torpedo boats which have not returned yet is unknown. The High Seas Fleet returned to our ports during the day.'[1] All this, with talk of rescuing 'portions of the crews of the sunk English ships, among whom were only two survivors of the *Indefatigable*', implied that their fleet was left in command of the sea, having suffered only slight losses.

At first the communiqué from the British seemed to neutral ears to confirm the German account of a great victory. A Basle newspaper even believed that 'Germany, before two or three months are over, will break the blockade and end the war'.[2] The Admiralty began by reciting the British losses, naming the three battlecruisers and three armoured cruisers and five of the destroyers sunk, and added that six other destroyers were 'not yet accounted for'. The implication so long after the fighting stopped must have been that the *Kaiserliche Marine* had sunk three more ships than in fact they had.[3] Though stating that, 'The enemy's losses were serious', it did not name any ships that were sunk, just ending hopefully, 'The exact number of enemy destroyers disposed of during the action cannot be ascertained with any certainty, but it must have been large'[4] – not a convincing report. The Navy was furious. Officers and men ashore were met with consolation instead of congratulation, as though it was they and not the High Seas Fleet, which had had to retreat in haste.

For the Germans the 'Battle of the Skagerrak' was a great victory, which laid the ghost of Trafalgar. They had seen British ships blow up, and the numbers of the admitted dead, 6,097 British to 2,551 German reinforced this.[5] The Emperor also appreciated the propaganda victory and rewarded the Head of the Naval Press Bureau, whose adroit turning of the British communiqué to his purpose had helped to raise a new War Loan.

Three days later, on 5 June, the Admiralty issued a further statement, which was more bullish, and in fact exaggerated the enemy's discomfiture. 'The losses were severe on both sides; but when the main body of the British fleet came into contact with the German High Seas Fleet, a very brief period sufficed to compel the latter, who had been severely punished, to seek refuge in their protected waters . . . the Admiralty entertain no doubt that the German losses are heavier than the British.'[6] In the haze and smoke of battle, ships often disappeared from view and if they did so after being seen to be hit, with an explosion of flame, it was a natural, if often false, conclusion that they had been sunk. The overstatement of German losses was probably due to Sir John Jellicoe, who reported 'after a most careful examination of the evidence of all officers who testified to seeing enemy vessels actually sink, and personal interviews with a large number of those officers', that two battleships of the dreadnought type had been seen to sink, as well as one of the Deutschland-type (*Pommern*). Five light cruisers and six destroyers were 'seen to sink' and one submarine was claimed. This made a total of sixteen German warships 'seen to sink' as opposed to eleven in fact sunk, while five others were 'seen to be so severely damaged as to render it extremely doubtful if they could reach port'.[7]

Gradually the full story came out. The *Admiralstab*'s first announcement rebounded. Why had they hidden the loss of the *Lützow*? What more was yet to be revealed? A Dutch paper now wrote, 'the English carried off the fruits of victory, and still rule the sea, in spite of heavy losses'.[8] In fact although both sides had lost roughly ten per cent of their fleets – the Germans losing eleven ships and the British fourteen with greater tonnage – the position of the High Seas Fleet was worse after the battle than before. Neither side had lost any of their modern dreadnoughts, but while Jellicoe was ready for battle next day with twenty-four almost untouched battleships, Scheer had only ten capital ships ready for action, including the sole battlecruiser capable of fighting. As a much quoted American newspaper aptly put it, 'The German navy has assaulted its jailer, but is still in jail'.

In the Royal Navy a post mortem was immediately begun.[9] Why had the battlecruisers blown up? If they had taken hits from 11-inch and 13-inch shells during the battle of the Dogger Bank and survived, why had three battlecruisers been destroyed so soon at Jutland? With their loss, to the guns of a weaker squadron, had gone the invincible name of the Royal Navy.

And why had more German ships *not* been sunk? Their battlecruisers had been given a terrible hammering, but none had blown up and only one had failed to get home. The finger pointed first at the qualities of German armour and British gunnery, but subsequent enquiries have disproved both, though too often British armour-piercing shell exploded or broke up before the projectile had penetrated.[10] The strength of Scheer's warships lay in two advantages. Because the German dry docks were wider, the ships could be broader in the beam. This, with the more cramped living quarters, allowed space for empty 'rampart compartments' along the ships' sides to absorb the force of an explosion.[11] Next, the lesser weight of the smaller calibre guns allowed for thicker armament on the sides, decks and turrets, and stronger bulkheads separating the compartments, so the German battlecruisers were almost as well protected as the British battleships – and far better than the British battlecruisers.

And it was a combination of three faults which made the British ships so vulnerable, and caused the huge and devastating explosions. First, to increase the speed of firing men relaxed safety procedures in the heat of battle, and where anti-flash shields were in place they were often not used, so explosions were caused by jets of flame coming down the ammunition hoists at enormous temperatures and under high pressure'.[12] Secondly, as a German naval officer wrote later, 'Your cordite charges were encased only in silk covers, while ours were enclosed in air-tight metal cases and covered in sand. The result was that if one of our shells got in among your cordite, the whole lot went up.'[13] Finally and most importantly, the chemical mix of the British cordite was less stable than the German version. Von Hase in the *Derfflinger* noted that 'the flames from charges burning in the (German) turrets spread to the case chamber – ten charges in all being ignited – but they only blazed. They did not explode as had been the case with the enemy. This saved the ship.'[14] It seems that the Battle of Skagerrak was won in the laboratories of Essen.

British technical committees studied every aspect of the battle and put forward a wide range of areas where improvements were required; range finders, fuses, armour-piercing shells, more armour for the battlecruisers and anti-flash barriers. Naturally, not only the *matériel*, but also the men came under scrutiny. Had Jellicoe saved the fleet, but lost its reputation? The Admiralty exonerated him. Was it Beatty's fault? That charismatic Admiral could do no wrong in the public eye. So was it the officers, their training, the naval system, which had led to the destruction of the battlecruisers? There were those who thought so.

More important, however, than the effect of the battle on opinion in the United Kingdom or the neutral countries, was its influence in German naval circles and on the views of the Commander-in-Chief himself. Scheer knew how close he had been to disaster. He had had a narrow escape and, with four dreadnoughts and all his battlecruisers badly damaged, was numerically in a weaker position than before. 'It is one of the ironies of naval history that Scheer's final report upon the Battle of Jutland plainly advised the Kaiser that Germany could not win the surface war in the North Sea against Britain.'[15] He even doubted whether a more successful fleet action would force the UK to make peace, admitting that, 'The disadvantages of our geographical situation as compared with that of the Island Empire and the enemy's vast material superiority, cannot be coped with to such a degree as to make us masters of the blockade inflicted on us.'[16] The conclusion was clear: victory could only come through 'the crushing of English economic life'[17] which required Germany to reimpose her U-boat blockade without restrictions. To that extent 'Jutland was as decisive as Trafalgar'[18] – though not in the way expected.

The stalemate on land pointed in the same direction. On the Western Front, while the battle of Verdun had shown the Germans again that they could not break through to Paris, the torrents of blood shed on the Somme had demonstrated that they could withstand the heaviest Allied 'pushes'. With no end of the war in sight the struggle at sea to strangle the enemy became of paramount importance if only to relieve the pressure the Central Powers were feeling. When Marshal von Hindenburg was summoned into the presence of his All-Highest War Lord at Pless behind the Eastern front on 20 August 1916, and appointed Chief of the General Staff of the Field Army with Ludendorff as his First Quartermaster-General, he recorded that 'the privations of daily life had increased. The middle classes in particular were suffering very severely from the economic situation, which affected them exceptionally intensely. Food had become very scarce, and the prospects of the harvest were only moderate.'[19] Germany's 'turnip winter' would be relieved by successes in the east – the victory over Romania brought in oil and cereals to Germany and Austria – but there would not be enough until the Russian storehouse could be raided, and that was still a long way off. German strategy therefore turned once again to an intensified submarine campaign in the hope of starving Britain of food and her allies of munitions, before the Central Powers were themselves brought to their knees by Britain's blockade. With good reason they looked once more to 'Germany's little swordfish which had already destroyed more enemy ships in a month than the cruisers had succeeded in sinking during the whole of their glorious but short-lived career.'[20] Admiral Scheer still did not accept the concept of a restricted U-boat campaign – especially now that there were more armed freighters and Q-ships about – but he was persuaded by his chief, Admiral Holtzendorff, head of the Naval Staff, to release his submarines for a new campaign against merchant shipping under the prize rules while continuing with Tirpitz and Holtzendorff to press for the withdrawal of restrictions.

While the policy of the German Navy was being debated, Admiral Scheer, contrary to the commonly held view that after Jutland the High Seas Fleet never emerged until it surrendered in 1918, made two more sorties into the North Sea. Scheer was emboldened by a false view of the outcome of Jutland, believing that his enemy suffered twice as much material loss as he did, that the Grand Fleet's formation had been broken before nightfall and that 'Jellicoe did not seek us out the following morning, although he possessed both the power and requisite speed to do so'.[21] The first sally, to attack Sunderland, was on the night of 18 August 1916, only six weeks after Jutland and before the battlecruisers *Seydlitz* and *Derfflinger* had been repaired. As usual the Grand Fleet was warned in advance, but, when the fleets were only thirty miles apart, Scheer was enticed away southwards by a mistaken report from a Zeppelin, and the *Admiralstab* called him back before Jellicoe could make contact. However Scheer had disposed five lines of submarines in the North Sea. HMS *Falmouth* passing over one of these on her way out was sunk by three torpedoes, and HMS *Nottingham* was torpedoed on her way back, finally succumbing to two more as she limped home.

The loss of these two light cruisers persuaded the British Commander-in-Chief to believe that the enemy had perfected a game which he had long expected them to play. Fearful of being drawn over submarine traps again, Jellicoe ordained that the Grand Fleet should not go south of Scotland or east of Belgium unless there was a real chance of catching the High Seas Fleet.[22] That meant that the Royal Navy would not guarantee coastal towns against bombardment or even interfere with the early stages of a landing by the German army. The dreadnoughts, which could steam several thousand miles without re-fuelling, were not now to go more than a few hundred miles from their base, unless the High Seas Fleet came out. So the day's events, which transpired so differently from the expectations of either side, did have important consequences.

The protection of the English coast was to be left to submarines, which were at the same time delivering the only blows possible against the *Kriegsmarine*. During the latest operations of 18–19 August the German battleship, *Westfalen*, had been torpedoed, but not sunk, by the *E23*, and when Scheer emerged again on 19 October 1916, without being allowed his U-boat advance guards which were then required once more for attacks on shipping, it was a submarine which inflicted damage on his fleet. His movements were as ever reported by the Admiralty, but this time Jellicoe merely put the Grand Fleet under short notice for steam, until more was known of the enemy's objective. Lieutenant Commander John de Burgh Jessop in the *E38* watched the whole German battle fleet pass him. He missed with his first attack, but hit the cruiser *München* with two torpedoes on the next attempt. Scheer returned to his base without having achieved anything.

Two weeks later the battlecruiser *Moltke* and the Third Battle Squadron composed of modern Kaiser-class battleships, accompanied by a half flotilla of destroyers, came out, not to attack, but on a bizarre defensive move. Two U-boats had become stuck on a Danish sandbank and were in danger of being either interned or attacked by British destroyers, which had been alerted after a radio signal from one of the distressed submarines had been picked up by Room 40. One of the submarines was no ordinary U-boat. It was the *U-20*, still captained by Schwieger who had sunk the *Lusitania*. To save that notorious craft from capture or destruction Scheer considered it worth risking the capital ships, which kept guard to seaward, while the destroyers tried unsuccessfully to tow the U-boat off. Whilst they were so engaged, Commander Noel Lawrence in the *J-1* fired four torpedoes, one of which struck the *Grosser Kurfürst* and another the *Kronprinz* – both of them dreadnoughts. Both got home, but the Kaiser was not amused and rapped Scheer over the knuckles for taking such risks, although for the Admiral it was now logical that 'the Fleet will have to devote itself to one task – to get the U-boats safely out to sea and bring them safely home again'.[23]

The North Sea had become a 'No Man's Sea'. The German Commander-in-Chief would not venture north without his submarine vedettes; Jellicoe would not move south for fear of them. The High Seas Fleet, which became weaker in manpower and morale as U-boat crews were drawn from it, was not to emerge again for nearly two years.

The new U-boat campaign under the prize rules, which had begun on 7 October 1916, was gathering pace. Losses were inflicted daily on the British merchant marine without intolerably antagonizing the United States, who at this stage saw Britain as a greater annoyance than Germany. Indeed so difficult had the relations between the US and the UK become by the spring of 1916, that Sir John Jellicoe considered the possibility that the US might enter the war against the Allies to be one of the factors requiring him to take extra care not to run risks with the Grand Fleet. (The forthcoming battle on the Somme, which was confidently forecasted to be a decisive Allied victory finishing the war, was another.)[24]

A US Naval Board had reported that merchant ships could be examined at sea without undue danger from submarines, and therefore the Royal Navy was unjustified in bringing them in to harbour for examination. American vessels were in essence being captured, whenever they were escorted by a Royal Navy ship into Kirkwall, even if they were soon released. Forcing fifty suspects off the SS *China*, a US ship, did not help the British case either. And Americans considered that their mails were seized lawlessly by the British and French. There was no proof that during censorship, confidential trade information was being obtained and used to gain an unfair commercial advantage, but mail delays aroused suspicions, and the British government was infuriatingly dilatory in replying to official protests: five weeks for an acknowledgement of a note sent in May 1916, and three months for a detailed reply was hardly courteous.

Great efforts had already been made to expedite the work of

censorship. A staff of three thousand men and women was involved in London and Liverpool, and mails taken off ships at Kirkwall were delivered at the Censorship Office within forty-eight hours. (Transatlantic post took a week in any event.) Stoppage of mail was prohibited by the Hague Convention XI, and the censorship, which inevitably caused delays, however expeditiously the huge organization worked, appeared to be a breach of the Convention even if it was not technically a stoppage. But Lord Robert Cecil asserted that it was vital to Britain's conduct of the war, as it was 'necessary to check espionage, prevent merchandize entering or leaving Germany and forestall efforts to promote uprisings by the circulation of seditious and inflammatory literature'.[25] The mail was sometimes used to run the blockade too, and Cecil quoted '168 packets of rubber goods'. When put more plainly as three and a half tons of raw rubber sent in small parcels to a Swedish firm in Gothenburg, which was known to be the centre of contraband trade, the stoppage sounded more reasonable. But just as important, the mail was filled with securities, money transfers and other documents used in maintaining German credit. That alone made censorship essential to the blockade.

Worst of all to the Americans was the blacklist of companies deemed to have relations with the enemy. Not only the ports, but all Allied coaling stations had the blacklist, and many more firms were added to it in July 1916, among them eighty-five more American concerns. Although the blacklist was not illegal – any country could forbid its nationals to trade with those whom it considered to be helping the enemy – US opinion saw it as regulating American trade with other neutrals. The *New York Times* described the blacklist as 'the most tactless, foolish and unnecessary act of the British government during the war'. The President agreed. 'I am, I must admit, about at the end of my patience with Great Britain and the Allies,' Wilson wrote to his adviser, Colonel House. 'This Black List business is the last straw . . . a stupid blunder. I am seriously considering asking Congress to authorise me to prohibit loans and restrict exportations to the Allies . . . Polk (counsellor to the Department of State) and I are compounding a very sharp note. I may feel obliged to make it as sharp and final as the one to Germany on the submarines. What is your own judgment? Can we any longer endure their intolerable course?'[26]

Britain's brutal mishandling of the Easter Rising in Ireland earned her more enemies in the USA and a Congressional Representative introduced an unsuccessful resolution to sever relations with the UK. Most dangerous of all, there were calls for American freighters to be convoyed by the US Navy. This could only have had one of two consequences: either Britain would abandon the blockade or there would be war with the United States. The spectre of the Anglo-American war of 1812 appeared with frightening clarity.

So in mid-1916 it seemed that irritants at sea might drive the USA to war against Great Britain as soon as against Germany. But Anglo-Saxon and French sympathies aside, commercial ties proved too durable. The Allies were by far the best customers of American business, they owed too much to American banks and they too could take commercial reprisals. US commerce at that time was expanding unbelievably fast and the President could not risk ruining industry and trade. So, though Wilson was given powers to take economic reprisals, he did not exercise them. The downwards spiral could have led to hostilities, and Wilson believed that President Madison had been too hasty declaring war in 1812. Besides, there was force in the British protest that such US reprisals would be a totally unjustified contrast to their failure to act against German submarine atrocities. Wilson recognized this, declaring in the autumn, '. . . property rights can be vindicated by claims for damages when the war is over, and no modern nation can decline to arbitrate such claims; but the fundamental rights of humanity cannot be. The loss of life is irreparable. Neither can direct violations of a nation's sovereignty await vindication in suits for damages.'[27] On the verge of an election campaign the President was reluctant to antagonize anyone. Congress, however, voted a huge naval appropriation on 8 September; the planned construction of 137 new ships of all types would make the US Navy second, and maybe even first, in the world. Once, when Colonel House was discussing their differences with Britain, Wilson had snapped, 'Let us build a bigger navy than hers and do what we please.'[28]

Then in October 1916, the actions of a German submarine, *U-53*, aroused a different flurry. This large U-boat crossed the Atlantic and appeared off Newport, Rhode Island. Then, having delivered mail to the German ambassador, and been well received by the port authorities, she promptly sank several ships within sight of the Massachusetts coast. The English press irritated the US administration by uncritically accepting rumours that the commander of the U-boat had learnt the movements of British ships while in Newport, and had ordered US destroyers to keep away while he sank the steamers. But the U-boat's actions roused anger in the US too. The destruction was committed under the noses of the US Coast Guard and, though outside United

States' territorial waters, some saw it as an affront to the US, and 'popular indignation is not easily subdued by quotations from books of maritime law'.[29]

Odium was further heaped on Berlin that month, when thousands of Belgian men were forced to go and work in Germany. The excuse that this relieved Belgian unemployment did not wash. The 'slavery' released Germans to fight in the trenches and so, in effect, made the Belgians fight against their own kith and kin.[30] Then on 15 November, the SS *Ancona* was sunk with the loss of twenty US lives, and a little later the liner *Persia* went down with many of her passengers. Both were victims of submarines (though one U-boat was Austrian).

Thus once again the belligerents were in equally bad odour in the eyes of Woodrow Wilson. He was still not prepared for hostilities. 'If my re-election as President depends upon my getting into war, I don't want to be President,' he had told his secretary, Joseph Tumulty.[31] His sympathies were being wafted one way and then the other, while he struggled to keep the nation out. Now though, as ships with Americans aboard were sunk almost every week, he was beginning to believe that 'the business of neutrality is over. . . . I mean this, that war now has such a scale that the position of neutrals sooner or later becomes intolerable.'[32]

It seemed that the only way of keeping the United States out of the conflict was to bring peace to the warring nations. Wilson redoubled his efforts to make 'peace without victory', but he was met on all sides with rejection. The timing was unfortunate for two reasons. The first was that Chancellor Bethmann-Hollweg had with 'lack of foresight and the first rudiments of diplomatic strategy'[33] forestalled the President by launching the German peace overtures only a week before, even though Ambassador Bernstorff knew that Wilson was about to make his moves. The consequence was that Wilson was made to look as though he was just endorsing the German initiative, which was unlikely to give him a favourable reception in the Allied camp. The second reason was that it came a week after Lloyd George took office as Prime Minister, and under his optimistic and pugnacious leadership the British were once again anticipating success on the Western Front. The French were adamant too, and they would not consider any such proposals while Germany squatted on a major part of industrial France and nine tenths of Belgium. Nor did the French want Wilson to hold the scales, a sentiment shared with the Germans, who were as confident as their, as yet undisclosed, war aims were ambitious.[34] Lloyd George declared that the fight must be to the finish. They were bold words for the country was running out of money. Ten million dollars a day went to pay US manufacturers. Cash and securities were near exhaustion. New unsecured loans, or credits secured only by the government's guarantee, were required, because much of Britain's treasure, accumulated over the past century, had been poured into ships and cargoes which now lay at the bottom of the sea.

The U-boat campaign had steadily grown in ferocity. It seemed that they could not be checked – not even prevented from passing through the Straits of Dover. Reginald Bacon, the Vice Admiral of the Dover Patrol, and a brilliant engineer, had laid a new barrier from the southern tip of the Goodwin Sands towards Dunkirk in September 1916. This was a wall of light steel netting with mines attached. The net wall only dropped sixty feet from its supporting hawsers and so rows of mines were laid below that depth at a safe distance. However, again the Channel storms wreaked havoc; the great length of netting chafed, parts of it tore and the whole gave constant trouble. Finally some mines dragged their sinkers and fouled the nets while work was going on, and the entire barrier had to be removed after only two months. The submarines coming out of Zeebrugge and Ostend were not greatly impeded either by the twenty-three mile long line of netting and mines, which Bacon had laid parallel to the Belgian coast that April.

Morale among the U-boat crews rose higher with their tally of sinkings. While sticking to the prize rules (around Britain and in the Atlantic, even if not in the Mediterranean) they decimated the unescorted merchant ships, appearing one by one over the horizon. Even round the coasts of Britain and Ireland enemy submarines still seemed almost immune. They could see a patrolling destroyer fifteen miles away, but because of their low silhouette could only be spotted within four miles, by which time they had slipped below the waves. The log of Hans Rose in *U-53* showed how freely they operated. Setting out from Heligoland on 20 January 1917 he passed uneventfully through the English Channel and two days later was on station off the Lizard. During the next fifteen days between the Scillies and the coast of France he sank ten vessels, six by bombs or gunfire and four by torpedo; he inspected and dismissed nine neutrals, even those exporting coal from Britain to Spain.

Rose and some of the other U-boat commanders showed that it was possible for a submarine to intercept passing ships, dividing the sheep from the goats, much as the warships of the Tenth Cruiser Squadron did. The difference was that if they found a vessel carrying contraband they sank her, instead of escorting her into port. However, Hans Rose, who came fourth in the list of German U-boat aces judged by tonnage sunk, was second to none in humanity. He noted in his log what happened to the crew of any ship he saw sink. Sometimes he merely observed as they sailed or rowed to the coast; on a couple of occasions he towed the lifeboats until they were near enough to the shore; twice he called up another ship by flare or even by firing towards a guard-ship and once he let a French schooner go because its sea boat was obviously unseaworthy. Rough weather rather than the navy's patrols, which he easily avoided, hampered his operations. Only three vessels escaped him, two because he could not get near enough in the tumbling seas, and one after it fought back with a gun.[35]

Armed merchant ships clearly had the best chance of survival and naval guns were for a time given priority over guns for the army. More guns were obtained from France and Japan and the number of armed ships doubled, with good effect. (During 1916 and January 1917 over 600 ships were attacked. Roughly half were armed. Of these seventy-six per cent escaped, twenty per cent being torpedoed and only four per cent being sunk by gunfire. But of the 302 unarmed ships only twenty-two per cent escaped, ten per cent being sunk by torpedo and no less than sixty-eight per cent by gunfire.) But neutral ships were not armed, so their losses came to equal the British victims. In the latter part of 1916, both British and world shipping losses trebled:

	British	World
May-June 1916	101,500 tons sunk	237,900
July-August	125,800	280,900
September-October	280,800	584,000
November-December	351,100	666,600

In November the balance of premiums received under the government's War Risks insurance scheme was for the first time insufficient to cover the payments to shippers. Although the country as a whole was kept in ignorance of the situation, Jellicoe had written to the Admiralty from Scapa Flow on 30 October of 'a serious danger that our losses in merchant ships, combined with the losses in neutral ships, may, by the early summer of 1917, have such a serious effect upon the import of food and other necessaries into the Allied countries as to force us into accepting peace terms . . .'[36] Germany was switching her shipbuilding resources to submarines. It was a signal of how seriously Jellicoe viewed this, when he agreed to withdraw destroyers from the Grand Fleet to protect merchant shipping.

While this second U-boat campaign round the British Isles was beginning to show alarming results, ships flying the Red Ensign were mysteriously disappearing again on the outer oceans too. Four commerce raiders set out from Germany in the winter of 1916–17. This time, since it would have been well nigh impossible for a regular cruiser to have escaped from the patrols of the Tenth Cruiser Squadron guarding the northern exit of the North Sea, disguised merchant ships were used. They were not so fast, but were economical with fuel and were more elusive.

The first to slip away was the *Möwe* (Seagull). Her captain, Count Nikolaus zu Dohna Schlodien, had already enjoyed one successful raiding cruise in her from the end of December 1915 to the beginning of the following March, returning safely home to a triumphal reception. In those nine weeks the *Möwe*, wearing many disguises and flying different flags, had sunk fourteen steamers with her four 15-cm (5.9-inch) guns, while five others, three trawlers and the greatest prize of them all, the battleship *King Edward VII*, had succumbed to the 500 mines she laid daringly close to the waterways of the Pentland Firth and the mouth of the Gironde.

The *Möwe* had been the only commerce raider at large in the early part of 1916. A week before she returned, another, the *Greif*, had set out, but her wireless signals had been intercepted and she had been sunk by the Northern Patrol after a sharp fight. There were no more surface raiders until Count Schlodien set out for his second foray on 23 November 1916. Keeping radio silence he again managed to evade the North Sea patrols, and thanks to his skill, cool head, courage and considerable luck succeeded in avoiding destruction by the twenty-four cruisers searching for him in the North and South Atlantic. He was away for four months. Owing to the precautions taken by the British naval authorities his activities were circumscribed, but he still managed to sink another twenty-two steamers and three sailing ships, before returning again unharmed to Kiel. The Count treated his prisoners with consideration, putting them ashore when it was safe to do so. He sent another 400 prisoners to Germany in the captured munition ship *Yarrowdale*, which was, in her turn, converted into a raider. (If the tonnage of ships sunk on the two cruises of the *Möwe* are added together, including the battleship, and credit is given for the two sailing ship victims of the *Theodore*, which he converted into the raider, *Geir*, Count Nikolaus zu Dohna Schlodien ranks after the top three U-boat aces in tonnage destroyed. Moreover the *Möwe* and her crew were provisioned at the expense of her enemies – from the coal, food and supplies plundered from Allied ships.)

The *Yarrowdale* was caught before she could escape out of the North Sea, but the *Wolf II*, a converted liner captained by Karl-August Nerger, was more successful, being escorted out by U-boats. She caused consternation by laying mines off South Africa, Colombo, Bombay and even New Zealand, holding the attention of Allied cruisers for fourteen months, at the end of which Nerger had accounted for 114,000 tons of shipping. Count Felix Luckner, out at the same time in the three-masted sailing ship, *Seeadler* was a more romantic pirate but with a meagre tally of thirteen sailing vessels and three steamers, before his ship, with some of the crew suffering from scurvy, was wrecked off a Pacific island.

Once more German commerce raiders in the outer oceans had come and gone. None of the three which had escaped into the open seas had been caught, but like their predecessors of 1914 and the spring of 1915, they had not been able to make a serious impact on the volume of shipping which sailed under the Red Ensign. Perhaps they deserved better; it had been warfare conducted again with gallantry and humanity, in the way that people liked to think that war, if it must be fought, should be fought. However, unless the *Kaiserliche Marine* had managed to pass more auxiliary cruisers out on the oceans at one time, they would never have had a chance to disrupt Allied ocean traffic. As it was, the raiders were a colourful digression, a footnote to the war at sea, not a major element in the blockade.

The predations of the U-boats were another matter. The British Government had been slow to realize that it could not continue to suffer shipping losses at the rate which occurred every month, unless something was done to increase the credit side of the balance sheet. More merchant ships had to be built or bought, and better use had to be made of the tonnage remaining. A Shipping Control Committee had been set up as early as January 1916. Their report in February showed that even allowing for the use of foreign shipping there would soon be a deficit of 3.3 million tons, concluding that the situation was extremely grave and called for immediate drastic action, but though the President of the Board of Trade wrung his hands, he took no effective steps. The losses increased in the longer days of spring and summer and became clearly unsupportable. If Britain, while building under 50,000 tons of merchant shipping a month, lost 150,000 tons per month, (as she was doing by the autumn of 1916) the drain would be fatal in the end. And the *Admiralstab* were beginning to think of sinking 600,000 tons *every month*.

With the destruction of British ships the whole Allied cause was in jeopardy. France used over a million tons gross of British shipping, which carried fifty per cent of her imported coal and forty-three per cent of her total imports. Italy needed almost as much, since Germany and Austria had supplied much of her coal and other imports before the war. Three quarters of her coal was now carried in British bottoms. Though victory or defeat hung on the shipping situation, the Coalition Government could not galvanize the country or itself into taking the necessary action. Prime Minister Asquith could not overcome his 'well-known dislike for kicking along laggard colleagues with academic qualifications'.[37]

On 5 December 1916 the Asquith administration fell, and Lloyd George, who became Premier, had no such inhibitions. On his first day in office he called up the Glasgow shipping magnate, Sir John Maclay, and asked him to become Shipping Controller in a new Ministry of Shipping. He was joined by three of the ablest shipping tycoons. To enable them to work near the Admiralty, the lake in St James's Park was drained and an unattractive row of concrete office buildings was erected in the middle. The wide powers over all British shipping given to the new ministry entailed taking some authority from the Admiralty, but Lloyd George saw the objections of the admirals merely as horror at 'the notion that brass buttons should be ordered about by bone'.[38]

The new Shipping Controller found a sorry state of affairs. Freight rates had risen tenfold, and with unfair effect. The owners of ships which had been requisitioned did not gain from the rise in rates, but those whose ships had escaped the government's powers made huge profits. The answer chosen was to requisition nearly all ships, and allow the ship owners the same level of profit as they enjoyed in an average year before the war.

Merchant shipbuilding had to take priority over the demands of the Royal Navy. Output had fallen from nearly 2,000,000 tons gross in 1913 to 650,000 tons in 1915 and little more than 500,000 tons in 1916. Under the new Ministry, vessels under construction were speedily finished; a standard pattern of freighter was introduced to shorten building times; and more ships were purchased abroad from the US and Japan. Creeks and harbours were scavenged for old hulks which could be restored. In some months as many as 150 ships were released from the repair yards.

Port congestion worsened the shipping shortage. Many of the dock workers had joined the colours, and at the same time unprecedented amounts of government stores had to be shipped in and out, while unscheduled prize cargoes were dumped on the quays. Add to that the shortage of railway wagons caused by the extra demands of war and ships being held in port when U-boats were known to be outside, and the consequence was great delays to cargo vessels in the ports and too many waiting at anchor outside. Matters were worse in French ports. Bordeaux was notorious. A ship could take five weeks to be turned round as opposed to the normal ten days. However, the French unions were not so hostile to bringing in foreign labour, which eased the situation. When these problems had been taken in hand, it was reckoned that the time saved was equivalent to adding another 3,000,000 tons to the available shipping.

More had to be done to conserve cargo space. Wherever possible, commodities were brought from nearer home to save time at sea. Australian wheat was replaced by North American; French wood was substituted for Scandinavian. Timber, which constituted over eleven per cent of British imports, was tackled first, because Britain imported ten times as much timber as the normal felling of her sparse forests produced. Wood kept all industry going. Without pit props there would be no coal – and the war demanded ever more British coal. The navies also required wood for shipbuilding; armies required it for hutments, ammunition boxes and duckboards in the trenches, to name just a few of its uses. To meet this new demand, lumberjacks were brought over from Canada to exploit English and Scottish woods and some of the best were stripped in the emergency. Alfred Rothschild offered his beech woods in the Chiltern hills as a gift, but it was only the great forests of France which satisfied the needs of the Allies.

These measures were taken none too soon, because the Allies were not the only ones to become apprehensive at this time. The Kaiser was again being pressed to take the consequences of Jutland to their logical, ruthless conclusion: if the battle fleet could not break the British blockade, nor the army break the Western Front, then if there was to be no negotiated peace, the U-boats must forget the rules to win the war.

The blockade was starting to cause serious distress in the Central Powers, as the aggregate yields of the wheat and rye harvests in 1916 fell by nearly twenty-four per cent from their 1913 level (due largely to lack of fertilizers), the potato crop in both 1915 and 1916 had been only half the 1913 yield, and the quota system dramatically cut German imports from the neighbouring Netherlands.

The decline in value of American exports to the Netherlands showed the effect of the quota (£000):

	1913–4	1914–5	1915–6	1916–7[39]
Netherlands	22,400	28,600	19,400	6,400

Consumption of meat and milk fell sharply in the towns and cities, and a range of products became scarce. An Austrian acquaintance of Albert Ballin believed their food supply would only last until March. 'With us at home', Ballin wrote, 'the paraffin question is becoming very serious. In country districts it may be possible to tell people to go to bed at curfew time, but the working population of our large cities will never consent to dispense with artificial light. Serious riots have already taken place in connexion with the fat shortage.'[40] More drastic for the war effort, the stockpile of manganese, which had been built up before the war, was run down and strong steel could not be made without it.

The German Admiralty produced a detailed and cogent paper arguing in favour of unrestricted submarine warfare. It brushed aside the objection that it would be impossible to starve out England because it only required five wheat ships a day to feed the country, and, since the *Kaiserliche Marine* could never close the Straits of Dover, the ships could be docked in France and the grain transported across the Channel. Wheat, it was pointed out, was not the only essential. Fodder, timber and iron ore were all vital if Britain was to continue fighting. France's rail system was already overworked, and could not transport all Britain's supplies. 'Without timber, and in particular pit-props, England cannot live, any more than she can live without wheat.'[41] Further, five-sixths of the iron ore for Great Britain came from neutral countries. France was in no better state. The basins of Briey and Longwy, which were now in German hands and being exploited, had yielded 15 million tons of ore out of the 18.5 million that France produced in 1912. Other mines were in the fighting zone and useless. But coal was the Allies' Achilles heel. Italy, which produced less than a million tons herself and now required 10 million tons a year from Britain, was in the worst position. 'France could probably not exist without England's coal; Italy certainly not', the *Admiralstab* gloated, adding, 'no branch of the British export trade is more exposed to our submarines . . . Its dislocation would enormously impair the military efficiency of our enemies. Its destruction would end the war.' The conclusion was that 'when [England] sees that in spite of everything, we are sending to the bottom a considerably greater number of tons than she can replace, she will give in. She must and will give in at any price; the surrender of valuable colonies, the payment of milliards of war indemnities, the surrender of all rights on the continent of Europe – all these are nothing to England, when compared to the consequences of a lost submarine war.'[42]

Notes

1. Newbolt, Henry, *Official History of the Great War, Naval Operations*, Longmans, Green, 1928, Vol. 4, pp.4–5
2. ibid. p.10
3. The German operations connected with Jutland are often said to have claimed another victim, more famous than any of those who died in the battle. On 29 May 1916 the submarine U-75 laid twenty-two mines on the western side of the Orkneys. A week later, on 5 June, Field Marshall Lord Kitchener set out on a mission to Russia and was drowned when HMS *Hampshire*, taking that route to shelter from an easterly gale, probably struck a mine and floundered with great loss of life. The mines were laid off Marwick Head because suspicious signals intercepted by the Germans indicated that an important ship would pass by that route. But why the signals were sent is a mystery and a German spy claimed to have paid two Irishmen to plant bombs on board.
4. Newbolt, op. cit. p.6
5. There were just over 500 wounded on each side. The casualties in both fleets at Jutland showed again one of the major differences between a sea fight and a land battle. On land there would normally be twice as many wounded as dead. (The British casualties, dead and wounded, made 8.8 per cent of the total ships' companies; the German 6.8 per cent. Strangely, those were roughly the percentages of tonnage lost too.)
6. Newbolt, op. cit. p.6
7. Wilson, H.W. and Hammerton, J.A., eds., *The Great War* series, Vol. 7, p.456
8. Newbolt, op. cit. p.11
9. The post-mortem continued with Bacon, Pastfield and others. See now Campbell, Tarrant, and Gordon.
10. Campbell, op. cit. See Campbell's detailed analysis from German

sources of the effect of every shell which struck the High Seas Fleet's capital ships. Some writers have drawn attention to the different methods of manufacturing the guns, but none of the British guns fired enough during the battle to come near to the end of their accuracy.

11. The High Seas Fleet was built for short-range actions in European waters, so the ships were 'made to fight not to be lived in'. It is a myth that they were more compartmentalized than the British, although they had fewer very large or small compartments. (See notes in Marder, op. cit. Vol. 3, pp.200–1)

12. Newbolt, op. cit. p.14

13. Flag-Commander G. Stapenhorst, quoted in Pastfield, Revd. J.L., *New Light on Jutland*, Heinemann, 1933, p.3

14. Von Hase, op. cit. p.198. Pastfield concludes that if the fleets had swapped cordite and methods of handling, they would have reversed the number of battlecruisers lost. It was surprising that the Admiralty had not enquired earlier into the instability of their cordite, especially at high temperatures. The battleship *Bulwark*, the cruiser *Natal* and the minelayer *Princess Irene* had already blown up in harbour.

15. Kennedy, Paul M., *The Rise and Fall of British Naval Mastery*, Allen Lane, 1976, p.246

16. Scheer, op. cit. p.169

17. ibid.

18. Herwig, op. cit. p.189

19. Hindenburg, Field Marshal Paul von, *Out of my Life*, Cassell & Co., 1920, p.167. The palace of the Prince of Pless, behind the Eastern Front, was chosen as the Kaiser's HQ, because it is in Upper Silesia over the border from Austria's HQ.

20. Lloyd George, op. cit. p.669

21. Scheer, op. cit. p.191

22. To be precise, the Grand Fleet should not go further south than Latitude 55 degrees 30' North (which cuts the English coast about twenty-five miles south of the Scottish border) nor east of the Longitude 4 degrees East (which cuts the Dutch coast just south of the Hague).

23. Scheer, op. cit. p.194

24. Marder, op. cit. Vol.3, p.10

25. Cecil, Lord Robert, *Why Mail Censorship is vital to Britain*, Jas. Truscott, 1916, p.1. As to the spying, Cecil did not know that the Censorship Office itself was vulnerable, and that Silber had penetrated it right from its inception.

26. Baker, op. cit. Vol.6, p.312.

27. Wilson's speech of Acceptance, 2 September 1916. (See Baker, op. cit. p.326)

28. House, op. cit. Vol.2, p.317

29. Newbolt, op. cit. Vol.4, p.249. The *U-53* had intended also to rendezvous with the *Bremen*, a huge, unarmed commercial submarine, but the *Bremen* had disappeared without trace. The *Bremen*'s sister, the *Deutschland* broke the blockade twice, carrying dyes and chemicals to America and mails and rare metals back.

30. In response to the Hindenburg Programme industrial leaders called for 400,000 Belgian workers. The first demand for 20,000 weekly was reduced to 8,000. (Fischer, op. cit. p.270)

31. Tumulty, Joseph P., *Woodrow Wilson as I Know Him*, William Heinemann, 1922, p.249.

32. Baker, op. cit. Vol.6, p.362

33. Lansing, op. cit. p.183

34. A memorandum by von Holtzendorff of December 1916, backed by Tirpitz and adopted by Hindenburg in his war aims, defined five areas in which Germany should acquire new territory, including the Belgian coast, the Danish Faeroe Islands, more of the Baltic coast, African colonies, and naval bases in various islands round the globe. The Wilhelmstrasse did not see any possibility of obtaining these ends through US mediation, and so did not want Wilson's intervention. (See Fischer, op. cit. p. 298ff) The President saw Allied war aims as exaggerated too.

35. For Rose's log of this patrol see Scheer, op. cit. pp.267–724. Another humane U-boat captain was Baron von Spiegel, who was recognized and thanked by the captain of one of his victims when he stepped ashore as a prisoner at Cobh.

36. Quoted in Lloyd George, op. cit. p.673

37. ibid. p.726

38. ibid. p.730. Later, all shipbuilding, whether for the Royal Navy or the mercantile marine, was put into one hand under the 'Controller of the Navy'. This grandiloquent title gave the holder a place on the Admiralty Board and he was made an instant Vice Admiral. The man selected was Sir Eric Geddes, a businessman who had been organizing transportation in France, where he held the rank of Major General. For a short time, Lloyd George noted, he 'enjoyed the amphibious distinction of being at once both a General and an Admiral – an unprecedented attainment for a civilian'.

39. Figures from July to July taken from Guichard, op. cit. p.83. The Netherlands suffered especially badly from the loss of their entrepôt

trade. US exports to Sweden and Norway were also down from their peaks of the previous two years, but were less changed from their pre-war totals.

40. Huldermann, B., *Albert Ballin*, Cassell & Co., 1922, p.262
41. *The German Admiralty's Views on Unrestricted Submarine War*, Berlin 30.1.17. PRO ADM 186/429, pp.3–35.
42. ibid.

CHAPTER TEN

The U-Boat Crisis

Few, either in the White House or in the German Headquarters, doubted that the resumption of the unrestricted U-boat campaign would bring America into the war against the Central Powers; and no one doubted that her intervention, once she had brought her enormous industrial power into play, would conclusively tilt the delicately balanced scales of the Great War. But how long would it take for the immense might of the USA to take effect? Could the Germans win the war by a 'sink at sight' U-boat campaign, before the huge resources of the peaceful giant could be mobilized? It was on this calculation that the decision of Field Marshal Hindenburg, as Chief of the General Staff, and ultimately the Kaiser, depended. And it was on their miscalculation that Germans may lay the blame for the loss of the war in 1918. As Winston Churchill wrote, 'How hard to condemn the war-worn, wearied, already outnumbered heroic German people to mortal conflict with this fresh, mighty, and once aroused, implacable antagonist!'[1]

At a conference at Pless on 9 January 1917 the decision was taken. The Chancellor, Bethmann-Hollweg, wiser but weaker than the naval and military leaders, had been against renewing the unrestricted campaign, when it had been demanded by Tirpitz and Scheer a year earlier. In the spring of 1916, besides the moral and diplomatic objections, they had too few submarines for decisive effect. Tirpitz had been rebuffed and had resigned once more. That time his resignation had been accepted by the Kaiser. But late in 1916 the pressure from the military was greater. There was stalemate on the Western Front, a negotiated peace was not an option, and the growing number of U-boats were achieving dramatic success, even under the restrictive prize rules. For a while, however, nothing was done until Romania's disastrous intervention on the side of the Entente had been crushed by Hindenburg and Ludendorff. That over, the German army again had troops enough to overrun Holland and Denmark, should those neutrals be provoked into war by the sinking of their ships. The increasing effectiveness of the British blockade and the 'rapidly growing destitution of the central nations'[2] then gave an urgency to the situation.

So the Chancellor, Bethmann-Hollweg, let himself be swayed, recognizing the U-boat campaign as the 'last card'. When the Kaiser, still nominally the All-Highest, the Supreme War Lord, ordered the intensified submarine operations, the Chancellor would endeavour to secure that America would remain out of the war. Certain concessions, previously discussed with the Naval Staff, would be made to the US. Bethmann-Hollweg was not sanguine about their effect, but he yielded, trusting the confident forecast of Admiral Henning von Holtzendorff, that they would have Britain at their mercy before the next harvest. The *Admiralstab* had reckoned that if 600,000 tons of shipping could be destroyed each month, and 1,200,000 tons of neutral shipping scared off the sea, the United Kingdom would be brought to its knees, and without its support France and Italy would collapse. Nine prominent German businessmen were asked how long it would take; eight replied six months and the other only three.[3] Surely the US could do little before the end of July. The Chancellor optimistically believed that on America's eventual entry into the war, her help would consist only of the delivery to England of food, financial assistance, aeroplanes and a force of volunteers. Hindenburg, now virtual ruler of the country, declared, 'We are already prepared to deal with that'.[4] There was no mention of naval assistance or the possibility that the whole manhood of the American nation, then some 120 million people, nearly twice the population of Germany and thrice that of France, might be subject to the draft, because they would not have time to fight. To Admiral Capelle, the successor to Tirpitz as Secretary of State for the Navy, it was inconceivable that the American army might be a threat. 'They will not even come, because our submarines will sink them.'[5] But if 100,000 got through, what difference could they make? A million men would be needed, and the US could not raise, equip, train, transport and deploy such an army in four or five months.

On 31 January 1917, in spite of pleas for postponement from Count Bernstorff, the Imperial Ambassador in Washington, Germany announced to the world that the unrestricted U-boat campaign would be resumed at midnight. In a zone round the British Isles, France, Italy and in the Mediterranean all navigation of belligerents and neutrals alike would be prevented. Corridors were left round the coasts of Norway, Denmark and Spain and through the Mediterranean to Greece. Otherwise all ships met within that zone, which stretched 400 miles west of Ireland, would be sunk. The reason given for the new merciless campaign was to shorten the war and preserve the lives of thousands of brave soldiers. 'The Imperial Government would not be able to answer before its own conscience, before the German people and before history if it left any means whatever untried to hasten the end of the war.'[6] The announcement also accused the British of abusing the privileges of hospital ships; any found in the Channel or the south-western part of the North Sea, from the Dutch border across to Flamborough Head on the Yorkshire coast, would be liable to be attacked.[7] As for the United States, they would be allowed to send one steamer a week into Falmouth, arriving on Saturday and leaving on Wednesday, provided that it was marked with red and white vertical stripes on the side, flew the American flag aft and red and white flags on the masts, and was well lighted at night – a concession which was viewed in the USA as a gratuitous affront.

President Wilson first heard the news via an Associated Press bulletin, brought to him by his secretary, Joseph Tumulty. 'Without comment I laid the fateful slip of paper on his desk,' Tumulty wrote, 'and silently watched him as he read and reread it. I seemed to read his mind in the expressions that raced across his strong features; first, blank amazement; then incredulity . . . Handing the paper back to me, he said in quiet tones: "This means war. The break that we have tried so hard to prevent now seems inevitable."'[8] Just three weeks before Wilson had presented his 'Fourteen Points' to Congress as a basis for peace; his last offer to bring about a conference had been dated 26 January, but he was informed that it had arrived too late, because the submarines had already left. Now his untiring struggle to deliver that peace, a mirage which had given him hope to the end, was shown to be in vain.

The President reacted swiftly. On 3 February he severed diplomatic relations with Germany, recalling the US ambassador and handing von Bernstorff his passport. But that was as far as he would go. Woodrow Wilson still did not want war. His Presbyterian instincts were pacifist at heart, believing war to be as destructive of morality as of the nation's finances. Like Jefferson he believed that the first and fundamental maxim of Americans should be never to entangle themselves in the 'broils of Europe'. He had remained aloof in spite of the sinking of the *Lusitania* and the scorn of many of his fellow citizens, because of his strict principles, and because many of the electorate, particularly the quiet, industrious German-Americans, the politically active Irish-Americans and other 'hyphenated-Americans' did not want war. Wilson sincerely believed that to declare war, 'based on neither judgement nor ideals, but merely on emotion'[9] would be a mistake; it would be a tragedy for civilisation. Lastly, US entry into the war would mean that 'Germany would be beaten and so badly beaten that there would be a dictated peace, a victorious peace',[10] which he had the wisdom to recognize would not last. His protests to the Kaiser's Government had been heeded in March 1916, when a Flanders U-boat had sunk the SS *Sussex*, a cross-Channel packet boat, with the loss of American lives. The stiff US note had resulted in an undertaking to curtail the ruthless campaign. That promise had now been broken, but the President still hoped that the German High Command would see reason again, now that the US had shown that they meant what they said. In this he was again disappointed. The Germans had hoped, but not expected, that the US would keep out. (In anticipation of war they had immediately disabled all their ships held in US ports.)

When on 1 February 1917 the Imperial Navy resumed unrestricted submarine warfare, it possessed little more than 100 submarines in service, of which only about thirty-eight were ready at any time,[11] but they were launching seven or eight a month, and against this only twenty-two had been sunk in the whole of the previous year. What was more, the U-boats had previously been attacking largely on the surface, sinking seventy per cent of their victims by gunfire. At once the ratio was almost reversed; within the war zone sixty per cent were torpedoed, most without warning regardless of nationality. Merchant ships, armed or not, went down often seeing only the track of the fatal missile coming into their side. With the sudden ruthlessness of the attacks losses soared:

Month	Ships Sunk	Total tonnage
January 1917	181	298,000
February	259	468,000

In addition to that the ships of Denmark, Holland and Sweden stayed firmly in port, while the food they would have carried went to Germany. Only the Norwegians dared put to sea. It seemed that the German businessmen were right, that the British had no way of stemming the haemorrhage. The submarines, now able to keep at sea for longer periods, moved from one area to another, wherever the patrols were weakest. The Admiralty had set in train a dozen methods of curbing the menace: more guns on merchant ships, more instructors to train their crews, smoke trials, patrolled sea lanes, air patrols, more Q-ships, submarines to hunt submarines, submarines escorting merchant ships, depth charges and bomb howitzers, hydrophones and paravanes, hunting patrols of destroyers and more and better mines to be laid in German waters. But arming freighters did not help when they were torpedoed without warning and most of the other measures would need time. For all the improved weapons against submarines and mines which the Royal Navy possessed, it was still crippled by shortages. Depth charges were the most significant addition to the escort's armoury, but in January 1917 each destroyer was only equipped with four. Often they dared not use these when going out to meet a merchant ship, for fear of having no means of attack when escorting her back.

U-boats found that they could operate close to the patrolled sea lanes in spite of scores of armed auxiliaries in the area; the sixty-two destroyers operating out of Plymouth and Portsmouth and the handful at Cobh did not sink one submarine in the first two months of the un-restricted campaign. In fact U-boats were blown up on their own mines as often as they were destroyed by their enemies. They operated most successfully in an area about 150 miles west of the south-west tip of Ireland, too far out for continuous patrolling to be possible. Prospects for the UK could not have looked more bleak. Which would she run out of first – ships or money?

The U-boat commanders sank at sight every type of ship inside the war zone, including the passenger liner *Laconia* and US vessels. Without a government sponsored war risks insurance scheme, US shipping came to a virtual halt. Then, just as the President was preparing to ask Congress for powers to arm American merchant ships, Captain Reginald Hall, Director of Britain's 'consummately efficient Naval Intelligence Service'[12] dropped a bombshell that neither His Imperial Majesty Wilhelm II nor the hawks among his advisers could have foreseen, one that would finally push America into the war.

The bombshell was the publication of a telegram from the recently appointed State-Secretary responsible for Foreign Affairs. Arthur Zimmermann, the new incumbent was, as former Chancellor Bulow put it, 'one of those Germans who mean so well, whose industry is so unquestionable, their virtues solid and apparent, but who never can manage to see that, in diplomacy, it is skill and the knowledge of "how to take people" that count.'[13] Colonel House, who enjoyed Zimmermann's company, considered him 'in some ways, the ablest, though not the most trustworthy man in the government'.[14] Shortly after taking office Zimmermann had assured James W. Gerard, the US Ambassador in Berlin that U-boat warfare would not be extended without an understanding having been reached with America, and in response the Ambassador had said at a banquet that German-American relations had never been more cordial. Yet in another ten days, on 16 January 1917, Zimmermann had sent to von Eckhardt, the German Minister in Mexico, a coded message which belied all that had been said. It went via Count Bernstorff in Washington, and by ten o'clock the next morning, long before it had been received by its addressee, the message had been partly deciphered by two of the strangely assorted staff of Room 40, Nigel de Grey, a former publisher, and the Revd. W. Montgomery, an Ulster parson. So far as they had then got, it contained the sentence, 'We propose to begin on the 1st February unrestricted submarine warfare. In doing this however we shall endeavour to keep America neutral.' The full text was not clear but it spoke of an alliance with Mexico and possibly Japan.[15] It was immediately clear to Captain Hall that he had dynamite in his hands, and he had two weeks to have the rest deciphered and to decide how to deal with it in conjunction with the Foreign Office.

Hall's agents in Mexico obtained a copy of the Zimmermann telegram as relayed from the German embassy in Washington, and on 20 February he was given permission by Arthur Balfour, Foreign Secretary after Grey's retirement, to handle the matter as he thought fit. He asked a friend in the American Embassy, Edward Bell, to call on him, and presented him with the full text, which now contained the following devastating words:

Decipher yourself
We intend to begin on the first of February unrestricted submarine warfare. We shall endeavour in spite of this to keep the USA neutral. In the event of this not succeeding we make Mexico a proposal of alliance on the following basis:
    Make war together
    Make peace together
Generous financial support and an undertaking on our part that Mexico is to reconquer the lost territory in Texas, New Mexico and Arizona.

It went on to suggest that the Mexican President should 'on his own initiative' invite Japan to adhere to this new alliance, and finished: 'Please call the President's attention to the fact that the ruthless employment of our submarines now offers the prospect of compelling England in a few months to make peace.'[16]

Nothing could have been more calculated to infuriate the Americans than the reconquest of its three states, and no plan could have been more inept. A Swiss citizen, walking beside Lake Lucerne, expressed it aptly, 'The notion of using little Mexico to assail such a Colossus as the States strikes me as much about the same as a project to sink the British fleet with the three pleasure steamers on this lake'.[17]

To hide the source of the information, Hall released the version of the telegram as relayed by Bernstorff to Mexico, and it was said to have been deciphered in America. In vain the German press claimed that the telegram was a forgery. They were believed at first. Nineteen out of twenty Americans at a dinner attended by Guy Gaunt, the British Naval Attaché, thought it was false. But then on 2 March Zimmermann himself admitted that the note was genuine. A statement broadcast over the German wireless read, 'The German Minister in Mexico was . . . instructed, should the United States declare war, to offer the Mexican Government an alliance and arrange further details. These instructions, by the way, expressly enjoined the Minister to make no advances to the Mexican Government unless he knew for a certainty that America was going to declare war. How the American Government received instructions sent by a secret way to Mexico is not known, but it appears that treachery (and this can only be the case) has been committed on American territory.'[18]

Anger in America welled up. US vessels had been sunk, American lives lost and now this. To add insult to injury the message had been dispatched over the private wire of the State Department, which the German Foreign Ministry had been allowed to use in code as a favour, because it was said to relate to the President's peace overtures. While this duplicity was being explained to him by the Secretary of State, Wilson could only exclaim, 'Good Lord! Good Lord! Good Lord!'[19]

For the President it was the last straw. He had held his hand in spite of many torments. Now he could not: he felt duped by an untrustworthy militarist clique. On 2 April Woodrow Wilson addressed Congress. He catalogued the events which had led to the crisis, the war at sea, the unarmed ships sunk without thought for those on board, even hospital ships: 'International law had its origin in the attempt to set up some law which would be respected and observed upon the seas, where no nation had right of dominion and where lay the free highways of the world . . . This minimum of right the German Government has swept aside under the plea of retaliation and necessity and because it had no weapons which it could use at sea except these, which it is impossible to employ as it is employing them without throwing to the winds all scruples of humanity . . . Civilisation itself seems in the balance, but right is more precious than peace, and we shall fight for the thing which we carry nearest to our hearts, for democracy, for the right of those who submit to authority to have a voice in their own government, for the rights and liberties of small nations, for the universal domination of right, for such a concert of free peoples as will bring peace and safety to all nations and make the world itself at last free.'[20] On 6 April 1917 the United States was at war.

While these dramatic developments were unfolding, the losses of merchant shipping continued to rise:

March 1917 325 ships sunk. Total tonnage lost – 500,000 tons.

Nor was March the worst month. As the German General Headquarters had foreseen, the effect of US intervention was not immediate. The United States did not yet have a large navy, and its military advisers neither knew how best to help, nor indeed how serious the situation was. The bluff, distinguished, anglophile Rear Admiral William S. Sims sailed incognito for England a few days before the US declared war to see what assistance was required, and was amazed to find that the shipping predicament was far worse than he and the people of Britain had been led to believe by the officially published figures. He had been reminded of the danger when his liner struck a mine outside Liverpool, but his subsequent interview with Jellicoe left him 'fairly astounded' – not only because he 'had never imagined anything so terrible', but because the First Sea Lord could see no way out, although they were doing all they could in the way of increasing anti-submarine forces.

> 'It looks as though the Germans were winning the war,' Sims remarked.
> 'They will unless we can stop these losses – and stop them soon,' Jellicoe replied.
> 'Is there no solution to the problem?'
> 'Absolutely none that we can see now,' was Jellicoe's dismal conclusion.[21]

There then occurred one of the most momentous and extraordinary battles of the naval war. Defeat or victory for the Allies hinged on its outcome. It was not fought at sea, but on land and not in Flanders, but in London at the Admiralty. On one side were ranged almost all the senior professional sailors and on the other David Lloyd George, backed by Arthur Bonar Law, and Sir Maurice Hankey, the Secretary of the War Cabinet. In short the dispute was whether it was better to defend the sea lanes or the ships themselves. Could the Navy best protect shipping by patrolling, trying to drive the submarines away from the shipping routes or by sticking close to ships and convoying; waiting until they were attacked? In hindsight the argument seems remarkable for the obstinacy of the Admirals' defence of practices, which had resulted in increasing losses for two years. But at the time it was not clear-cut. The one thing about which there was no dissent was the seriousness of the situation.

When Admiral Sir John Jellicoe wrote to Asquith on 30 October 1916 about the U-boat threat to merchant shipping, he had immediately been invited down to London to attend a meeting of the War Cabinet. Jellicoe had no solutions to offer, but then as C.-in-C. of the Grand Fleet he was not responsible for the defence of the mercantile marine. When Lloyd George raised the question of convoys at that meeting, the then First Sea Lord, Admiral Sir Henry Jackson, and the Chief of Naval Staff, Vice Admiral Sir Henry Oliver, were both strongly against them. All the naval arguments still seemed to condemn convoys. They would present too large a target; the French had tried convoys of more than one or two vessels and had lost ships, the Navy did not have enough ships to escort every vessel and tramp steamers could not keep station in large groups. The President of the Board of Trade added that convoys would be wasteful of shipping, because each crossing would be slowed down. A conference of the Sea Lords and other senior naval officers was convened after the War Cabinet's meeting, and as a result a special Anti-Submarine Division was formed at the Admiralty, but convoys were not even discussed.

It had been all change at the Admiralty in December 1916. Arthur Balfour, then First Lord, offered the position of First Sea Lord to Sir John Jellicoe, who after a few days' delay on account of flu took up office on 5th. Then as Asquith's Ministry collapsed and Lloyd George was appointed Prime Minister, Balfour himself was replaced by the eminent lawyer, turned politician, Sir Edward Carson. Jellicoe with his great talents, had been expected to produce fresh ideas to deal with the submarine menace. However, the new First Sea Lord was no more persuaded of the merits of convoys than the other members of the Board of Admiralty. An official pamphlet issued by the Naval Staff in January 1917 affirmed, 'Whenever possible, vessels should sail singly, escorted as considered necessary. The system of several ships sailing together in a convoy is not recommended in any area where submarine attack is a possibility. It is evident that the larger the number of ships forming the convoy, the greater is the chance of a submarine being enabled to attack successfully, the greater the difficulty of the escort in preventing such an attack.'[22] Who could doubt that a submarine lying in wait ahead of a slow moving convoy was almost bound to hit one or more ships, if it simply fired its torpedoes into the middle of them? In the light of these opinions of the senior naval professionals, it would need a bold man to take issue with them or to retract them.

Jellicoe hoped that more destroyers coming off the slipways, more depth charges, more mining in the Heligoland Bight, more defensively armed merchant ships and all the extra efforts that were now being put into the struggle by the Royal Navy would in time bear fruit. But there was no time now. Even if some scientific device had been invented to curb the submarine menace – and thousands of suggestions, some possible, others ludicrous, poured into the Admiralty every year – by the time that it had been developed, produced and installed in the ships the war would have been over.

Lloyd George wanted Carson to insist on trials of the convoy system but, faced by the Admiralty experts, the redoubtable advocate was at a loss. 'In dealing with them Sir Edward Carson's forensic gifts could not be brought into full play,' the Premier realized. 'He could hardly cross-examine his First Sea Lord and show him up in the presence of his colleagues as if he were a hostile witness.'[23] Lloyd George therefore invited Carson, Jellicoe and Rear Admiral Alexander Duff, the head of the Anti-Submarine Division, to a breakfast meeting at Downing Street on 13 February 1917. They discussed a memorandum drawn up by Sir Maurice Hankey after consultation with Lloyd George. This proposed the 'entire reorganisation of the Admiralty's present scheme of anti-submarine warfare.' It not only advocated convoys, but the concentration on them of 'the whole anti-submarine craft allotted to the protection of our trade routes' and 'every means of anti-submarine warfare – the gun, the submarine, the net, the depth charge, the mortar, the hydrophone, and wireless telegraphy.'[24] In other words the Admirals were asked to acknowledge that they had been totally wrong in their methods up till now. This was too much for the First Sea Lord to do. He protested again that a large convoy would present too much of a target and they did not have enough escorts to convoy one or two ships at a time.

Rear Admiral Sims believed that he had never met a 'more approachable, more frank, and more open-minded'[25] man than Jellicoe, and in justice to Sir John it should be said that the United States Naval

Department agreed with the British Admiralty, as Sims himself had done when President of the American Naval College at Newport. But it is hard to see why Jellicoe did not try out a convoy or two in view of the growing shipping crisis. A seductive argument in favour of the existing system of patrols had been that attack was the best method of defence and the patrols were taking the attack to the U-boats rather than passively defending ships in convoy. That however, was to miss the essence of the situation. The few destroyers were playing a game of blind man's buff. They rarely saw a submarine, even when it had been on the surface, because the submarine could spot them first, dive, wait till they had passed and then sink the next merchant ship to come along. The sub hunter, especially if it was a slow trawler, was left to rush back and drop its few depth charges in the wide area in which the U-boat might by then be. The only real hope of a successful attack lay in being on the spot at the time when the submarine loosed off its 'tin fish'. The destroyer could then turn towards the easily visible track of the torpedo and drop depth charges with some chance of a kill. That, however, meant escorting ships. Admiral Beatty, the new Commander-in-Chief of the Grand Fleet, used his influence in favour of convoys. Sims now agreed and a few less senior officers pressed for them.

On 21 February 1917 Jellicoe, still unconverted, drew up a paper for the information of the War Cabinet, which did not mention convoys. He recognized that they were not winning the U-boat war, but believed that 'the only immediate possible remedy is to increase by every means in our power the number of patrol craft used for the protection of trade routes'. There was a shortage of about 240 trawlers and 120 destroyers or sloops. Sir John called for more and claimed that, 'The only means by which they can be made available is the reduction of the military forces employed in the East'.[26] If the Salonika campaign was terminated and troops withdrawn from the Middle East, losses could be cut and it would release 333 steamers aggregating over 1,250,000 tons for the essential Atlantic routes. The destruction of shipping sent through the Mediterranean to supply these 'secondary', and at that time indecisive, campaigns was now too much of a drain on Britain's maritime resources.

The availability of escorts was only one issue that worried the Admiralty. However many escorts there were, would the merchant ships be able to keep together in convoy? Jellicoe had his doubts, but convened a meeting of captains in the merchant navy to obtain their opinion on the feasibility of convoys. He also agreed to abide by the results of two experiments which were already in progress. In response to French appeals, convoys of a kind had been started on 7 February to curtail the sinkings on the cross-Channel coal trade, and similar trials were to be made on the dangerous Scandinavian route.

Two days after the War Cabinet meeting the masters of ten merchant ships met at the Admiralty to give their views. The First Sea Lord led them along. He first pointed out that the best formation would be for the ships to sail in line abreast. This was because 'a submarine would not dare to attack any except the wing ships as she would stand a chance of being run down if she attacked in the centre'.[27] Good station keeping would be essential. Or the ships might steam in line ahead, if in two columns of not more than four ships each. When he asked the ships' masters whether eight merchant ships differing in speed by about two knots would be capable of keeping station 500 yards behind each other in two columns 1,000 yards apart, 'the masters were quite emphatic that this would be impossible . . . By night, without lights, the masters said that an organised convoy . . . would be quite out of the question.'[28] 'The merchantmen themselves are the chief obstacle to the convoy,' Jellicoe concluded.[29]

Lloyd George was scathing in his refutation of all these arguments. To withdraw the troops from the Middle East would show the world that the Turks with German help had beaten the British Empire. The Suez Canal and Egypt would fall into Turkish hands. The pressure on Austria and Bulgaria exerted via the Mediterranean would be released. All this would be conceded to save only as much shipping tonnage as the Germans expected to sink in a couple of months! As to the surprising opinions of the masters of ocean liners, 'It is simply the arrogant sense of superiority which induces the uniformed chauffeur of a Rolls-Royce to look down on the driver of what is contemptuously stigmatised as a "tin Lizzie".'[30] (To be fair, which Lloyd George was disinclined to be, the ships' masters had pointed out that 'the troubles would not only be on the bridge but in the engine room as regards regulating speed'.[31] The freighters had differing standards of engine room telegraphs and other equipment, and fuel of varying quality.)

The most foolish conflict arose over the belief that convoys would require very many more escorts than the Navy had, bearing in mind the demands of the Grand Fleet, while the High Seas Fleet remained in being. First it was maintained that a ratio of one escort to one cargo ship was necessary, and when that was contested, the huge number of ships entering and leaving British ports was adduced to show how impossible convoying would be, however many ships were escorted by one vessel. The number compiled by the Customs authorities was 5,000 per week, but this included all movements of vessels above 300 tons. One coaster, leaving her home port, going in and out of another harbour and tying up for the night in a third, would be shown as four movements of shipping. These figures were given out to show that whatever the rate of losses, Britain's merchant fleet still moved about without hindrance. The remainder were secret. The emergence of the relevant statistics was due to younger officers, Commander Reginald Henderson and Commander K.G.B. Dewar. When Dewar was given the job of writing a weekly appreciation of the naval situation for the War Cabinet, he set about trying to find accurate data of the U-boat campaign. He wanted to compare the sinkings with the number and tonnage of ships entering and leaving the UK and the amount of traffic passing through different areas. Neither the Operations Division nor the Trade Division of the Naval Staff could tell him. They only knew the number and tonnage of ships sunk. For the rest he was directed to Customs.

However, once Dewar had been formally permitted to speak to the Ministry of Shipping, he found them most helpful. The weekly arrivals and departures of British ocean-going ships was given in his second appreciation as about 200, a figure so low that it was taken by the First Lord of the Admiralty to be a *daily* total. Sir Edward Carson was a lawyer, new to the job, and might be forgiven, but Dewar took the view that 'no responsible naval officer can have imagined that the weekly return of the Customs was any criterion of escort requirements. It seems more likely that the authorities did not want figures which might prove the possibility of convoying the general trade.'[32]

If Dewar's figures for arrivals and departures in the ocean trade were low, those obtained by Commander Henderson from the Ministry were lower still; 120 to 140 per week. These would require only seventy destroyers. Thus it was that, in the words of the Official Historian, 'After long investigation and consultation with the Ministry of Shipping they succeeded in revising the table of relevant facts with surprising results'.[33]

In April disaster loomed: 419,600 tons were sunk in the first two weeks. On 21st and 22nd alone a total of 57,000 tons were lost. The next day and again on 25 April the War Cabinet discussed the critical situation at sea. The First Sea Lord said that convoys were under consideration, but gave no indication of when, if ever, they would be introduced. The Prime Minister then determined to act. He would beard the Admirals in their den. He announced that he would visit the Admiralty 'and take peremptory action on the question of convoys'. He demanded to call in whatever officers he needed to give information, whatever their rank. (Since there was no one above the heads of generals and admirals to whom Lloyd George could turn for advice, he frequently went 'below their feet', talking to relatively junior officers. He boasted that he had 'more converse with fighting officers and men, untabbed with scarlet, straight from the trenches, than had any member of the Staff either at General Headquarters or at the War Office.'[34]) The PM was now supported in his views by the experience of Commander Reginald Morrison, who had been very effectively organizing the cross-Channel sailings of the French coal trade. Morrison had lost on average only three colliers in more than 1,300 crossings a month to Brest, Cherbourg and Le Havre, though the escorts consisted only of armed trawlers.[35]

In view of these events at sea Admiral Duff wrote a paper for Jellicoe on 26 April, minuting: 'It seems to me evident that the time has arrived when we must be ready to introduce a comprehensive scheme of convoy at any moment. The sudden and large increases in our daily losses in merchant ships, together with the experience we have gained of the unexpected immunity from successful submarine attack in the case of the French coal trade, afford sufficient reason for believing that we can accept the many disadvantages of large convoys with the certainty of a great reduction in our present losses.' The losses of merchant shipping of the world by the end of that month were indeed staggering:

April 1917:   423 ships sunk.   849,000 tons lost.   1125 lives lost.

In the three months since the unrestricted campaign had begun over 1,000 ships had been sunk, an average of eleven a day, and 470 of them were ocean-going. One in four of the ships which left the United Kingdom did not return, and the *Admiralstab* target of destroying 600,000 tons of shipping per month had been achieved. Admiral Sims spelt it out bluntly to Ambassador Page: 'This simply means that the enemy is winning the war. There is no mystery about that. The submarines are rapidly cutting the Allies' lines of communication. When they are cut, or sufficiently interfered with, we must accept the enemy's terms.'[36]

Freighters were being sunk, but U-boats were not. At any time there would be on patrol twenty-one U-boats from the German North Sea ports, eight out from Flanders and thirteen more in the Mediterranean. Of all these only two had been lost in April. The morale of the U-boat crews was at its zenith. 'Yes, you've got us,' a captured commander would say, 'but what difference does that make? There are plenty more submarines coming out. You will get a few, but we can build a dozen for every one that you can capture or sink. Anyway, the war will be over in two or three months and we shall be sent back home.'[37]

The situation was now desperate: famine or defeat threatened not only England, but France and Italy with her. If the shipping losses continued, there would soon be just enough capacity to feed the people, but none to transport her troops, munitions, coal, raw materials and all the other essentials for conducting the war. No hope was coming from the Western Front, where the Canadians' advance had halted after capturing Vimy Ridge and Nivelle's offensive had met with such disaster on the Chemin des Dames that his *poilus* were near mutiny. There could be no doubt that 'the crisis of the naval war' was at hand. It seemed that the deaths of millions of men on land, on the Western and Eastern Fronts, would be in vain, because Britain was losing the war at sea. The Germans had forecast that the end would come in July; English officials with whom Admiral Sims came in contact differed only about the month. They 'placed the date at November 1st – always provided, of course, that no method were found for checking the submarine.'[38]

So, when the Prime Minister arrived at the Admiralty on 30 April, he believed he 'found the Board in a chastened mood'.[39] It was agreed to start convoys. Lloyd George triumphantly reported to the Cabinet, 'I was gratified to learn from Admiral Duff that he had completely altered his view in regard to the adoption of a system of convoy, and I gather that the First Sea Lord shares his views, at any rate to the extent of an experiment'.[40] Faces were saved by Duff's finding that the number of ships needing to be convoyed was more manageable than he had thought and by mention of destroyers coming from the USA. The first six, new 1,100 ton ships of the Eighth US Destroyer Division, were to arrive on 4 May under Commander Joseph K. Taussig, who had fought alongside the British before. (He and John Jellicoe had been in adjoining beds when wounded in the Boxer Rebellion.) Two more flotillas of six ships would cross later in the month. They would all go straight to the south-west of Ireland, where they were placed under the command of Vice Admiral Bayly at Cobh. For him the US warships made all the difference. His sloops were too few for the large convoys of freighters and too slow for the fast troopship liners – and no one wanted to take more destroyers from Scapa or Harwich even at that perilous juncture – so that without the US destroyers, he believed, 'when the convoy system was at last introduced it would have been quite impossible . . . to carry it out'.[41]

Jellicoe later wrote huffily, 'It has frequently been erroneously stated that the Admiralty decision in this matter was the result of pressure brought on the Admiralty from the War Cabinet and civilian quarters. Possibly this idea has arisen from the proceedings at the War Cabinet of April 25, . . . but it is quite incorrect. The views of experienced naval officers on a technical question involving the gravest responsibility could not possibly be affected by outside opinion, however high the quarter from which that opinion emanated.'[42]

Still the naval authorities on both sides of the Atlantic were hesitant. The first Scandinavian convoys were not well run and suffered losses, and the US Navy Department objected to convoys of more than four merchant ships together. It was not until 17 May that the Admiralty appointed a committee of four naval officers and a representative from the Ministry of Shipping to draw up a complete organization for a general system of convoy. By then, however, the first convoy from Gibraltar had set off. Before they came to the danger zone they practised steaming in formation and zigzagging together, and finally arrived quite intact on 20 May. None were more pleased than the masters of the merchant ships. 'They had suddenly discovered,' as Sims suspected, 'that they could do practically everything which, in their conferences with the Admiralty, they had declared that they were unable to do.'[43] On 24 May a convoy of twelve ships set off along the vital Atlantic route from Hampton Roads on the US east coast. Not only did it arrive safely, but the Royal Navy captain in command reported that 'the station keeping was excellent and that he was prepared to take charge of thirty vessels in stead of twelve'.[44] One vessel had been torpedoed, but she was brought in with the loss of only part of her cargo.

It took some time for the system to be fully introduced, but the results were startling. Fourteen convoys, averaging seventeen ships, were escorted across the Atlantic in the next six months. After the convoy system had become properly organized, one sailed every other day from Hampton Roads, New York or Halifax, Nova Scotia for the remainder of the war. Less than one in a hundred ships was sunk. It was now that the tracking of U-boats could be utilized. As their commanders obligingly spoke to each other or reported to base, the British Direction Finding system pin-pointed their positions; they were marked up on the huge wall map at the Admiralty, and wireless operators guided the convoys round them. Further, it was found that the delays experienced by the ships were not much longer than when they were sailing individually under war conditions. Steaming alone, they had had to take long routes round danger areas or had to wait to approach them in darkness, and were frequently held up by the presence or scares of U-boats. Also the delays in unloading convoys were lessened, when the arrival of more US escorts enabled the sailings to become more frequent.

The convoys were a success wherever they were run and the Admiralty gradually spread their operation over more sea routes, from Australia, the Cape and South America. Admiral Sims saw the arrival of the first convoy from Gibraltar as one of the great turning points of the war. 'That critical voyage meant nothing less than that the Allies had found the way of defeating the German submarine . . . In fine, it meant that the Allies could win the war.'[45]

Notes

1. Churchill, op. cit. p.1120. Fate also took a hand by delaying the Russian Revolution until after the Germans had undertaken the U-boat campaign. Churchill believed that, 'If the Allies had been left to face the collapse of Russia without being sustained by the intervention of the United States, it seems certain that France could not have survived the year, and the war would have ended in peace by negotiation or, in other words, a German victory.' But the German GHQ did not foresee the speed of the political events in the Russian Empire, which would release German armies for a final onslaught in the West.

2. Newbolt, op. cit. Vol. 4, p.265

3. Gibson and Prendergast, op. cit. p.121

4. Ludendorff's *The General Staff and its Problems* quoted in Churchill, op cit. p.1116.

5. The US had a fine battle fleet, thanks largely to Theodore Roosevelt, but few escorts.

6. Gibson and Prendergast, op. cit. p.137

7. The German declaration had been accompanied by twenty-three annexes of 'trustworthy reports' and sworn statements, which constituted 'only a small part' of the evidence in their possession. Some were no doubt due to mistaking the khaki uniformed Royal Army Medical Corps for soldiers, and their stores for munitions, but others needed explaining.

8. Tumulty, op. cit. p.254

9. Seymour, op. cit. p.48

10. Baker, op. cit. p.490

11. Hurd, op. cit. Vol.3, p.3. Opinions on the number of available U-boats vary between 105 and 111.

12. Baker, op. cit. Vol.6, p.473

13. Bulow, op. cit. Vol. 3, p.263. Von Jagow, the previous State

Secretary, had been against the resumption of unrestricted submarine warfare, and was replaced by his assistant, Zimmermann, in November 1916.

14. House, op. cit. Vol.2, p.143

15. James, op. cit. p.136. The message was cabled via Stockholm and Buenos Aires to Washington, so Hall's organization, tapping into the British owned international cable network, received it two days before Bernstorff.

16. PRO CAT HW7/8. The Mexican territories had been lost after the US-Mexican war of 1848.

17. Bulow, op. cit. Vol. 3, p.264. It should be remembered that US relations with her southern neighbour had been strained for some years; Wilson had almost gone to war, and it was only on 5 February 1917 that the last 10,000 of General Pershing's cavalry rode out of Mexico after an abortive pursuit of Villa, the political leader turned warlord.

18. James, op. cit. p.148. Hall and his staff were amused to read subsequent protests of innocence in cables between the Mexican ambassador and his masters in Germany. On the other hand it must have been galling to hear comment about how much smarter the US intelligence service was than the British. Hall's reward came later in a note from Colonel House, 'I cannot think at the moment of any man who has done more useful service in this war than you, and I salute you.' (House, op. cit. Vol.2, p.457)

19. Lansing, op. cit. p.228. To ensure the telegram got through, Zimmermann had sent it by two other channels.

20. Quoted in Baker, op. cit. pp.510–14

21. Sims, Rear Admiral William Sowden, *Victory at Sea*, John Murray, 1920, p.7

22. Newbolt, op. cit. Vol.V, p.5

23. Lloyd George, op. cit. p.685. Lloyd George was himself a solicitor.

24. ibid.

25. Sims, op. cit. p.5

26. ADM 1/8480,f.1. (See Patterson, A. Temple (ed), *The Jellicoe Papers*, Navy Records Society, 1966, Vol. II pp.145–9)

27. ibid. p.149

28. ibid. p.150. In practice ships in convoy came to steam closer than this.

29. Sims, op. cit. p.88

30. Lloyd George, op. cit. p.682

31. Patterson, op. cit. p.150

32. This seems a harsh view, but later, after the first few convoys had

arrived safely, Dewar's belief was reinforced, when remarks favourable to convoys and the suggestion that they should also be used for outward-bound ships were deleted from his Weekly Appreciation. His second Weekly Appreciation had also felt the scissors. Dewar's suggestion of attacking German ships carrying Swedish iron ore as they passed outside Dutch territorial waters was deleted, and he was told, 'not to give the politicians so much ammunition.' Dewar, always a trenchant critic, believed that Admiralty reluctance to introduce convoys might also be because it fixed them with direct responsibility for losses. If a ship sailed independently, the Master chose its course and responsibility fell on him. (See Dewar, Vice Admiral K.G.B., *The Navy from Within*, Victor Gollancz, 1939, pp.213–28)

33. Newbolt, op. cit. Vol. V, p.18

34. Lloyd George, op. cit. p.697

35. To be fair, the small colliers were not really in convoy. They steamed in batches, often at night, and were held back when a U-boat was known to be prowling. As the distances were short, good station keeping was not required.

36. Sims, op. cit. p.52

37. ibid. p.13

38. ibid. p.14

39. Lloyd George, op. cit. p.692

40. ibid.

41. Bayly, op. cit. p.242. Also, his coal-burning sloops wasted one day a week refuelling.

42. Jellicoe, Admiral of the Fleet Viscount, *The Submarine Peril*, Cassell, 1934, p.130. Professor Halpern agrees. Duff's paper accepting convoys had of course been written and approved in the five days between the Prime Minister's announcement of his intended visit and his arrival at the Admiralty. However, it looked like a deathbed conversion. Commander Dewar, who saw the debate from within the Admiralty wrote, 'The idea that they were really in favour of convoy, and only waited a favourable opportunity to introduce it, is neither borne out by the facts nor by their own memoranda.' (Dewar, op. cit. p.221)

43. Sims, op. cit. p.96

44. Ministry of Shipping Report on Convoys.

45. Sims, op. cit. p.96–7

CHAPTER ELEVEN

The Pendulum Swings

No one now doubts that the convoy system proved the salvation of the Allies, but it did not put an end to the destruction of shipping, and for several months the issue hung in the balance with the advantage in Germany's favour well into the summer of 1917. Frustrated in the Atlantic, the U-boats came closer to the coast. Freighters continued to be sunk as they steamed to the point of assembly, were taking up position (which might take several hours) or after the convoys had dispersed. Coastal shipping was still vulnerable. Mediterranean traffic was not convoyed for some time and neutral ships were not escorted with British ships, because the authorities were afraid to divulge to them the time, course and tactics of the convoys.

And all the time the number of enemy submarines increased. The commissioning of U-boats was so rapid in early 1917, that the boats operating out of German ports doubled to ninety-eight in the four months to the end of May (in which month an unrepeated thirty new submarines were launched). Between thirty and forty of these boats could be on patrol around the United Kingdom at any time that summer. Besides them ten more would be out from the Flanders bases and as many again in the Mediterranean. A few huge cruiser submarines carried the attack into the open Atlantic and marauded around the Canary Islands and the Azores, where they were beyond the range of the patrols. Displacing nearly 2,500 tons when submerged, and as long as a light cruiser (over a hundred yards) they could be out for three months. Their two 5.9-inch guns outranged many escorts, their torpedoes had a charge three times as powerful as earlier marks, they could communicate under water by submarine telephone and with new attack periscopes, less than two inches in diameter, they could approach to torpedo with less warning than ever.

To counter the U-boat threat, hunting flotillas were deployed round the coast with hydrophones, but even when guided by observers in kite balloons, they mostly arrived too late on the scene of an attack to do more than harry the U-boat for a matter of hours. Submarines regularly passed under a line of hydrophone vessels without being heard. (Not surprisingly the Admiral in charge at Milford Haven in south-west Wales considered his hydrophone patrols 'a waste of useful ships'[1], and preferred to use his hunting flotilla to convoy ships across the Irish Sea.) It was only in October 1917 that the 'fish' hydrophone, which indicated the direction of the submerged U-boat, began to be fitted, and only at the very end of the war that the more efficient pinging ASDIC system was developed.

Moreover, although in the Western Approaches the greatest threat to sea traffic was always the torpedo speeding suddenly towards the unsuspecting side of the merchantman, on the east coast of England the mine was equally to be feared. The incessant visitations from the UC boats (minelayers) out of Zeebrugge, quickly depositing their payload within a few miles of the shore and returning home to Bruges, were stepped up during 1917. Till then sweeping 178 mines in one month was a record: in 1917 that figure was exceeded every month. On average ten mines were swept up every day, a third of them in the mouth of the Thames and round the East Anglian coast to Lowestoft. Some ships were saved by streaming the 'otter' gear on either side of their bows. (The otter was pulled at the end of a cable. It had a cigar-shaped body and fins which kept it below the water and pulled it away from the ship. When it caught a mine's anchor cable, it kept the mine away from the ship's hull, and cutters on the otter cable then severed the mine from its mooring.[2]) But however adept the forces hunting the mines and minelaying U-boats, the volume of coastal traffic was so great – over 2,000 vessels passing Lowestoft in April 1917 alone – that inevitably there were losses. Less than four per cent of the mines struck a ship during the first six months of the year, but they still sank or damaged ninety merchantmen.[3]

The row of lightships and buoys which marked the swept war channel for coastal traffic helped the U-boats to fix their position, and sometimes, as an area was cleared and buoyed, they would lay their mines in the wake of the sweepers. The most difficult was the delayed-action mine, which rose from the seabed one or two days after being laid. Chain sweeps were employed, but they were unreliable over rocky ground. That the shipping losses were not greater was due to the 'race of hardy, skilful and courageous men'[4] who crewed the minesweepers. The job required unflinching bravery: ten minesweepers were sunk or damaged by mines every month of 1917, and in a boat as small as a trawler the crew were lucky to escape the explosion unhurt.[5]

So losses of merchant shipping did not fall at once; 596,600 tons (well over half British) were sunk in May and 687,500 in June. Though the U-boats were never again to achieve that destruction of tonnage which had occurred in April 1917, the *Admiralstab* was still on target. No wonder that as late as 29 June, Rear Admiral Sims, writing to the Secretary of the Navy, Josephus Daniels, had to rehearse the arguments for convoys: arming freighters was no use against a torpedo (even battle-ships needed a destroyer screen); convoys were *not* just defensive, they concentrated forces at the point where an attack could be made; large numbers of destroyers need not be retained in the US, because nothing would be more fatal to the German campaign than for them to divert their forces on long trips across the Atlantic to harry trade along the US coasts; hesitancy would be disastrous.

The Admiralty now put outward voyages under escort, assembled the vessels earlier and dispersed them nearer their ports.[6] The organization which this required in the major ports should not be underestimated. Convoy departures were like train timetables and assembly instructions had to be sent via British consulates all over the globe to masters of ships, who opened their sealed orders when a hundred miles out at sea and steamed to the convoy rendezvous. By the end of September, eighty-three ocean convoys had come safely home. Only eighteen ships had been lost in 1306 crossings, and only ten of those, one vessel in every eight convoys, had been sunk while escorted.[7] In October three escorting warships were sunk, but by then convoys were arriving daily in UK ports, four or five hundred ships a month, having traversed the ocean, some crawling at seven knots, most at nine or ten and a few as fast as twelve and a half knots.

There were always too few destroyers and sloops, but by 5 July there were thirty-four US destroyers in western Ireland, allowing the Royal Navy's ships to be deployed elsewhere. The American craft looked sleeker and could keep at sea longer than the British destroyers, though they were slower and could turn less quickly. Small US submarine chasers were to follow.

Vice-Admiral Sir Lewis Bayly welcomed the US captains, passed on tips from British experience and laid down priorities: first to destroy submarines, second to protect merchant shipping and third to save lives.

They must not stop to rescue crews if it risked letting a U-boat escape or being themselves torpedoed. They should never steer a straight course, steam less than thirteen knots, nor show lights or use search-lights at night, positions should be reported every two hours, periscopes should be shelled and not rammed in case they were dummies with mines attached. There came to be ninety-two US ships under Bayly's command between May 1917 and the end of the war. In fact, when he took a week's leave and the dark blue flag of Admiral Sims was seen on the flagstaff, the rumour went round that Ireland had been handed over to the USA!

The disciplined, crusty, sixty-year-old Bayly had come into his own at Cobh, and might have been chosen for his ability to get on with the new transatlantic allies. He had spent time as Naval Attaché in Washington, had no 'side', displayed a friendly sense of humour with ready repartee, and treated the men of both nations equally. The teetotal table, physical fitness, and businesslike manner of 'Uncle Lewis' were well received by the Americans. Then there was his Australian niece, Violet Voysey, who presided over Admiralty House and whose charm and flair for hospitality made it a home for the hard-worked officers. Equally solicitous of the needs of the U-boat victims, the Admiral and his niece would break off from dinner to tend to them in a large hall in the Custom House. Admiral Sims, similarly 'free of speech, frank in praise and criticism,'[8] developed a great respect for them both and always kept 'a vivid recollection of this kindly gentleman, Admiral Sir Lewis Bayly, K.C.B., K.C.M.G., C.V.O., Royal Navy, serving coffee to wretched British, American, French, Italian, Japanese or negro sailors, with a cheering word for each, and afterward, with sleeves tucked up, calmly washing dishes in a big pan of hot water.'[9]

For the first eight months of 1917 the Allies destroyed only three or four submarines a month, while German yards were launching twice that number. Turning to every available method of combating the submarine menace, Bayly sent out Q-ships from Cobh, two or three at a time, whenever U-boats were known to be about. The Admiralty had established a special department to select suitable craft, crews and disguises for the decoys. In the middle of the year there were about eighty ships, steam and sail, of between 200 and 4,500 tons, employed as submarine traps. It was the time of their greatest activity.

The ships were an odd assortment of craft. Since U-boat comman-ders were no longer ordered to surface and obtain the ship's papers before attacking, the decoys had to be small enough to be hardly worth wasting a torpedo on, and as large guns cannot be easily hidden on a small ship (and could not at first be spared), their guns were often too small for decisive action with the enemy they were hoping to attract. The bravery and discipline of the crews of the Q-ships was proverbial. The 'mystery ships' could not actively stalk a submarine; their task was to make the U-boat stalk them. They had to take punishment without showing any sign of life, other than the lowering of a 'panic party' into boats to give the impression that the ship was deserted. In between moments of terrifying suspense there were weeks or months of boredom. Yet the chance of action, the fun of disguising yourself and your ship and the independent command ensured that there was never a shortage of volunteers.

There were amazing examples of cool heroism. One of the finest was on board the three-masted schooner *Prize*, commanded by a New Zealander, Lieutenant W.E. Sanders RNR. On 30 April 1917 she was under sail in the Atlantic, moving slowly in the light breeze when her captain saw a large modern U-boat running parallel with her. This was the *U-93*, commanded by *Freiherr* von Spiegel. He had already sunk eleven vessels on that maiden patrol of his new command, and was returning home. As his two 10.5-cm guns (4.1-inches) opened up, the panic party got into the *Prize*'s boat and rowed off, while the remainder of the crew hid. Shells crashed into the schooner, two of them on the waterline, bursting inside, putting the engine out of action and wounding two of the crew. There was no reaction from the men at the guns, who were crouched down out of view. The gunnery officer lay at the foot of the foremast, with his ear to a voice pipe leading to where the captain was peering at the submarine through slits in the wheelhouse.

For twenty minutes von Spiegel circled half submerged round the slowly sinking ship, once so close that he touched her stern. Still the crew waited for orders. 'They could see nothing, they could not ease the mental strain by watching the enemy's manoeuvres or inferring from what direction the next shot – perhaps the last – would come.'[10] Finally when the U-boat surfaced only seventy yards away, where the *Prize*'s guns could bear, Sanders gave the order, 'Down screens! Open fire!' Shells hit the conning tower, the forward gun and the hull of the *U-93*. It seemed that there was a fire on board and she slowly disappeared. Three men were plucked from the water by the 'panic party'. Among them was von Spiegel himself. 'The discipline of the German Navy is wonderful,' he told Sanders, 'but that your men could have quietly endured our shelling without reply is beyond belief.'[11]

The victor and vanquished were now literally both in the same boat, which was sinking, but finally reached Cobh. Lieutenant Sanders was awarded the Victoria Cross and, for a later action in the *Prize* the DSO. Courageously he refused to accept another posting. But two other U-boats had escaped the clutches of the *Prize* after she had opened fire, and the three-masted topsail schooner was a difficult ship to disguise. She was carefully stalked by the *U-48*, and torpedoed one night, when she sank with all hands.

Von Spiegel was the author of *The War Diary of U-202*, which contained a chapter describing how the British had used hospital ships to carry troops, so Captain Reginald Hall, hearing that he had been captured, had him brought to London for interrogation, and particularly asked about the origins of the notorious piece. Von Spiegel admitted that he had not himself witnessed the use of a hospital ship to carry arms, but he had heard it from another submariner. (His retraction was widely published in Britain and America, but Germany continued to believe that the immunity of hospital ships was being abused. Six or more clearly marked ships were attacked in 1917 and 1918.)

Commander Gordon Campbell was the most successful captain of 'mystery ships', and his crew in the *Farnborough* (*Q-5*) were suicidally brave. His officers countersigned his order that 'Should the Officer of the Watch see a torpedo coming, he is to increase or decrease speed as necessary to ensure it hitting'! The ship's company were all warned of this and given the chance to leave. None did. Campbell sank three U-boats and was awarded the VC, but it was in the *Dunraven* in August 1917 that his men gave their most astounding display of coolness. The Q-ship had been given a gun aft, because most tramp steamers were defensively armed by this time. With this she carried on a deliberately uneven fight with a pursuing U-boat. Campbell then stopped the ship, as though her engines had been hit, and waited. A shell from the submarine had penetrated the poop, where depth charges were stowed and one of them exploded. Lieutenant Bonner was blown out of his control position, but crawled into the gun hatch on the poop deck. The position of Campbell's men, as he described it, was parlous. 'They there remained at their posts with the fire raging in the poop below and the deck getting red hot . . . and all the time they knew that they must be blown up, as the secondary supply and magazine were immediately below; . . . they also knew they would spoil the show if they moved, so they remained until actually blown up with their gun.'[12] But their endurance was in vain. The explosion, when it came, was catastrophic; the 4-inch gun was catapulted over the bridge and fell down in the well deck; the gun-crew and projectiles were hurled all around. What was more, the action hooter had gone off, so the White Ensign had been run up and one gun had been fired ineffectually at the U-boat. The enemy was warned and dived. The men, though wounded, had to lie still, awaiting a final explosion, if not from their own ammunition, then from a torpedo. The torpedo duly arrived, hitting the *Dunraven* near the engine room. For nearly an hour the submarine circled like a shark. The scrutiny over, the U-boat surfaced and again shelled the ship and played a Maxim gun on the men in the boats. Campbell replied with two torpedoes, but both missed, and the U-boat made off when a US warship and two British destroyers arrived. This time the Q-ship capsized before she could be towed home.

The *Dunraven* was one of six Q-ships lost during August 1917. U-boat commanders were becoming more circumspect. They learnt to shell from a distance or torpedo any ship which might be a decoy. Several carried an ex-merchant seaman to spot the uncharacteristic points in a freighter, which might indicate a trap – too many men on deck, clothes hung up man-of-war fashion, a man climbing up a ladder too briskly. But it was still not all one way. It was a Q-ship which sank the *U-88*, captained by Walther Schwieger, who had sunk the *Lusitania*. He perished with his whole crew, when the conning tower hatch jammed.[13]

Q-ships sank five submarines in 1917, but after that autumn not one when acting alone. However, the Admiralty never abandoned the 'mystery ship' concept. During the war 180 in all were commissioned, their tricks and disguises becoming more sophisticated with time. For fear of spies in Cobh a vessel might leave harbour with three masts and, when at sea, drop one mast or have a different coat of paint. When any vessel made an unsuccessful attack, she was ordered back to port, given a new appearance and sent out again. In the whole war Q-ships claimed only eleven of the U-boats sunk by naval action (about six per cent of the total), but they damaged eighty more, and a submarine which was holed and unable to dive would not dare to make any more attacks before returning to base. Q-ship warfare was a unique episode, unrepeated in the Second World War and so largely forgotten now, but Sir Henry Newbolt, the Official Naval Historian, believed at the time that it 'had been waged with a skill and endurance which had provoked the admiration of the entire naval service; and its story will always form one of the most brilliant chapters in our naval annals'.[14]

Nonetheless, just as some Britons viewed the German submariners as pirates, some in the *Kriegsmarine* thought the same of the men in the Q-ships, and a few U-boat commanders became vicious, killing the crews of merchant ships, whatever their nationality, without mercy. In April 1917 when Werner in *U-55* sank the *Torrington* (5,600 tons), he took the master prisoner, ordered the crew out of their boats and had them line up on the deck of his submarine. He then submerged. None of the men was seen again. Four days later he did the same when sinking the *Toro*. Paul Wagenfuhr emulated this atrocity in July. On another occasion the British submarine, *C-23*, came across a Dutchman riddled with shell holes and apparently abandoned, but there was a man on board, whom they rescued just as the ship was sinking. He was the second mate and had gone back for his sextant when all the rest of the crew were in the lifeboats. He became the sole survivor. The rest of the crew were fired on; shelled till they were all dead in their boats.[15] A similar fate awaited the crew of the Norwegian barque *Eglinton* when they took to their boats. One man survived to tell the tale. These were not the only incidents. Though prisoners were not infrequently shot on both sides of the Western Front, to seafarers such barbarity was 'ruthlessness which in pre-war days would have been regarded as beyond the bounds of human conscience'.[16]

It should, however, be recorded that there were also examples of chivalrous behaviour on the part of U-boat captains, such as when *Kapitänleutnant* Otto Steinbrinck, having sunk the submarine *E-22* with a torpedo, paused to pick up two survivors, even though three other British submarines were pursuing him on the surface. 'It was a very gallant deed, and one much admired by his opponents.'[17] Again, Hans Rose called up Cobh and gave the position of a destroyer which he had sunk, so that her crew could be picked up. The report involved his own craft in little danger, because he could be far enough away before any destroyer reached the site, but the output of depth charges was constantly being increased and was beginning to tell.

The fight back had begun. A range of weapons was available in the summer of 1917 for the anti-submarine war. In the Channel, French and British aeroplanes and airships patrolled from bases along the coasts, giving warning of submarines, and sinking a few with bombs. Submarines were most successful hunting U-boats in spite of earlier doubts. (Too few British submarines however, perhaps ten out of the eighty-six which were available, were employed in attacking or patrolling in the enemy's waters; the remainder were kept for coastal defence or 'ready to meet an imaginary danger of invasion'.[18])

The monthly strength of active U-boats peaked at 140 in the autumn. Ten had been sunk in September by various means and at the beginning of October a large-scale anti-submarine operation of a different kind – fishing for U-boats – was undertaken with some success. It had been observed that submarines returning to bases in the German rivers had become accustomed to take a defined route home through the minefields of the North Sea. Their path lay through a 300 mile funnel-shaped track, which narrowed to forty-five miles wide at the southern end. At this end drifters laid a line of mined nets twenty-five miles long, while two dozen trawlers and twenty destroyers at a time patrolled the surface along the route to keep the U-boats down. This watch was maintained in spite of the most appalling weather which dogged the operation. As the storm gathered, the nets could not be laid exactly as required, and during the gales of the next ten days the destroyers were often driven back into harbour by the mountainous waves, or had to cease patrolling and turn their bows into the wind and seas just to keep afloat. However, the trawlers held their positions and lowered their hydrophones over the side and listened, while the tempest roared around them. From time to time underwater explosions were heard, but these could have been mines fouling the waving nets and detonating each other. On three occasions they heard the sound of a submarine's motors, followed by an explosion and then silence. After ten days of buffeting by the waves the nets were so torn as to be useless and the project was abandoned, but the German authorities acknowledged that three U-boats were in fact lost in the North Sea at that time.[19]

In spite of these successes the destruction of merchant shipping continued apace. In the first eight months of the campaign 4.5 million tons was sunk – as much as in the preceding thirty months of the war. Five or six vessels worldwide were lost to enemy action every day in the second half of 1917. The gross tonnage lost in the third and fourth quarters, 15,270 and 12,500 tons, though nowhere near the appalling figure for April to June, was still greater than the shipping launched. The loss of tankers had reduced the country's reserves of oil from eight months' to eight weeks' supply. This restricted the Grand Fleet's movements, and when the US offered battleships to join the Fleet, coal-fired ships were requested. Moreover the strength of the currencies of Great Britain and France was sapped as the ships and munitions sank. In the summer Balfour was pleading with Colonel House, 'We seem on the verge of a financial disaster which would be worse than defeat in the field. If we cannot keep up exchange neither we nor our Allies can pay our dollar debts. We should be driven off the gold basis, and purchases from the U.S.A. would immediately cease.'[20] Multi-million dollar credits were arranged, and the US replaced the UK as banker of the Allies.

At home in Britain some foodstuffs were running short and prices were rising, causing industrial unrest. Because of the excellent harvests in Canada and Australia in 1915, plans to increase Britain's cereal output had been shelved, but now drastic action was vital. A Food Controller had been appointed by Asquith's coalition administration, but little else had been done. However, on 1 January 1917, Lloyd George's cabinet had set up a Food Production Department in the Board of Agriculture and Fisheries and had promptly given it powers more draconian than any previously issuing from the Mother of Parliaments. One million acres of grass land were to be put under the plough, unproductive farmers were dispossessed, implements and stock could be commandeered, prices and rents were fixed, the wages of farm workers were raised and pegged and, horror of horrors, in the absence of shooting parties, 'the autumnal massacre of the pheasantry'[21], tenants were even authorized to poach, since the birds had multiplied and were gobbling the corn.

The Prime Minister gave a rousing call for yet more potatoes to be grown and farmers responded by beating all records. 'The potato grower,' he declared, 'is in the front line of the fight against the submarine.'[22] But army recruitment had thinned the ranks of the farm labourers. The shortage gave birth to the Women's Land Army early in 1917 and finally 30,000 prisoners of war were drafted in to work the land. Steam engines and over 9,000 tractors, mostly Fordsons assembled at Manchester, increased farm production. The British too produced new fertilizers to take the place of nitrates, which were required for explosives, and the potash which had previously come from Germany.

Yet all this effort to increase output was not enough: consumption had to be reduced too. Ultimately food supplies had to be controlled. It began with sugar. Britain was badly placed for sweetening, because she had virtually no sugar beet industry before the war. Worse, eighty-five per cent of her imports of beet had come from her enemies, Germany and Austria. Sugar cane accounted for only a small part of the total sugar consumed. An artificial sweetener called Saxin was produced for tea and coffee, but as early as January 1917 confectioners were forbidden to make more than half their previous production of sweets. Sugar and chocolate coverings of cakes and pastries were prohibited. Then pastries, muffins, and teacakes were banned altogether. The curtailing of sweetmeats was a gentle introduction to the tightened regime. For some months rationing was deferred by appeals for voluntary restrictions on consumption, and when in February German propaganda in the USA announced that Britain only had enough food for another month, it was not contradicted at home to encourage frugality, though vigorously denied in America. Prices rose steadily through the summer. The wholesale and retail prices of essential foods, meat, butter, flour, potatoes and milk, had to be fixed in September. This caused food queues, which lengthened in December. The nation was warned that from New Year's Day 1918 no meat in any form could be sold on one day a week. (In an act of fellow feeling the US encouraged its citizens to have a meatless day too.) Rationing could not now be deferred in Britain. It would start at the end of February with sugar, fats and meat, first in London and the Home Counties, and later all over the country. At the same time beer was reduced in strength. France, with its huge loss of manpower from the fields, was in still greater trouble and Italy, which had been slow to recognize the danger, suffered too.

These worries were now dwarfed by sudden disasters on the Continent. In October 1917 the Austrians, reinforced by German divisions, had broken through the Italian front at Caporetto, advanced eighty miles in eleven days and captured a quarter of a million prisoners. At the same time the Bolshevik Revolution had finally destroyed Russia's will to fight, and released fifty seasoned German divisions to fight in the west. Once again the General Headquarters, using the internal lines of communication of the Central Powers, was able to shift troops to wherever strategy demanded. Allied leaders waited and worried. Next spring the Germans would have superior numbers on the Western Front. Would they attack the British, who were exhausted after the carnage of Passchendaele, and seize the Channel ports, or would they assail the French army, many of whose divisions had refused to return to the trenches in 1917, and push to Paris? Defeat was staring the Allies in the face unless the Americans crossed the Atlantic much faster than had been planned. US troops had not been rushed into the line in 1917: there were then few to send. By the end of 1917 there were no more doughboys in France than there had been Tommies in 1914. A new army was to have been steadily built up ready for victory in 1919. However, the collapse of Russia had changed the situation. It would be a race against time. The main problem now was not the lack of training of the raw American recruits, but the shortage of transports. The loan of tonnage was demanded of neutrals in return for keeping them supplied with food. Allied tonnage had to be pooled and trooping was given priority. General Tasker Bliss, the US Chief of Staff called for 'every ton of shipping that can possibly be taken from trade . . . The one all-absorbing necessity now is soldiers with which to beat the enemy in the field, and ships to carry them.'[23] Shipbuilding took priority over shells in the queue for American steel.

The great transatlantic liners were being converted to troopships, but would these huge targets be sunk like the *Lusitania*? The torpedoing of one US troopship with the sacrifice of thousands of young lives would have been a double disaster. American opinion might have held back further assistance until crossing was more secure. Lloyd George was impatient that no offensive action was being taken by the Royal Navy against the U-boat bases and his feud with the First Sea Lord continued during 1917. Jellicoe for his part considered that the Premier's suggestions 'were of such a nature that they could never have emanated from the brain of a Naval officer . . . They were not, however,' he generously conceded, 'so strange as the one sent to me in 1917 by a gentleman, who said that the obvious solution to the (U-boat) danger was to fill the North Sea with Eno's Fruit Salt, which would, he said, force the submarines to the surface.'[24] It was a measure of the desperation of the admirals that at an Inter-Allied conference in September 1917 there was a serious proposal to block all the German harbours with forty old battleships and a similar number of cruisers contributed by all the Allies. It was rejected as both impracticable and a waste of ships, but the idea of closing the North Sea with several lines of mines right across from Scotland to the Norwegian waters was approved. The US Navy Department ordered 100,000 mines as a start. However, this enormous output, even with the massive manufacturing capacity of the United States, would take time. Surely more could be done meanwhile?

The Royal Navy's inactivity seemed more shameful, when surface raiders of the *Kaiserliche Marine* managed to bring off two coups in the North Sea towards the end of 1917. In mid-October Naval Intelligence became aware of the impending movement of German surface warships. Admiral Beatty therefore ordered out a large force of three cruisers, twenty-seven light cruisers and fifty-four destroyers. They spread out in eight patrol cordons over the southern and eastern areas of the North Sea, expecting a minelayer and destroyers. In fact the enemy consisted of only two ships, but these were the 34-knot light cruisers *Brummer* and *Bremse*. They sped north during the moonless night of October 16–17 without being sighted by any of the British forces, located the Scandinavian convoy, sank its two escorting destroyers and then picked off nine of the twelve merchantmen, before returning home in daylight.

The sudden attack did not deter the masters of Scandinavian convoys from continuing their daily runs in one direction or the other, though it did cause a political stir. (When British forces achieved much the same, it was rather taken for granted, as when on 15 July that year Commodore Tyrwhitt's light cruisers and destroyers crushed a German convoy which had ventured outside Dutch territorial waters. After sinking the escort, they captured four merchant ships, which were sent in to Harwich, and drove the remaining two ashore.)

Emboldened by success Scheer attacked again two months later in December 1917. This time he employed two Half Flotillas of four modern destroyers each. One struck at the eastbound convoy just as it was approaching the Norwegian coast. The two British destroyer escorts were at a disadvantage and one, HMS *Partridge* was sunk, along with all six of the escorted freighters. Only the damaged HMS *Pellew* escaped. The destruction had been wrought in forty-five minutes, and when British cruisers came up they were too late. The Germans had retired, having suffered little damage. (One had been hit by a torpedo which failed to explode.)[25] Their other Half Flotilla missed its target, the convoy down the east coast of England, but sank two other ships.

This escapade again made the Royal Navy look impotent. They were now in a very difficult position in the North Sea. Single merchant ships would be picked off by submarines; convoys could be equally easily destroyed. It was particularly hard to defend convoys on the eastern side of the North Sea without exposing whatever escorts they used to an even greater force coming out from the German bases. The whole Grand Fleet could not escort a convoy, but any lesser force was tempting fate, as Beatty was well aware.

Recognizing the Royal Navy's dilemma, Admiral Scheer one day, in the spring of 1918, surreptitiously moved the High Seas Fleet north for a potentially cataclysmic sortie. His U-boats had reported that the Scandinavian convoys were being supported by battleships and cruisers. 'To take the High Seas Fleet to the coast of Norway to sink another convoy and its escorting cruisers under the eyes of the neutral skippers; to overwhelm a battle squadron almost within sight of the Norwegian coastguard stations and lighthouse keepers, and to do all this whilst the British armies in Flanders were reeling under the German onslaught, would be a success of the first order,'[26] as the Official History recognized. It would be of much greater value than the propaganda victory of Jutland. More British capital ships would be destroyed without the chance of doing much damage to his own ships, and, with the threat of easy repetition, it would stifle the Scandinavian trade, even if, with the American intervention, it could never now level the balance of power in the North Sea. Such care was taken to keep radio silence that Room 40 was quite unaware of the battle fleet's movement. They reported that there was no action in the Heligoland Bight, even as the German battle-cruisers were steaming beyond Horns Reef.

Early in the afternoon of 22 April 1918 a large convoy of thirty-four merchant ships set out with the light cruiser, *Duke of Cornwall*, and two destroyers as escorts. To the south steamed the Second Battlecruiser Squadron and the Seventh Light Cruiser Squadron, a powerful cover-ing force for a convoy, but no match for ships which were on their way to intercept them. Scheer's fleet stopped for half an hour when fog covered the North Sea, and set off again slowly through the minefields, still without breaking wireless silence. Ironically a British submarine saw the fleet pass, but crassly believing them to be RN minelayers, sent no report.

However, luck was not with Scheer that day. Nor did he deserve it, for he had failed to ascertain just when the convoys sailed, and that was something which a German consul in Norway, had he been asked, would have found out for him. The result was that Hipper's reconnais-sance group was a day too late and the convoy was already nearing the British coast, when he arrived off Stavanger. It is possible that the east-ward bound convoy might have sailed into his clutches, if he had waited there longer, but fate took a hand. At 8 a.m. the battlecruiser *Moltke* reported, 'Grave damage, speed four knots'.[27] She had suffered a serious accident in her engine room, and was ordered to fall back on Scheer's battle squadrons. However, when the *Moltke* came to a halt and had to be towed back the whole operation was aborted. Later, as she was going slowly under her own steam, she was torpedoed by the *E-42*, but eventu-ally reached port. What was more, when the problem with the *Moltke* was radioed to Scheer, the message was intercepted by Admiral Hall's eavesdroppers. The Grand Fleet was ordered to sea from Rosyth. In all thirty-one battleships (including four US ships under Rear Admiral Rodman), four battlecruisers, two cruisers, twenty-four light cruisers and eighty-five destroyers weighed anchor and steamed hopefully east. As had happened once before, luck had saved units of the Grand Fleet in the first part of the operation and had protected their foes later on. Never again after that April foray was there to be the possibility of a battle between major parts of the surface fleets.

Coincidentally 23 April 1918 was also the date of the last major oper-ation by British naval forces. In response to Lloyd George's plea for more aggression, the ardent Rear Admiral Roger Keyes had been brought down to head the Admiralty's Plans Division. From there he initiated an attack, which he ultimately led, to block in the U-boats and destroyers which were based in the inland docks at Bruges. The plan was to seal up simultaneously the exits of the two canals from which the enemy emerged at Zeebrugge and Ostend. The blocking attempt, though heroically executed, was only partially and temporarily successful. The stark courage of the attack at Zeebrugge immortalized the event and was a boost to the nation's morale, but it was the other project, the Dover mine barrage, for which Keyes was responsible as commander of the Dover Patrol, that made a definite contribution to beating the U-boats.

After the failure of the nets and mines in the Straits of Dover the only deterrent to U-boats had been the ships of the Dover Patrol and the occasional lurking British submarine, so in September 1917 the larger North Sea U-boats were again ordered to run through the Straits so as to have extra time on station. To keep the Dover Patrol in ignorance of this, U-boats were ordered to show themselves openly as they went round Scotland, but to keep well submerged as they passed through the Straits. It was not till these instructions were found on raising the sunken *UC-44* that action was taken.

The British had by now copied the German mines almost exactly, and at last had an efficient weapon, which they and the Americans were producing in huge numbers. In the Heligoland Bight 25,000 of the new Mark H2 mines had been laid, but these minefields had been a disappointment, because the Royal Navy could not prevent the Germans from using Dutch and Danish territorial waters, nor from sweeping paths through the minefields and buoying the channels. A deadly battle of wits developed, as the British laid mines at the end of the swept channels and the Germans laid mines in the paths of the minelayers, creating an ever widening danger area. The German minesweeping forces were attacked in October 1917, but without success, partly because of the sound defensive tactics of Admiral von Reuter, and partly because Beatty's staff had not given Admiral Napier the latest maps of the minefields. Nevertheless the continual visitations by British minelayers cost the Germans prodigious efforts and daily losses among their minesweepers and U-boat escorts, the latter being down to four boats at one stage.

A mine barrage which could not be swept up by the enemy could, however, be laid across the Straits of Dover. Before he was superseded by Keyes as Vice Admiral at Dover, Bacon had devised a deep minefield to be laid between Folkestone and Cap Gris-Nez with several rows of mines laid at various depths. A gateway was left at Dover for commercial traffic, but it was scanned for submarines by acoustic devices. To force the submarines to dive into the minefield the barrage was brilliantly illuminated at night from drifters and trawlers guarded by patrol boats and old 30-knot destroyers. From 19 December 1917, when it was first illuminated, the barrage accounted for nineteen enemy submarines.[28] After the loss of the *U-109* in January 1918 the large submarines from the Heligoland Bight were ordered to go north round Scotland, but it was not until September 1918 that the smaller UB boats and UC minelayers from the Flanders Flotilla were forbidden to attempt the Dover Straits.

This effectively confined the small U-boats to the east coast of England, where safe channels were regularly swept and patrolled. All round the coast the minesweeping force had expanded enormously. By the end of 1917 there were several hundred fast minesweepers, mine-hunting trawlers, drifters, yachts, paddle steamers and motor launches working out of a score of harbours round the British Isles, so that in the second half of the year the number of merchantmen falling victim to mines declined to forty-nine, and only eight merchant ships were lost to mines round the British Isles in 1918.

By April 1918 the convoy system and other anti-submarine measures had cut the shipping losses to a third of the peak twelve months before. On the vital Atlantic crossings few ships were sunk. Even the best U-boat commanders seemed to find that a convoy in good formation had an 'extraordinary and baffling power of evasion'.[29] Between 10–25 May, for instance, there was methodical collaboration between eight German submarines off the Irish coast, but they enjoyed minimal success. On one day nine convoys passed through without one ship being sunk. Next day one was torpedoed, but two U-boats were sunk, one by ramming and the other by a hunting submarine. On another occasion thirty-five vessels in nine parallel columns passed a U-boat close enough for it to fire two torpedoes. Neither struck home and the submarine did not get another chance. By June convoys were substantially reducing losses even in the restricted waters of the Mediterranean and total tonnage lost was down to the level of January 1917, before the second unrestricted U-boat campaign began.

This would still have been crippling, had not more freighters been launched by then, but by the second quarter of 1918 UK shipbuilding on its own had overtaken losses for the first time in two years. United Kingdom yards built 140,000 tons each month as against 170,000 lost, but ship repairing put back a hundred thousand tons or more each month.[30] And if Britain had increased her shipbuilding capacity dramatically, the growth in the United States, after a slow start, had been phenomenal. At newly constructed yards they came to build a merchantman in seventy days, from laying the keel to launching the ship. From April 1918 the graph of available shipping was always pointing upwards.

And finally more German submarines were being sunk, (although at no stage in the war were they destroyed faster than they were built). The number of active U-boats declined between October 1917 and July 1918, as sinkings, repairs and the training of raw crews took time. The men were no longer all volunteers; every month 500 were drafted from the Fleet to the submarine school at Kiel. Their training was less thorough, their commanders less expert. Morale declined and they began to surrender more easily when a boat was damaged. The log of *U-110* recorded what could be expected in the North Sea in 1918. Depth charges exploded near her on twelve consecutive days until finally one damaged her hydroplanes and she was rammed by a destroyer while struggling to submerge. The order was given to abandon her, but she was under fire and there was a panic rush to the hatch, which jammed and several men drowned.[31]

By the end, over half the 360 U-boats employed had been lost. Minelaying U-boats, which had to work near the coast, were especially vulnerable.[32] 'This dateless victory at sea was decisive according to the strictest definitions of decisive victory,'[33] concluded the Official Naval Historian. However, it was not achieved without the allocation of enormous resources. There were a couple of hundred escorts and innumerable auxiliaries (dropping 2,000 depth charges each month towards the end of the war), nearly 700 aeroplanes and 100 airships watching for submarines.

The last nail in the U-boats' coffin was intended to be the Northern Barrage. Only the US could have envisaged and executed such a gigantic project – laying a minefield at varying depths for 230 miles from Scotland towards Norway. At first it seemed a stark impossibility, even though it would not be necessary to ensure that every submarine which attempted the passage came to grief. (If one in four were damaged that would be more than enough. The U-boats would have to pass the minefield twice on each patrol and if fifty per cent were damaged going in or out, they would soon abandon the attempt.) However, the number of mines needed was cut by three quarters, when an American engineer devised an antenna with a small metal buoy which, when touched, transmitted a current to detonate the mine. Nonetheless, the statistics of the Northern Barrage are stupendous:

500 contractors in the USA alone manufactured 1,000 mines a day with their mine cases, wire ropes and mine anchors.

25,000,000 lbs of TNT were automatically poured into the mine cases.

1,200 mines a day were assembled in Inverness and Invergordon.

5,400 mines were laid on each of thirteen escorted minelaying 'excursions' on dark nights starting in June 1918. Four or five 'planters' (converted excursion steamers) would drop one mine every fifteen seconds, as they steamed without lights towards Norway.

In the end 70,000 mines were laid, eighty per cent by the Americans and the remainder by British crews, the process creating a barrage several miles wide, which would have been extended month by month, had the war continued. (Compare this with the 11,000 German mines laid round the British Isles during the whole war.)

Some of the hastily manufactured Northern Barrage mines detonated prematurely, but the destruction of seven out of the thirteen U-boats lost in August and September 1918 has been attributed to the Northern Barrage,[34] while others boats returned to base after suffering damage there. The mine barrages incidentally completed the control of international merchant shipping. 'From that time forward no neutral merchant ship, even if she escaped bunker control, blacklists, export restrictions and search in harbours could, without an Allied permit, hope to reach a port in a rationed neutral country,' as Vice Admiral Sir Roger Keyes pointed out, adding with irony, 'which final denial of all neutral rights at sea was another contribution of America'.[35]

Had the U-boats been confined to the North Sea and the Mediterranean – where the Otranto barrage at the heel of Italy was growing in efficiency – it would have spelt the end of the German blockade of the United Kingdom, but the long term effect of the barrages cannot be known, because by the late summer of 1918 events on land had moved to their climax.

Notes

1. Newbolt, op. cit. Vol.5, p.196
2. Naval ships had 'paravanes', invented by Commander Usborne, who

observed that the bow wave prevented a mine from hitting the stem of a ship, but the mine's mooring made it swing back to hit the side. Paravanes were more sophisticated than 'otters', having their depth controlled by rudders actuated by hydrostatic valves. They worked well. Once as Vice Admiral Tupper's ship 'discovered' a minefield, she was saved by her paravanes, which cut three mines loose to be destroyed on the surface.

3. Figures from Jellicoe, op. cit. pp. 183–94

4. Jellicoe, Admiral of the Fleet Viscount, *The Crisis of the Naval War*, Cassell, 1920, p.188

5. During the war enemy action by mine, gun or torpedo, accounted for over 200 trawlers and drifters and forty-two other minesweeping vessels. Another fifty-five were lost to the perils of the sea or other causes.

6. From 17 August outward bound ships were organized into convoys, assembling in the wide waters of Milford, Falmouth, Devonport, Lough Swilly and Lamlash on Arran.

7. Wheat convoys from Argentina were particularly successful, only one ship being lost in 307 passages. Nevertheless, the method of presenting the figures, (even after the war) exaggerated the efficacy of convoys and was reminiscent of the false accounting which had led the admirals to think that convoying was impracticable. If twenty ships sailed together to the USA and back five times, they would of course be counted as ten convoys, but 'the number of ships convoyed' would invariably be given as 200, not twenty, so if two ships were sunk the percentage lost would be given as one per cent, not ten per cent. In the convoys traversing the North and South Atlantic from 26 July 1917 to 5 October 1918 there were 14,968 passages and only 118 ships were casualties. This is given as a loss of 0.79 per cent of the ships convoyed. (See Gibson and Prendergast, op. cit. Appendix IA) But it is difficult to find out just how many ships were involved in the Atlantic trade. If there were only 600 ships en route to and fro or unloading at any time, should not the loss really be shown as twenty per cent over the period?

8. Seymour, op. cit. p.198

9. Sims, op cit. p.60

10. Chatterton, E. Keble, *Q-Ships and their Story*, Sidgwick & Jackson, 1922, p.147

11. ibid. p.150. Amazingly, von Speigel's submarine had not been sunk. Her First Lieutenant managed to plug her holes, bring her to the surface and return to Germany without diving again.

12. Chatterton, op. cit. p.207

13. After twelve patrols Schwieger had become a U-boat ace with a tally of 190,000 tons of shipping sunk.

14. Newbolt, op. cit. Vol.5, p.112

15. Edwards, op. cit. p.300

16. Hurd, op. cit. Vol.3, p.8

17. Gibson and Prendergast, op. cit. p.94. Steinbrinck was also a U-boat ace, sinking 200,000 tons of shipping.

18. Newbolt, op. cit. Vol.4, p.328

19. One, the *U-50*, had, with the *U-49*, destroyed nineteen ships in the Bay of Biscay in one cruise in November 1916; another, von Bothmer's *U-66* had put the first two torpedoes into HMS *Falmouth*, and the last, the *U–106*, was one of the latest 1,000 ton U-boats.

20. Cable to House of 29 June 1917. (House, op. cit. Vol.3, p.106)

21. Lloyd George, op. cit. p.764

22. *Annual Register*, 1918, p57

23. House, op. cit. p.312.

24. Jellicoe, Admiral of the Fleet Viscount, *The Submarine Peril*, Cassell, 1934, p.36 Another 'cunning scheme' was that British submarines should spread bread on the water to attract seagulls. Then gulls would flock round the U-boats too in the expectation of finding food, and give their presence away.

25. It is appalling to think of the waste of effort when a torpedo failed to explode; all the skills of design and manufacture which culminate in the efficient submarine weapon system, and all the training followed by weeks of patient patrolling, ruined by a defective component, such as the detonator. Lieutenant Musters in the submarine *C 4* was particularly unfortunate, because the logs of German submarines, which were obtained after the war, showed that he had hit two U-boats with non-exploding torpedoes.

26. Newbolt, op. cit. Vol. 5, p.232

27. Scheer, op. cit. p.321

28. This includes five U-boats, which, according to German records, left Zeebrugge to attempt the passage of the Dover Strait, but were not heard of again. (See Keyes, op. cit. Vol.2, p.380) The Flanders Flotillas were losing a boat a week from all causes in 1918, and by the end of the war eighty had been sunk with the loss of 145 officers and over a thousand men. (See Gibson and Prendergast, op. cit. p.284)

29. Newbolt, op. cit. Vol.5, p.281. The U-boats had not yet learnt the art of hunting in packs, which brought such success in the Second World War.

30. See Fayle, C. Ernest, *Seaborne Trade*, John Murray, 1924, Vol.3, p.467

31. PROCAT HW 7/1

32. Out of the twenty-nine U-boats from the Flanders Flotilla that were sunk during 1917, twenty were UC minelayers.

33. Newbolt, op. cit. Vol.5, p.299

34. The number of German submarines sunk in the Northern Barrage is admittedly taken from a British source, Newbolt. Scheer thought that none were sunk there but his figures, notably for tonnage sunk, are not always reliable, and the U-boat Commodore Michelsen, gives the fate of at least four U-boats lost in September 1918, as mined in the North Sea.

35. Keyes, op. cit. Vol.2, p.97

CHAPTER TWELVE

Collapse

During the eighteen months while the second U-boat campaign waxed and waned, the blockade of the Allied navies continued its work without restriction and with new efficiency. Long before the mine barrages were complete, control of imports from the US, coupled with the British, and now American, coal bunkering policies, led to progressively tightening quotas for the north European neutrals and ensured almost watertight control of seaborne trade without any fear of retaliation. In mid-1917 contraband came to be cleared at the departure quays rather than at sea, and the wearisome work of the Tenth Cruiser Squadron was wound down.[1] All humanitarian restraint had already evaporated from both the German and British blockades; all diplomatic restrictions were removed with the entry of the United States into the war. At this stage neither side had anything to lose from infringements of the international law which had, until then, imposed some check, though of variable force, on their activities, and American officials now endorsed what they had previously condemned as flagrant violations of law. Polk of the US State Department told Arthur Balfour, 'It took Britain three years to reach a point where it was prepared to violate all the laws of blockade. You will find that it will take us only three months to become as great criminals as you are.'[2]

The blockade was, however, subject to new and fundamental influences, during the second U-boat campaign. True, the Allies had greater control, but they also had greater needs, the need above all for merchant shipping tonnage. The British Empire, which had begun the war with more than 12,000,000 tons, forty-eight per cent of the world's total, lost

231

to torpedo, mine and gun over 2,400 merchant ships and 640 fishing craft[3] during the next four and a quarter years – two vessels for every day of the conflict and nearly eight times the losses of the next largest sufferer, Norway. But Norwegian losses were proportionately as heavy. When the unrestricted campaign started in February 1917 all the neutrals save Norway had kept their ships in port. In the first three months of that year her bravery had cost her 240 ships totalling 356,000 tons – fourteen per cent of her fleet. No wonder the others needed coaxing to put to sea again. If ships reached the neutrals courtesy of London, they left courtesy of Berlin. Exploiting the U-boats' dominance, the *Admiralstab* issued safe conducts to approved voyages of neutral merchantmen, but at a price. When Nansen, the Norwegian Arctic explorer, negotiated a deal for US food supplies, Norway had to apply for a safe conduct to the Germans, who demanded a loan of money in return. But confidence in these arrangements was shaken, when six Dutch ships, sailing together under a safe conduct, were met by a U-boat returning from the Mediterranean. Unaware of the *Admiralstab*'s promise, the U-boat sank the lot.

In spite of the risk to their vessels, the neutrals had eventually to come to terms with the Allies. If they would not send their agreed produce, not only would they not get any coal from Britain, they would not receive their other quotas, which the US had already made more stringent. But there was some hard bargaining. The Danes, who continued to send all their produce over the German border, replied to the US proposals that 'the figures of the Danish quota would of course be taken into consideration, but . . . there certainly must be some telegraphic error; obviously 5,000 tons of mineral oils were meant and not fifty, and similarly the United States must surely have meant to write 3,000 tons of rice instead of 300'.[4] It was the hardest time for the neutrals, caught between the devil and the dark North Sea. By the end of 1917 they had all imposed rationing of some goods – butter, coffee and paraffin in Denmark, bread in Sweden, Switzerland and the Netherlands. There were riots in Amsterdam and Rotterdam the following spring when the bread ration was reduced to 200 grams a day.

All the neutrals except Switzerland were minor maritime powers, and one of the terms of any agreement would concern tonnage. During the summer of 1917 both Britain and the US had exercised the old right of 'angary' (allowing a belligerent to make use of neutral property), by taking up Swedish, Danish and Dutch ships, which had been clogging their quays. The move was not unpopular with the shipping companies, because the ships, which had not been earning their keep for six months or so, were hired at generous rates. After protracted negotiations the Allies reached new agreements about supplies and the remaining tonnage – but not before the draft terms had been submitted to Berlin, who threatened to view the cession of too much shipping as unneutral conduct, and always managed to insist on receiving a certain amount of food. For instance Denmark's agreement of December 1917 listed all the imports she was allowed, and permitted the Allies to charter 200,000 tons of shipping in return for supplying the Danes with 100,000 tons of coal a month, but Denmark continued to supply cattle to Germany.

Negotiations with the neutrals continued while the fighting raged in 1918, but among the Central Powers the shortages had already begun their deadly effect. Two months after the February Revolution in Russia, the new Austrian Emperor, Karl, had seen the threat of similar events at home, writing to the Kaiser, 'We are now fighting against a new and more dangerous enemy than the Entente: social revolution. It is an enemy that finds the strongest possible ally in hunger.'[5] Austria wanted peace, if only because her war aims were satisfied: Serbia had been crushed and Russian supremacy in the Balkans was over. The deprivation which threatened the integrity of the Empire had no purpose now. Field Marshal Hindenburg, wearied with propping up his disintegrating ally, complained that the mutual aversion of the different races of the Austro-Hungarian Empire was intensified by maladministration and inequalities in the distribution of food, 'Vienna was starving while Buda-Pesth had something to spare. German-Bohemia was almost dying from exhaustion while the Czechs lacked practically nothing.'[6] However, at that time the U-boat campaign seemed unstoppable, inevitably leading to victory, and the anxieties were stilled for a while, but by July 1917 Social Democrats in Germany too were proposing peace negotiation under the Russian slogan, 'No annexations or indemnities'. Hindenburg recognized that behind this resolution 'the great disappointment at the course of military events and the visible results of our U-boat campaign played a large part'.[7] Some foresaw revolution at the German door. Chancellor Bethmann-Hollweg, who was suspected of being ready to make concessions to the Allies, resigned on 14 July.

Five days later the first of several minor naval mutinies broke out. On board the dreadnought *Prinzregent Luitpold* the unrest arose out of food grievances. The stokers declared that they 'would gladly eat whatever food was given them if the officers would do the same'.[8] The revolt smouldered on in other ships, but the disturbances were finally brought under control by a combination of conciliation (increasing the bread ration of the sailors to 100 grams a day) and punishment (hanging two ringleaders and sending three to penal servitude). Before they subsided, however, it became clear that political organizations had been formed in the High Seas Fleet. Only the submarine service was unaffected by these troubles. They had the high morale of close-knit units successfully engaged in fighting for the Fatherland they loved, and also often enjoyed the advantage of being able to take necessities and even luxuries from enemy ships before they sank them. The artist Klaus Bergen described the scene on a U-boat in which he took passage in 1917: 'The crew in their leather kit, and among them the officers keeping strict order: on deck a medley of boxes and chests of cocoa, coffee and expensive tea, sacks of wonderful American meal, fresh butter and globes of margarine . . . fine white English bread, English marmalade, ham and bully-beef, bacon and beans, two bars of good soap, tobacco and various oddments. All these things, which were completely strange to us, we had removed from a few paltry enemy fishing boats, while in Germany the women and children were starving and dying from inanition, or supporting life on vile, injurious almost uneatable food substitutes. The poor in Germany thought of the old days as they sat over their watery turnips; while in the cabins of these trawlers . . . were plates piled . . . such as we only saw in dreams.'[9]

In the second half of 1917 the rations of the German army deteriorated further; those of the civilian population had always been worse. At the end of January 1918 a million hungry, war-weary workers were involved in strikes. Food supplies might be secured from the granaries of Russia after February's crushing Treaty of Brest-Litovsk, but there was no sign of them yet. It had long been clear, even to the *Admiralstab*, that their submarines were not winning the war. Three months after the inception of the unrestricted campaign, it had looked as though Britain must surely give in; after six months it still seemed quite possible; but after a year there was no reasonable hope, even though the Imperial Navy had as many submarines at its disposal as before. For the Central Powers hopes were now all pinned on Ludendorff's land offensive, which must be the final fling. Could it break through the Allied armies, before fresh American soldiers could fill the gap? If so, victory would be theirs.

The long expected onslaught on the Western Front was launched on 21 March 1918 with shattering success against the British line where it joined the French. After three weeks, with the Fifth Army pushed right back, Sir Douglas Haig was issuing a desperate order to hold every position to the last man. The attack then swung against the French armies, bringing the enemy to a position from which Paris could again be threatened – and, to general amazement, was shelled.[10] With Ludendorff still attacking in June the Prime Ministers of France, Great Britain and Italy jointly cabled Wilson that General Foch had presented them with 'a statement of the utmost gravity', pointing out that 162 Allied divisions were opposed by 200 German, and there was 'a great danger of the war being lost'[11] unless American infantry and machine guns came soon in large numbers. At the same time the Allies were frantically trying to agree a formula for intervening on a new front in Siberia, which would be a life-saving diversion, so long as it did not antagonize the Russians into joining the Central Powers. Without some intervention there too, the British Government feared, 'we have no chance of being ultimately victorious, and shall incur serious risk of defeat in the meantime'.[12] No one in London guessed that the end was only five months away. The speed and immunity of the transportation of US troops took both foe and friend by surprise.

The U-boat arm, which had so nearly won the war for the Reich in 1917, completely failed to stop the Allied armies from winning it in 1918. To receive the men and materials of war, new harbours had been constructed on the west coast of France, with docking facilities and railway lines, sheds and camps. In a remarkably short time St Nazaire grew from a fishing village into a major port, Bordeaux had a mile of new docks and Brest harboured as much shipping as Hamburg. Troopship convoys were arriving from America every four days in the summer. Men came in their thousands, guns by the hundred and munitions by the thousand tons. A third of a million men had crossed the Atlantic by March 1918, a million by June, and another million were to follow, pouring in at an ever increasing rate:

April	118,642
May	245,945
June	278,664
July	306,350[13]

Over half the Americans sailed in British ships, and at first they were escorted by the Royal Navy too, but since the Kaiser had not extended unrestricted submarine warfare to the American coast, few US freighters were sunk there, and the Navy Department was able to send 120 submarine chasers and almost all the US destroyers over to British waters. The US Navy then took over guarding most of the troopships, and their soldiers could see the Stars and Stripes flying on the escorts. To the dismay of Albert Ballin, head of the Hamburg-Amerika Line, his gigantic, 50,000 ton liner *Vaterland* was renamed *Leviathan* and converted into a troopship. She could carry 14,000 men at a time across the Atlantic. The crossing was no vacation for them, however, 'packed as they were like sardines three and five decks below the waterline, brought up in shifts to catch a brief taste of fresh air, and assailed at once by homesickness, seasickness, and fears of drowning like rats in a trap'.[14] But only one eastbound troopship was torpedoed and, including those drowned in a collision, only about 600 men were killed in crossing (less than one in every 3,000 transported). So much for Admiral Holtzendorff's boast that 'They will not even come'.

Ludendorff's attacks in June were soon checked. His fifth and final thrust on 15 July against the French was quickly followed on the 18th by a counter-attack, the second battle on the Marne, which signalled the end of the German offensive and the start of the Allies' great advance. It could no longer be held back. The British evicted their enemies from secure positions near Amiens on 8 August, the 'black day' for the German army. The following month the Americans, fighting for the first time as a separate US Army under General Pershing, inflicted a serious defeat at St Mihiel and so it continued.

The Allied armies had enjoyed artillery and air superiority and deployed a plethora of tanks, not just the earlier, vulnerable, lumbering leviathans, (which could be effective enough when sensibly used with close infantry support), but hundreds of an improved type, and small Whippet and Renault tanks, capable of eight miles an hour, which exploited gaps in the enemy defences. The munitions were landed in western France without impediment, while the raw materials continued to struggle through to Britain. Scheer, realizing that once again their best hope, now their only hope, rested on the Navy, planned to build 300 U-boats in 1919, but that was next year. Now there were not enough U-boats both to deny Britain its resources and to block the flow of American men and armaments into France, and the *Admiralstab* unwisely still concentrated on starving out Britain. No wonder that, when Ludendorff finally lost his nerve, he included the Imperial Navy in his rage against the Kaiser, the *Reichstag* and the home front.

Criticism of the home front was grossly unfair. For so long 'the dogged will of the united German nation'[15] had held fast, as the people suffered increasing deprivation in patient silence. Otherwise Germany would have collapsed much earlier. Farmers might still have their hidden sacks of potatoes, but people in the cities could starve, while 'even competent persons, qualified to point out the food distress of the nation . . . stood by in silence, though sometimes foaming with rage. They simply would not raise their warning, cautioning voice, or in fact – under the control of military commands in Germany – were not permitted to do so.'[16] As the promise of victory at sea was broken, as their armies were pushed back, as the prospect of corn from the Ukraine proved a mirage in the chaos of revolutionary Russia and the bread ration was further reduced, there was nothing to sustain optimism, and despair took control on the home front as on the fighting fronts. While June saw food riots in Austria, Anna Eisenmenger in Vienna received a letter from her soldier son, Karl, 'Life here is unworthy of any human being. I ask myself again and again how the motley collection of older men and young boys in these front positions endure this life. Insufficient food, tattered shoes and uniforms. No possibility of keeping oneself clean. P.S. See that you get in food supplies, for Vienna will be eaten out of house and home by the soldiers when they come back. I too suffer from chronic hunger.'[17] The poor citizens of the capital could not, however, obtain enough food for themselves. Those who could went into the country to buy from farms, because the smugglers charged exorbitant prices, and children foraged lawlessly in the fields.[18]

Though civilian sacrifices and industrial ingenuity kept the German armies supplied with munitions and basic food, almost all commodities were scarce at home. The output of cotton textiles which was, by 1915, already down by seventy per cent, had continued to fall steadily, and was only partly and pitifully replaced by paper fabric. There was little wool available. Leather was so short that window straps disappeared from the trains and pieces were cut out of the backs of the seats. New shoes had wooden soles and cardboard uppers; children went barefoot in the summer. The plight of young mothers was extreme. Lina Richter reported, 'It has become almost impossible to procure the necessary baby linen . . . for cotton goods have almost entirely disappeared . . . many mothers have had to wrap their new-born babies in newspaper.'[19] Babies born during the blockade averaged only between four and five pounds in weight. Towards the end of the war milk, which was always unrationed in Britain, was limited to one litre per week in Germany and only a third of a litre in Austria. Sometimes it was unavailable and 'milk delivered was almost always considerably watered'.[20] As the fats used in soap had all gone to make glycerine for explosives and propellants, soap was mostly clay and resin, and the alternative of a rather abrasive soap powder was strictly limited, so hygiene was less thorough. Where there was only one towel for the family, contagious diseases spread.

Many children had abnormal hearts or suffered from eye defects or goitre. Tuberculosis, which had been almost eradicated, appeared again, as farmers were reluctant to kill tuberculous cows, and the windows of ill-heated homes were kept fast shut. Finally the influenza pandemic, which swept the world in the latter half of 1918, killing hundreds of thousands in every major country, took a greater proportion of lives among the weakened populace than in the still well-fed states of the Allies.[21]

The distress at home affected soldiers on leave and was carried back to the trenches. At the same time the Allies added propaganda to their armoury.[22] Millions of leaflets were dropped by balloon over the enemy lines, driving home the loss of the U-boat campaign, the hopelessness of fighting a million fresh American troops, who were crossing the Atlantic without hindrance, and promising peace if the men would go home. German troops had already seen the falseness of their own propaganda about starving the British into surrender, when, having captured British trenches in the great offensive of March 1918, they found stores of food such as they had not seen for months.[23] The temptation to eat, drink and plunder had helped slow the advance, and when the tide was turned on the Western Front, German soldiers, disappointed and demoralized, gave themselves up in thousands and finally, like the Austrians on the Italian front, deserted in thousands.

As Jellicoe later noted, 'The decisive effect of the Blockade did not become apparent until the end, when the final crash came, and it was seen how supreme an influence on the result of the war this powerful weapon had exercised. Even those who during the war had been asking what the Navy was doing, recognised at the last how victory had been achieved, largely as the result of the silent pressure of Sea Power.'[24] It may be that the effect of the blockade has been exaggerated by both sides – by the British who were keen to show that their tactics, though questionable, had not been mistaken, and by the Germans to excuse the defeat of their army and to add force to their pleas for relief after the war. But while it is impossible to say how great its influence was on the outcome, what was the effect of the lack of rubber, lubricants, non-ferrous metals, soap, cloth, fats and food, it is also 'impossible to deny that the enfeeblement of Germany by reason of her economic encirclement was one of the main factors of victory'.[25] The blockade may also have had effects which are not always recognized. Why for instance did the Germans produce only twenty tanks in 1918 (though they made use of 170 captured Allied ones)? Was it due to a lack of materials and skilled men or a misdirection of effort, for which the naval situation was again responsible? Having gambled on victory at sea, German heavy industry continued to concentrate on submarines, vainly depriving it of skilled manpower and materials required for the war effort elsewhere. (During 1918 some eighty-one U-boats were launched and the same number were sunk, so the number in service remained at 169, but Scheer, calling for 69,000 skilled workers, planned to have twice as many in service in 1919, so that there were 226 boats being built at the end of the war, while another 212 were projected.)[26]

When the dam broke at last, it took everyone by surprise. On 12 September the general view among military chiefs in France was reported to be that, 'with great effort the war might be ended in 1919,'[27] but a week later the Salonika 'side-show' finally paid off. The Franco-British army broke through the lines held by the Bulgarians and Germans, and Bulgaria, at the end of its resources called for a truce. With the Austro-Hungarian flank exposed, her young Emperor Karl I renewed his approach to President Wilson. Already, a year after the crushing Austro-German rout of the Italians at Caporetto in north Italy, the tide had turned against the Austrians on the River Piave, and the many nations of the Austro-Hungarian Empire were beginning to declare themselves republics. Meanwhile, on 1 October, with the Germans being pushed steadily back, Ludendorff urged Prince Max of Baden, the third Chancellor since Bethmann-Hollweg's resignation, to appeal for an armistice on the basis of President Wilson's Fourteen Points. The army, though still in good order, 'could not wait forty-eight hours longer,'[28] he believed, if it was to remain a fighting force and a bargaining counter. For the Allies a ceasefire would be too soon – enemy troops were still on Belgian and French soil – and besides, the British could not accept one of Wilson's points, 'the Freedom of the Seas', which would ban unilateral blockades.[29]

Though the Central Powers were collapsing, the struggle at sea continued with unabated ferocity. On 10 October the torpedoed Irish mail boat, SS *Leinster*, had sunk in seven minutes, taking down with her 176 men, women and children. President Wilson demanded that all inhuman acts must cease, and on the 21st the German Emperor's Headquarters ordered that U-boats were not to attack passenger ships. This was again too much for Admiral Scheer, who two months before had succeeded Admiral von Holtzendorff as Head of the Naval Staff, but with new powers as Supreme Commander of the Navy too. He immediately ordered all his submarines back from commerce raiding but only, as in 1916, to play the old game.

The powerful dreadnoughts and other surface ships of the High Seas

Fleet were still intact and their officers were loyal. On 27 October 1918 Reinhard Scheer issued orders for Admiral Franz von Hipper, who was now C.-in-C., to make a last bid to redeem the name of the Imperial Navy. Hipper had plans ready. The fleet was to attack shipping in the Thames estuary on the 30th. Seven Zeppelins would give warning when the Grand Fleet steamed south in pursuit; to reduce its strength hundreds of mines would be surreptitiously laid by submarines in its path, twenty-five more U-boats would be lying in wait in six lines and torpedo boats would attack at night. Eventually the High Seas Fleet might meet the weakened Grand Fleet on even terms. (The Admiralty was soon aware that something was afoot. Six U-boats were detected opposite the mouth of the Forth, yet no attacks on shipping were reported, and Beatty's ships had found and swept the secret minefield.)

Sound though Scheer's plan was, it was too late. The fighting morale of the German fleet was no more. When the sailors heard that their ships were to sail on what they saw as a death-or-glory attack on the Grand Fleet, many of the crews of the great battleships refused duty. 'We should not be asked to fight a battle after the war is lost,'[30] a spokesman protested. In Schillig roads off Wilhelmshaven the sailors of the *Thüringen* and *Ostfriesland* openly mutinied. The U-boat ace, Johannes Spiess, was commanded to take his cruiser submarine, *U-135*, to the scene and await further orders. Spiess asked for those orders in writing, but no one, not even Hipper himself, dared give him that. Nevertheless, Spiess escorted two boat-loads of troops to the ships, and the mutiny was suppressed. But this was not like the mutinies of 1917. Now, though 180 men from the battleship *Margraf* were marched to prison, the officers were unable to keep control. German seamen, other than the U-boat and destroyer crews, had been infiltrated by red agitators, and the mutiny spread rapidly to all the naval ports.

The government shrank from taking drastic action for fear of exacerbating the situation, but it was already out of hand. The old order was crumbling under revolutionary agitation. There was open insurrection at Kiel, where officers had their medals and side arms stripped from them, and on 3 October, when the mutineers went round the fleet demanding that the Red Flag be raised, only the battleship, *König*, resisted; her captain and two officers were shot and the rest overpowered. The destroyer flotillas too were forced to surrender to the Soldiers' Councils, similar to the Russian councils (soviets) of workers and soldiers. The Kaiser's brother, Prince Henry, escaped Kiel incognito and the men then met the new port commandant, Admiral Souchon, the hero of the battlecruiser *Goeben*'s escape to Turkey in

240

1914. Souchon hesitated to send for troops, and agreed the first five demands: the same food as the officers, the right to public meetings, no saluting off duty, the release of the men from the *Margraf*, and no aggressive operations at sea. Their last two demands were beyond Souchon's powers: that the Kaiser should go and the *Bundesrat*, the Upper House, should be abolished. Sailors then seized rifles and machine guns. Many of the officers were incarcerated; others, fearing a repeat of Bolshevik terror, fled in cars, by bicycle or on foot. As the blue-jackets spread out through the country, one city after another fell to a handful of men in red armbands. In Cologne the garrison of 45,000 soldiers laid down their arms at the call of a few sailors.

There was no 'unconditional surrender' of German forces, only an armistice – for a month at first – but it was in fact a surrender and the terms reflected the facts. They were the subject of discord, not only between the hostile delegations, but also between the British and French Allies and the Americans (who did not call themselves 'allies', but only co-belligerents). All were determined that the Second Reich should not be in a position to resume warfare, but there were squabbles over whether the German army should be allowed to keep some of its guns or go home, as Petain wished, 'without a cannon or a tank',[31] whether the Rhine bridgeheads should be occupied and what to do with the Imperial Navy. None wanted to risk a resumption of the submarine campaign, but the British insisted that the High Seas Fleet should be immobilized too – interned in a neutral port, if a suitable one could be found. The soldiers led by Foch saw no need for that. But the French did want 'reparation for damages', and Clemenceau slipped that in at the last minute. The citizens of the Central Powers anxiously awaited the outcome, hearing, like Frau Eisenmenger in Vienna, that 'the terms of the Armistice are incredibly cruel and exorbitant, but we shall be forced to agree to everything in order to put an end to the blockade'.[32]

Eventually the Naval Armistice conditions included the British demands, 'Surrender to the Allies and the United States of America of all existing submarines (including all submarine cruisers and minelayers), with their complete armament and equipment, in ports which will be specified by the Allies and the United States of America'.[33] Also most of the High Seas Fleet's ships – six battlecruisers, ten battle-ships, eight light cruisers, including two minelayers and fifty destroyers of the most modern types – were to be disarmed and interned abroad, and the remainder disarmed in German naval bases under Allied super-vision. Further, the terms stated, 'The existing blockade conditions set up by the Allied and Associated Powers are to remain unchanged, and all German merchant ships found at sea are to remain liable to capture'.[34]

President Wilson's reply to German peace feelers had clearly indicated that the Hohenzollerns would have to go, but the Kaiser had long ceased to be in command. Albert Ballin, visiting him that autumn had found him 'very misinformed as usual'. News of the failure of the last offensive was 'dished up to the poor Kaiser in such a fashion that he remains perfectly blind to the catastrophic effect of it'[35], but the truth could not be hidden. On 9 November Scheer belatedly advised his Emperor that the fleet was no longer to be relied on, and when on the same day a similar warning was given about the army, the last of the German monarchs crossed into Holland, never to return. He wrote a brief, revealing letter to his son, the Crown Prince:

My Dear Boy,

The F.M. (Hindenburg) can no longer assure me that I am safe here, and refuses to guarantee the loyalty of the troops. I have therefore, after a hard inner struggle, decided to leave the army, which has gone to bits. Berlin is completely lost, in the hands of the Socialists, and already two rival governments have been formed there . . . I advise you to stick to your post till the armies retreat into Germany, and prevent the dislocation of the troops. We shall meet again, by God's will! General von Marschall will tell you more.

Your deeply afflicted father, William.[36]

Two days later the Armistice was signed, and on 20 November, in accordance with its terms the first U-boats crossed the North Sea to surrender at Harwich, followed next day by the major part of the High Seas Fleet, its guns disarmed, to be interned in the bleak waters of Scapa Flow.

Notes

1. By then 15,660 vessels had passed by the northern route. Nearly eighty-three per cent (ten ships a day) had been intercepted and boarded by the Tenth Cruiser Squadron; thirteen per cent went voluntarily into port and four per cent eluded the patrols.
2. See Fischer, op. cit. p.1138
3. Figures taken from Gibson and Prendergast, op. cit. pp.333–4. It should not be forgotten that, besides the Naval personnel, over 14,000

seamen and other civilians lost their lives in British ships. No maritime neutral was immune. Norway in 1914 had the fourth largest mercantile marine. By the end of the war she had lost 929 ships and a thousand Norwegian sailors had died. Denmark lost ships to U-boats, and a fifth of the Spanish tonnage was destroyed. Spain's protests did her no good. Germany offered to give safe conduct to selected Spanish ships, but the French promptly announced that they would consider any Spanish vessel holding such a permit to be in German service and so liable to be captured. (See Kenworthy and Young, op. cit. p.87)

4. Guichard, op. cit. p.171. Danish reply of 21 February 1918.

5. Newbolt, op. cit. Vol. 5, p.61

6. Hindenburg, op. cit. p.320

7. ibid.

8. Daniel Horn, quoted by Werner Rahn in Cecil and Liddle, op. cit. p.129

9. Neureuther and Bergen, op. cit. p.51

10. The gun in question, 'Big Bertha', was a prodigy, capable of firing seventy-five miles. This was achieved by virtue of its high elevation and muzzle velocity, which carried the shells into the thinner air thousands of feet above the ground.

11. House, op. cit. Vol.3, p.461

12. ibid. p.422

13. ibid. p.463

14. Seymour, op. cit. p.197. Ironically the British had agreed that all the Hamburg-Amerika ships interned in the US could be withdrawn for use by the Belgian Relief Committee, but the German civil authorities dallied. After the war *Vaterland*'s sister-ship, *Imperator*, was given to Cunard and the *Bismarck*, renamed *Majestic*, to the White Star Line. Ballin took an overdose.

15. Introduction to Rubman, Max, *Hunger! Effects of Modern War Methods*, Georg Reiner, Berlin, 1919

16. ibid. As to the number starving and the decline in births see Peter Loewenburg in Cecil and Liddle, op. cit. p.556

17. Eisenmenger, Anna, *Blockade, the Diary of an Austrian Middle Class Woman*, Constable, 1932, diary entry of 25 October 1918.

18. Ruth von der Leyen, head of the women missionaries at the Berlin Children's Courts, reported that in three months in Stuttgart, 273 children of twelve to fourteen were convicted of theft from the fields.

19. Richter, Lina, *Family Life in Germany under the Blockade*, National Labour Press, 1919, p.17

20. ibid. p.22

21. The flu pandemic was no respecter of friend or foe. It killed 228,000 Britons during 1918, 400,000 Germans, 450,000 Americans and probably 16,000,000 in India.

22. The newspaper tycoons, Lord Northcliff and Max Aitken, ennobled as Lord Beaverbrook, were made directors of propaganda, and the author, John Buchan, amongst other literary notables was pressed into service for the campaign.

23. Compare the effect on Russian visitors at the end of the 'cold war' of seeing the groaning shelves of a Western supermarket.

24. Jellicoe of Scapa, Admiral of the Fleet Viscount, *The Grand Fleet, 1914–1916*, Cassell, 1919, p.76

25. Guichard, op. cit. p.311

26. Gibson and Prendergast, op. cit. Appendix III. There were dreams of U-boats with four 6-inch guns and twenty torpedoes. (See Freiwald, Ludwig, *Last Days of the German Fleet*, Constable, 1933, p.39)

27. Lord Reading, the special Ambassador to the USA, in cable to Sir William Wiseman.

28. House, op. cit. Vol.4, p.74

29. Point II: 'Absolute freedom of navigation upon the seas, outside territorial waters, alike in peace and war, except as the seas may be closed in whole or part by international action for the enforcement of international covenants.' (House, op. cit. Vol.3, p.336)

30. Schubert, Paul and Gibson, Langhorne, *Death of a Fleet 1917–19*, Hutchinson, 1933, p.87

31. House, op. cit. Vol.4, p.114. It was agreed that the German army should be left a third of its artillery and half its machine guns (which might be required to quell Bolshevism).

32. Eisenmenger, op. cit. p.74

33. Article XXIII, see Newbolt, op. cit. Vol.5, p.416. Among the 176 U-boats actually surrendered to the Allies eighteen were newly completed. Two hundred and eight unfinished boats were broken up. (See Gibson and Prendergast, op. cit. p.364)

34. Article XXVI, Newbolt, op. cit.

35. Huldermann, op. cit. p.283

36. Bulow, op. cit. Vol. 3, p.2

Postscript

'Probably the greatest problem which will be presented to us upon the cessation of hostilities,' Colonel House had cabled the President, 'is the furnishing of food and other essential supplies to the civilian population,'[1] – both of their allies and their enemies. A relief organization was set up under Herbert Hoover, but the only surplus food was in the Americas, so House suggested that Germany should put her entire merchant navy at its disposal until the peace treaty was signed. There was an urgent need to save life and stabilize governments. However, as the solidarity of the wartime alliance gave way to separate ambitions for the peace, obstacles rose up in the way, and as late as March 1919 Germany still refused to turn her shipping over until there was an agreed plan for supplying her food until the next harvest.

Meanwhile at Versailles outside Paris the Allied leaders were absorbed in drafting peace terms which were designed, not only to solve the problems arising out of Europe's recent tragedy, but to prevent further wars. When President Wilson arrived at the Conference in mid-December they started debating the subject closest to his heart, the League of Nations, and in mid-February 1919, after the Covenant of the League had been adopted, he sailed home leaving Colonel House to discuss with the other European leaders the tremendous questions thrown up by the war. They had got peace: now they wanted security, and finally they would want payment.

Four great empires, German, Austro-Hungarian, Ottoman and Russian had collapsed. The Europeans had boundaries to define and protect, and scores to settle. France sought security in an independent

245

buffer state between her border and the Rhine; Italy sought it in pushing her boundary north to the ridge of the Alps; Britain sought it for her Empire by deals over the German colonies, navy and merchant marine. The colonies and the Ottoman provinces in the Middle East were to become mandated territories of the League. But what were the victors to do with the helpless but potentially powerful German High Seas Fleet? The French and some of the weaker maritime nations wanted to share out the German warships to increase their fleets, but Colonel House and Lloyd George agreed that, though the ships should be divided up, the UK, the USA and Japan should sink their share to prevent a new arms race between the Allies.

The US wanted no territory, and having suffered no invasion and lost few lives, wanted no indemnity. They stood for moderation. But when Wilson returned to Versailles after a month's absence, he had been forced by the Senate to require amendments to the Covenant to preserve the Monroe Doctrine. In this weakened position, looking worn and tired, he bargained concessions and could not keep the demands for reparations within reasonable bounds. It was not to be expected that the peace terms would be magnanimous after a war of such unprecedented suffering and hatred, but whatever their personal feelings, the victorious leaders found that the democracy in which they had gloried now ensnared them. Just as even the German leaders, had they so wished, would have been unable to offer acceptable terms in 1917 or 1918 because their citizens had been led to expect profitable annexations, now the Allied leaders were bound by the unrealistic expectations of their electorates to press for unsustainable terms from Germany.

When ultimately on 7 May 1919 the peace terms were delivered, the German government at Weimar, socialist and democratic, branded them as 'surpassing the most pessimistic forecasts' and 'dictated by hate'.[2] Philip Scheidemann, the Premier, declared to tumultuous cheering in the Reichstag, 'This Treaty, in the opinion of the Government, cannot be accepted'.[3]

During all this time the major part of the High Seas Fleet had lain in Scapa Flow. As the ships had been interned, not surrendered, the crews were still German under Admiral von Reuter. He was kept informed of the peace negotiations only through the British newspapers which found their way to him. When he read that the terms had been rejected, he expected that war would break out again. If so, he would consider himself bound by the order of the Imperial Navy to 'sink defenceless ships rather than let them fall into the hands of the enemy'[4] He therefore sent home those sailors who might not obey an order to open the seacocks – and waited. On 21 June he heard that the German Foreign Minister, having returned from Versailles with only small concessions, had pronounced the terms still unacceptable. Von Reuter now saw war as inevitable, and when the British Battle Squadron, which had been guarding the High Seas Fleet, steamed out of the Flow for delayed torpedo practice, he assumed it was to take up their war stations and gave the secret signal, 'Paragraph 11 – Acknowledge'.[5] So, on that quiet Saturday while school children were being taken on an excursion round the fleet, the German ships were scuttled – to the fury of the Allies generally, but to the secret relief of some.

There was, however, no way out for the Weimar Government. Foch was ready to march across the Rhine and the machinery of the blockade was still in place, although Woodrow Wilson, Colonel House, General Smuts and some of the other Allied leaders would not have agreed to use it to enforce the peace terms. Already in the post-war chaos on the continent many, many millions of Europeans faced the worst famine since the Thirty Years War of the seventeenth century. Scheidemann resigned, and the Treaty of Versailles was signed on 28 June 1919. On 12 July, nearly five years after the blockade began, it was formally ended. 'If suffering were a communicable experience,' wrote one observer, 'another such blockade would be impossible.'[6]

Notes

1. House to the President, 8 November 1918. (See House, op. cit. Vol. 4, p.420)
2. House, op. cit. Vol. 4, p.475. It was pure coincidence that the terms were presented on the anniversary of the sinking of the *Lusitania*.
3. Scheidemann, Philip, *Memoirs of a Social Democrat*, Hodder & Stoughton, 1929, p.628
4. Schubert, Paul and Gibson, Langhorne, *Death of a Fleet 1917–19*, Hutchinson, 1933, p.250
5. ibid. p.261
6. Arnold Forster in PRO ADM 186/603

Bibliography

Arnold-Forster, W., *The Blockade 1914–1919*, Clarendon Press, 1939

Bacon, Admiral Sir Reginald H., *Life of Lord Fisher of Kilverstone*, Hodder & Stoughton, 1929

—— *The Jutland Scandal*, Hutchinson & Co., 1933

Baker, Ray Stannard, *Woodrow Wilson, Life and Letters*, William Heinemann, 1938

Baty, T. and Morgan, J.H., *War: Its Conduct and Legal Results*, John Murray, 1915

Bayly, Admiral Sir Lewis, *Pull together!*, George G. Harrap, 1939

Bennet, Geoffrey, *Coronel & The Falklands*, Pan, 1967

Bingham, Commander the Hon. Barry, *Falklands, Jutland and the Bight*, John Murray, 1919

Bonnett, Stanley, *The Price of Admiralty*, Robert Hale, 1968

Bowles, Thomas Gibson, *Maritime Warfare*, W. Ridgway, 1878

Boyle, William H.D., Earl of Cork and Orrery, *My Naval Life 1886–1941*, Hutchinson, 1942

Brown, Malcolm and Meehan, Patricia, *Scapa Flow*, Allen Lane Penguin Press, 1968

Buchan, W., *The Log of HMS Bristol*, The Westminster Press, 1916

Bulow, Prince von, *Memoirs*, Putnam, 1932

Campbell, Rear Admiral Gordon, *My Mystery Ships*, Herbert Jenkins, 1919

Campbell, N.J.M., *Battle Cruisers – Warship Special No.1*, Conway Maritime Press, 1978

—— *Jutland, An Analysis of the Fighting*, Conway Maritime Press, 1998

Carl, Ernst, *One Against England*, Jarrolds, 1935

Carr, W.G., *By Guess and by God*, Hutchinson, 1930

Cecil, David, *The Cecils of Hatfield House*, Constable, 1973

Cecil, Hugh, and Liddle, Peter H., *Facing Armageddon*, Leo Cooper, 1996

Cecil, Lord Robert, Interview entitled *Black List and Blockade*, Eyre & Spottiswoods, 1916

—— Interview entitled *Why Mail Censorship is vital to Britain*, Jas. Truscott, 1916

Chatfield, Admiral of the Fleet Lord, *The Navy and Defence*, William Heinemann, 1942

Chatterton, E. Keble, *The Big Blockade*, Hurst & Blackett, 1932

—— *Gallant Gentlemen*, Hurst & Blackett, 1931

—— *Q-Ships and their Story*, Sidgwick and Jackson, 1922

Churchill, W.L.S., *The World Crisis 1911–1918*, Odhams Press, (Revised in 2 Vols.) 1938

—— *Thoughts and Adventures*, Odhams, 1932

Consett, M.W.W.P., *The Triumph of Unarmed Forces*, Williams & Norgate, 1923

Copplestone, Bennet, *The Secret of the Navy*, John Murray, 1918

Corbett, Sir Julian, *Official History of the Great War, Naval Operations, Vols.I–III*, Longmans, Green, 1920

Deacon, Richard, *A History of the British Secret Service*, Granada, 1980

De Chair, Rear Admiral Sir Dudley, *How the British Blockade Works*, Sir Joseph Causton & Sons, 1916

Dewar, Vice Admiral K.G.B., *The Navy from Within*, Victor Gollancz, 1939

Edwards, Lieutenant Commander Kenneth, *We Dive at Dawn*, Rich & Cowan, 1939

Eisenmenger, Anna, *Blockade; the Diary of an Austrian Middle Class Woman*, Constable, 1932

Eksteins, Modris, *Rites of Spring*, Bantam Press, 1989

Falkenhayn, General von, *General Headquarters and its Critical Decisions 1914–16*, Hutchinson & Co., 1919

Fayle, C. Ernest, *Seaborne Trade*, John Murray, 1924

Ferguson, Niall, *The Pity of War*, Allen Lane, 1998

Fischer, Fritz, *Germany's Aims in the First World War*, Chatto & Windus, 1967

Fisher, H.A.L., *A History of Europe*, Edward Arnold, 1936

Fremantle, Sydney R., *My Naval Career 1880–1928*, Hutchinson, 1949

Freiwald, Ludwig, *Last Days of the German Fleet*, Constable & Co., 1933

Geiss, Imanuel, *July 1914 – Selected Documents*, B.T. Batsford, 1967

Gerard, James W., *My Four Years in Germany*, Hodder & Stoughton, 1917

Gibson, R.H. and Prendergast, Maurice, *The German Submarine War 1914–1918*, Constable, 1921

Gooch, G.P. and Temperley, Harold, *British Documents on the Origins of the War 1898–1914*, HMSO, 1927

Goodenough, Admiral Sir William, *A Rough Record*, Hutchinson & Co., 1943

Gordon, Andrew, *The Rules of the Game*, John Murray, 1996

Grant, Robert M., *U-Boat Intelligence*, Putnam, 1969

Granville, Wilfred, and Kelly, Robin P., *Inshore Heroes*, W.H. Allen, 1961

Gray, Edwin A., *The U-boat War*, Leo Cooper, 1994

Guichard, Lieutenant Louis, *The Naval Blockade 1914–1918*, Philip Allen, 1930

Hale, John R., *Famous Sea Fights*, Mellifont Press, 1937

Halpern, Paul G., *A Naval History of World War I*, UCL Press, 1994

Hampshire, A. Cecil, *The Blockaders*, William Kimber, 1980

Hase, Commander Georg von, *Kiel and Jutland*, (Translated by Chambers and Holt) Skeffington & Son, 1921

Herwig, Holger H., *Luxury Fleet – The German Imperial Navy 1888–1918*, George Allen & Unwin, 1980

Hezlet, Vice Admiral Sir Arthur, *The Submarine and Sea Power*, Peter Davies, 1967

—— *The Electron and Sea Power*, Peter Davies, 1975

Hindenburg, Marshal von, *Out of my Life*, Cassell & Co., 1920

Hislam, Percival A., *The North Sea Problem*, Holden & Hardingham, 1913

Hoar, Allen, *The Submarine Torpedo Boat*, D. Van Nostrand, New York, 1916

Hogan, Albert E., *Pacific Blockade*, Clarendon Press, 1908

Hohenzollern, Prinz Franz Josef of, *Emden*, Herbert Jenkins, 1928

House, Colonel E.M., *Intimate Papers*, (4 Vols. arranged by Charles Seymour), Ernest Benn, 1926

Huldermann, B., *Albert Ballin*, (English translation), Cassell & Co., 1922

Hurd, Sir Archibald, *Official History of the Great War – The Merchant Navy*, John Murray, 1921

James, Admiral Sir William, *Admiral Sir William Fisher*, Macmillan, 1943

—— *The Eyes of the Navy*, Methuen, 1955

Jane, Fred T., *Fighting Ships*, Sampson, Low, Marston, 1914

—— *The British Battle Fleet*, (2 Vols.), The Library Press, 1915

Jellicoe of Scapa, Admiral of the Fleet, *The Crisis of the Naval War*, Cassell & Co., 1920

—— *The Grand Fleet, 1914–1916*, Cassell & Co., 1919

—— *The Submarine Peril*, Cassell & Co., 1934

Keegan, John, *The First World War*, Hutchinson, 1998

—— *The Price of Admiralty*, Hutchinson, 1988

Kennedy, Paul M., *The Rise and Fall of British Naval Mastery*, Allen Lane, 1976

Kenworthy, Lieutenant Commander the Hon. J.M. and Young, George, *Freedom of the Seas*, Hutchinson, 1928

Kerr, Mark, *Land, Sea and Air*, Longmans, Green, 1927

Keyes, Admiral of the Fleet, Sir Roger, *Naval Memoirs*, Thornton Butterworth, 1934

King-Hall, Lieutenant S. (Etienne), *A Naval Lieutenant 1914–1918*, Methuen & Co., 1919

King-Hall, Commander Stephen, *My Naval Life*, Faber & Faber, 1952

Kipling, Rudyard, *The Fringes of the Fleet*, Macmillan, 1915

Kock, Nis, *Blockade and Jungle*, (Translated by C.P. Christensen) Robert Hale, n.d.

Lambi, Ivo Nikolai, *The Navy and German Power Politics, 1862–1914*, Allen & Unwin, Boston, 1984

Lansing, Robert, *War Memoirs*, Rich & Cowan, 1935

Lauriat, Charles E., *The Lusitania's Last Voyage*, Houghton Mifflin Co., 1915

Lauterpacht, H., *International Law*, Cambridge University Press, 1970

Legg, Stuart, *Jutland*, Rupert Hart-Davis, 1966

Lloyd George, David, *War Memoirs*, Odhams New Edition, 1938

Lutz, Ralph H., *The Causes of the German Collapse in 1918*, Stanford University Press, 1934

McCormick, Donald, *The Mystery of Lord Kitchener's Death*, Putnam, 1959

MacDonald, Lyn, *1915, the Death of Innocence*, Headline Book Publishing, 1993

Mahan, Captain A.T., *The Influence of Sea Power upon History*, Samson Low, Marston, 1892

Marcus, Geoffrey, *Before the Lamps Went Out*, George Allen & Unwin, 1965

Massie, Robert K., *Dreadnought*, Jonathan Cape, 1992

Natkiel, Richard and Preston, Anthony, *Atlas of Maritime History*, Bison Books, 1986

Neureuther, Karl and Bergen, Claus, eds., *U-Boat Stories*, Constable & Co., 1931

Newbolt, Henry, *Official History of the Great War, Naval Operations, Vols. IV & V*, Longmans, Green, 1928

Nicolson, Harold, *Sir Arthur Nicolson, Bart., First Lord Carnock*, Constable, 1930

Parmelee, Maurice, *Blockade and Sea Power*, Hutchinson, 1924

Pastfield, Revd. J.L., *New Light on Jutland*, William Heinemann, 1933

Patterson, A. Temple, ed., *The Jellicoe Papers*, Navy Records Society, 1966

Picton, Harold, *The Better Germany in War Time*, The National Labour Press, 1918

Richter, Lina, *Family Life in Germany under the Blockade*, National Labour Press, 1919

Riddell, Lord, *War Diary 1914–1918*, Ivor Nicholson & Watson, 1933

Rintelen, Captain von, *The Dark Invader*, Frank Cass, 1997

Roskill, Stephen, *Admiral of the Fleet Earl Beatty*, Atheneum, New York, 1981

Rossler, Eberhard, *The U-Boat*, Arms & Armour Press, 1981

Rubman, Max, *Hunger! Effects of Modern War Methods*, Georg Reiner, Berlin, 1919

Salomon, Ernst von, *The Answers*, Putnam, 1954

Scheer, Admiral, *Germany's High Sea Fleet in the World War*, Cassell & Co., 1920

Scheidemann, Philip, *Memoirs of a Social Democrat*, Hodder & Stoughton, 1929

Schoen, Freiherr von, *Memoirs of an Ambassador*, George Allen & Unwin, 1922

Schubert, Paul and Gibson, Langhorne, *Death of a Fleet 1917–19*, Hutchinson, 1933

Seymour, Charles, *Woodrow Wilson and the World War*, Yale University Press, 1921

Silber, J.C., *The Invisible Weapons*, Hutchinson & Co., 1932

Simpson, Colin, *Lusitania*, Longman, 1972

Sims, Rear Admiral William Sowden, *Victory at Sea*, John Murray, 1920

Smith, Thomas A., *What Germany Thinks*, Hutchinson, 1915

Spiegel, Adolf von, *The Adventures of U-202*, Century Co., New York, 1917

Tarrant, V.E., *Jutland, The German Perspective*, Arms & Armour Press, 1995

Terraine, John, *Business in Great Waters*, Leo Cooper, 1989

Thomas, E. Lowell, *Lauterbach of the China Seas*, Doubleday, Doran, New York, 1930

—— *Raiders of the Deep*, William Heinemann, 1929

—— *The Sea Devil*, William Heinemann, 1928

Thomson, Sir Basil, *The Scene Changes*, Victor Gollancz, 1939

Triana, S. Perez, *Some Aspects of the War*, T. Fisher, Unwin, 1915

Tschuppik, Karl, *Ludendorff, the Tragedy of a Specialist*, George Allen & Unwin, 1932

Tuchman, Barbara, *The Zimmerman Telegram*, Constable, 1959

Tumulty, Joseph P., *Woodrow Wilson As I Know Him*, William Heinemann, 1922

Tuohy, Captain F., *The Secret Corps*, John Murray, 1935

Usborne, Vice Admiral C.V., *Blast & Counterblast*, John Murray, 1935

—— *Smoke on the Horizon*, Hodder & Stoughton, 1933

Warner, Philip, *World War One*, Arms & Armour, 1995

Wood, Walter, *Fishermen in War Time*, Samson Low, Marston, 1918

Young, Filson, *With the Battle Cruisers*, Cassell & Co., 1921

Magazines and newspapers

Chalmers, Robert, ed. *The World's Work*, William Heinemann, Dec 1914 to May 1915

Illustrated London News 1914–1918

The Naval Review, 1914

The Times History of the War, (illustrated series in 21 Vols.), 1914–1919

The Times Documentary History of the War, Vol. III – Naval, Parts 1–3

The Times, London, 1914–1918

Wilson, H.W., and Hammerton, J.A., eds., *The Great War*, (Weekly series), The Amalgamated Press, 1914–1919

Other sources

Battle of Jutland Official Despatches, HMSO, 1920

Brocklebank, Joan, ed., *Captain H.C.R. Brocklebank, notes and letters*, Greenwich Maritime Museum Library, 1974

Contributions to the History of German Naval Warfare 1914–1918 (PRO CAT HW7/1-3)

Intercepts from German Naval Intelligence Centres (PRO CAT ADM 137/4177)

Telegrams between Stockholm and Swedish Legation, Mexico (PRO CAT HW7/7)

The Zimmerman Telegram (PRO CAT HW/8)

Various personal accounts of actions in the libraries of The National Maritime Museum, Greenwich, and the Imperial War Museum.

Index

Note: Names of ships are shown in italics, followed by SS for merchant steamships, HMS for British warships, SMS for German ones and USS for American. The type of other vessels is indicated in the entry.

261